No Forgiveness

Copyright © 2025 by Daniel H Neal
All rights reserved. No part of this book may be reproduced in any manner without written permission from the publisher.

ISBN: 978-1-7334897-7-5
First edition paperback

Library of Congress Control Number: 2025909041

Editor: Renée C. Tafoya
Front cover: D.S. Neal's children a few days after his murder. Historic map of southeastern Idaho. Both images courtesy of the Neal family.
Back cover: Photograph of Mormon men imprisoned in the Utah Territorial Penitentiary in November 1888. Photographer: Charles Savage. Courtesy BYU Digital Collections.

WordsWorth Publishing
Cody, Wyoming
www.wordsworthpublishing.com

Truth is not crystalline and clear. It lies in pieces, and you have to pick them up as best you can.

Anthony Lane, *The New Yorker*

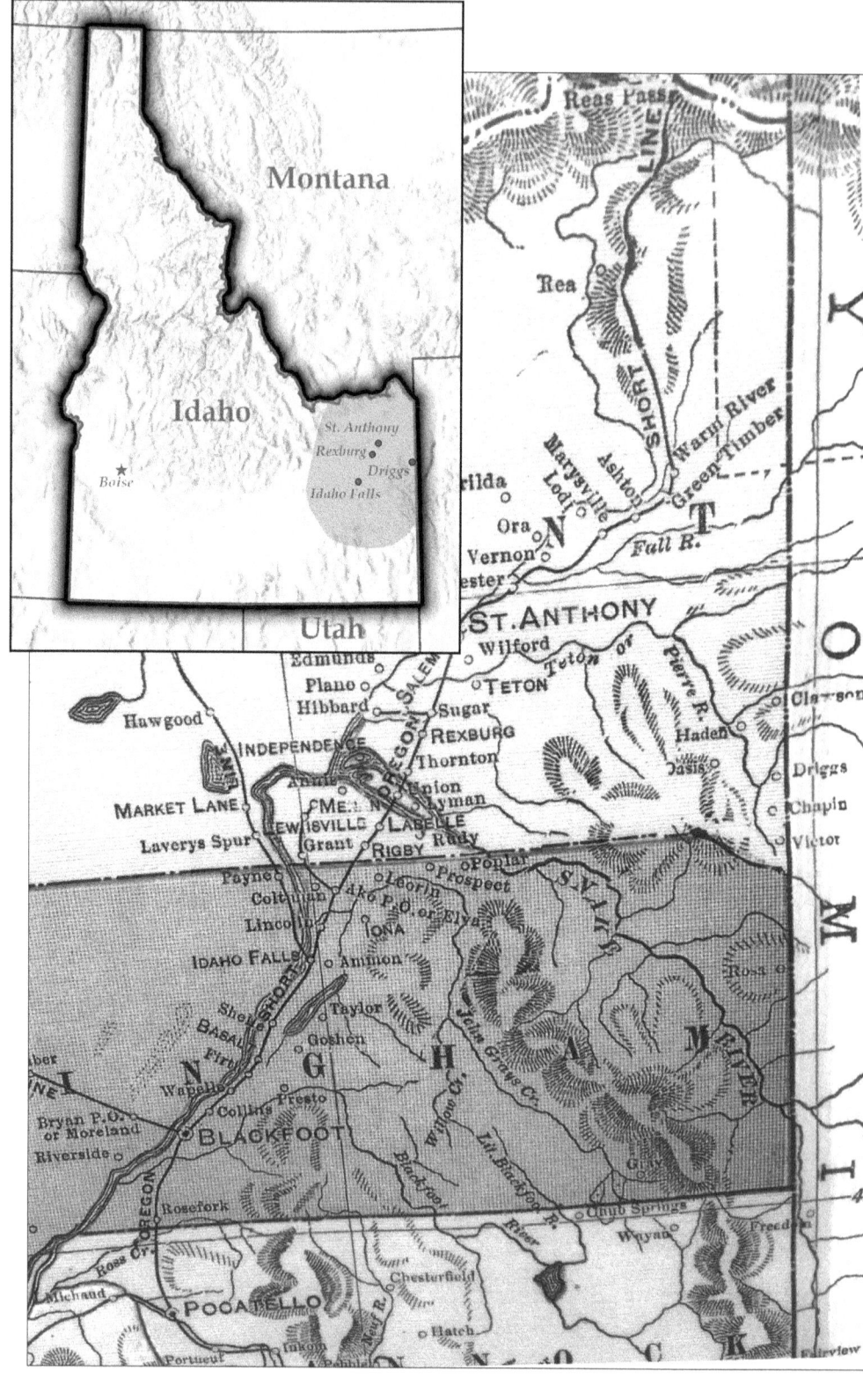

No Forgiveness

*Family, Polygamy, Murder, and Justice
among Idaho's pioneering Mormons*

By Daniel H Neal

✱
WordsWorth Publishing
Cody, Wyoming

Contents

Acknowledgments 9

A note on terms and story telling 10

The principal players 11

CHAPTER ONE
Murder on a still morning 15

CHAPTER TWO
First accounts of the murder 20

CHAPTER THREE
Smith arrested 26

CHAPTER FOUR
He looked very natural 30

CHAPTER FIVE
Roots in Mormon Zionism 35

CHAPTER SIX
Doctrine and Confrontation 40

CHAPTER SEVEN
Exaltation? Or marriage overdone? 47

CHAPTER EIGHT
Faith and polygamy in the Lewis and Neel families 57

CHAPTER NINE
Daniel Lewis flees Utah 70

CHAPTER TEN
It caused a breeze 75

CHAPTER ELEVEN
Cornering the church while it awaits Jesus 85

CHAPTER TWELVE
The education of May Lewis 90

CHAPTER THIRTEEN
College Days and a new way to spell Neel 95

CHAPTER FOURTEEN
A plural wife complains 106

CHAPTER FIFTEEN
David and May together 110

CHAPTER SIXTEEN
Interstate immigrants 124

CHAPTER SEVENTEEN
Settled and teaching in Darby 128

CHAPTER EIGHTEEN
Ellington Smith and Nick Wilson 135

CHAPTER NINETEEN
Charley Wilson's account 142

CHAPTER TWENTY
May in the aftermath 147

CHAPTER TWENTY-ONE
The wheels of justice grind away 152

CHAPTER TWENTY-TWO
The Holdens plan an insanity defense 164

CHAPTER TWENTY-THREE
The trial of Ellington Smith and David S. Neal 174

CHAPTER TWENTY-FOUR
Smith imprisoned 198

CHAPTER TWENTY-FIVE
How to get out of prison *208*

CHAPTER TWENTY-SIX
A new governor and prison reform *215*

CHAPTER TWENTY-SEVEN
Ellington bides time while May fends for her family *222*

CHAPTER TWENTY-EIGHT
Smith and friends push for a pardon *228*

CHAPTER TWENTY-NINE
Ellington pleads his case for reprieve *238*

CHAPTER THIRTY
May remarries and Ellington's niece tries again *250*

CHAPTER THIRTY-ONE
Ellington engulfed *263*

CHAPTER THIRTY-TWO
Smith's last months *271*

CHAPTER THIRTY-THREE
Last stories and a burial mystery *274*

Epilogue *281*

Endnotes *286*

Bibliography *302*

Acknowledgments

The descendants of David S. and May Lewis Neal started my thinking about writing this book at a family reunion on Teton Creek in 1992. Once I started seriously working on it, many family members assisted me, especially my cousin Diana Black. Diana offered unstinting support though she worried that the book might be viewed as critical of her beloved Mormon Church. She did not live to read it. Others willingly provided family papers, photographs, and copies of May Lewis Neal's correspondence.

The murder was a taboo topic among Ellington Smith's descendants until his great granddaughter Susan Foster learned that he had died in the Idaho State Penitentiary. She obtained penitentiary records that she shared with her relatives and with Diana Black. The documents opened a window on the past for both the Smith and Neal families. She willingly cooperated with me and has my deep gratitude for it.

For assistance with research: Archivists Jim Riley and Owen Prout with the Idaho State Archives and Research Center in Boise; the staff of the Research Center of the Utah State Archives & Utah State History; the staff of the Church History Library; Eva and Abby of the Reference Desk of the L. Tom Perry Special Collections at the Harold B. Lee Library at Brigham Young University; Heidi Stringham at the Research Center of the Utah State Archives; Davia Sullivan, Courtney Vick and Joshua Baxter of the Stockton Archives at Cumberland University; Tina Kirkham of the Marriott Library at the University of Utah; and Adam Luke at the BYU-Idaho Library.

Many, many other friends and family members gave encouragement and help. You are not forgotten.

Thanks especially to my wife Judy, who finds great meaning in family history and who keeps me on course in the present.

A note on terms and story telling

I grew up in Idaho Falls, Idaho, in the 1950s and 1960s. We lived on Wadsworth Drive, a neighborhood of twenty-two cinder block homes in which virtually all the families were Mormons. Officially, we were members of the Church of Jesus Christ of Latter-day Saints.

We proudly called ourselves Mormons and saints and referred to one another as "brother" or "sister." The church referred to itself as the Mormon Church and its members as Mormons until 2018, when its leaders called for ending use of the term in favor of its legal name. Given the common use of the term Mormon, I use the label freely in this book as well as the word "saints" to describe members of the church. For the same reason, I occasionally use the word "gentiles" to note people who were not members of the church.

The church doctrine of plural marriage is referred to here both as polygamy and as cohabitation. Practitioners gently were referred to as "cohabs" and not so gently as polygamists or worse.

I am related to many of the people in the book. D.S. Neal and his wife May Lewis Neal were my grandparents. Their son David Lewis Neal was my father. Readers will find that at a number of points in the book I present my own memories of my father and his stories recalling his mother. I likewise recall a few of my own experiences growing up deep inside the Mormon culture of southeastern Idaho.

During the years the events in this book took place, the institutions in Idaho for the treatment of mental illness officially were named "asylums" for the insane. People treated there might be called inmates, patients, or the insane. I use all these terms in this book. Now the same facilities are known as hospitals that treat the behavioral health of their patients, among other services.

No offense is intended in the use of these historical terms.

This book relies upon family letters and papers, newspapers of the time, archives in Utah, Idaho, and Tennessee, interviews of a few descendants of the pioneering Mormons, and other sources to establish the main facts and many details of the story. There are points in the story when the lack or the inadequacy of records requires informed, reasonable assumptions and I have made them.

The principal players

THE LEWIS FAMILY TREE

Daniel Lewis, born Sept. 22, 1834, Cayo, Wales.

Daniel Lewis had two wives:
   First wife – Mary Davis, born in 1827,
      married Lewis on May 10, 1860, in Illinois.
      Her Mormon community referred to her as Mary D.
      The children born to Lewis's second wife called her Auntie Mary.
   Second wife – Karen Marie Sorensen, born Sept. 12, 1843,
      Love, Denmark. Married Lewis Nov. 5, 1866.
      Her family and Mormon community called her Mary K.

Daniel and Karen Marie (Mary K) Lewis had nine children:
   Mary Elizabeth Lewis, born May 8, 1860, Kamas, Utah.
      Her siblings referred to her as Lizzie.
      She married Peter Sorensen
   Daniel Lewis, Jr., born Feb. 6, 1870, Marion, Utah.
   Sarah Lewis, born Feb. 7, 1872, Kamas, Utah.
      She married Joe Delaney.
   David Morgan Lewis, born July 12, 1874, Kamas.
   Clara Lewis, born March 22, 1875, Kamas.
   Eleanor Lewis, born Nov. 15, 1877, Kamas.
   Carrie May Lewis, born May 17, 1879, Marion.
      Called May by her family and friends.
   Eleazer Lewis, born June 19, 1881, Marion. Known as Elie.
      He married Roxie.
   Edward Lewis, born May 19, 1883, Marion.

No Forgiveness

THE NEEL / NEAL FAMILY TREE

John Neel, Jr., born Sept. 17, 1810, Madison, Kentucky. He and his wife Clemency had 11 children. Two of their sons figure in this book:

John Austin Neel, born Feb 9, 1845, Carthage, Illinois;
Joshua Wriley Neel, born Nov. 11, 1850, Ray, Missouri.

John Austin Neel had three wives:
    First wife – Theresa Amelia Quarm;
    Second wife – Ellen Christiana Stevens;
    Third wife – Emeline Augusta Stevens, sister of Ellen.

John Austin Neel and Ellen Christiana had six children:
    William Austin Neel, born Dec. 16, 1871, Randolph, Utah;
    John Marion Neel, born Nov. 3, 1872, Peoa;
    James Monroe Neel, born Oct. 18, 1874, Peoa;
    Charles Hugh Neel, born June 7, 1877, Peoa;
    Franklin Samuel Neel, born Sept. 20, 1879, Peoa;
    David Stevens Neel, born May 3, 1881, Peoa.

All six sons later changed the spelling of their surname to Neal.

David Stevens Neal married Carrie May Lewis on June 1, 1903. David and May Neal had five children:
    Melba May Neal, born Feb. 15, 1904, Honeyville, Utah;
    Ilah Aleene Neal, born Sept. 16, 1905, Marion, Utah;
    Carmen Neal, born May 2, 1907, Darby, Idaho;
    Lelia Ellen Neal, born Oct. 23, 1908, Darby;
    David Lewis Neal, born April 1, 1910, Darby.
        (Father of the author.)

ELLINGTON SMITH FAMILY TREE

Ellington Estle Smith, born Feb. 7, 1861, Bountiful, Utah. He married Hannah Louise Wilson.

Ellington, known as "Ton," and Hannah Smith had five children:

Joseph Ellington Smith, born Sept. 16, 1887, in Idaho;
Earl Octavus Smith, born March 16, 1889, Montpelier, Idaho;
William Eugene Smith, born Sept. 23, 1890, Salem, Idaho;
Zora Matilda Smith, born June 3, 1892, Darby, Idaho;
Mabel Melissa Smith, born Jan. 8, 1896, Darby.

OTHER PLAYERS OF NOTE

Alexander, Moses – governor of Idaho, 1915-1919.

Berntson, Kate – niece of Ellington Smith.

Cannon, George Q. – famous 19th century Mormon apostle.

Dalby, Oliver C. – Fremont County Probate Court judge.

DeKay, Frank – warden, Idaho State Penitentiary, 1917 and 1918.

Driggs, Don Carlos – founder of Driggs; Teton Stake president.

Fisher, Ray – doctor; Fremont County health officer; prosecution insanity expert at Smith trial.

Givens, John W. – doctor; directed both Idaho asylums; insanity expert at Smith trial.

Gwinn, James G. – Ninth District Court judge.

Holden, Ed – Darby farmer.

Holden, Harry, Edwin, and J. Wesley – defense attorneys for Smith.

Larsen, Andrew "A.C." – Darby farmer, friend of D.S. Neal.

Miller, B.H. – Fremont County attorney who prosecuted Smith.

Morgan, William – judge and corrections system reformer.

Murphy, Patrick C. – Idaho pen inmate 2338; author of *Behind Gray Walls*.

Pickett, John – Fremont County deputy; transported Smith to jail.

Poole, C.W. – Fremont County state senator and attorney; handled Smith's first pardon application.

Poole, Frances – doctor; director of state asylum in Blackfoot, Idaho; defense insanity expert at Smith trial.

Smith, Octavus – nephew of Ellington Smith also known as "Octave" and "Tave."

Smith, Zoyara – sister of Ellington Smith.

Snook, John – warden, Idaho State Penitentiary, 1909 - 1917.

Wilson, Charles, "Charlie" – author of *The Return of the White Indian*; son of Nick Wilson.

Wilson, Nicholas "Uncle Nick" – author of *Among the Shoshones;* father of Hannah Louise Wilson Smith; a Mormon bishop.

CHAPTER ONE

Murder on a still morning

On the morning of July 5, 1911, David S. Neal left his house south of Sorensen Creek in Idaho's Teton Valley to irrigate the field he had rented from Charles Christensen. He had milked his cows and put them out to pasture, then ate the breakfast cooked by his wife May. Their five young children were asleep in their beds after celebrating Independence Day in town the day before.

Dave and May talked about their good time in Driggs enjoying the parade and fireworks. Most of the valley's residents took the day off to celebrate America's independence. The Neals had bumped into their good friends, Alma Hansen and his family. Hansen, like Dave, taught in a rural public school and was a farmer. They had a lot to talk about. Top of mind for Dave was his neighbor Ellington Smith. The two had been feuding. Neal considered Smith mentally unstable.

When Dave left May after breakfast, he picked up his shovel and walked around the north side of their house, hoping to avoid running into Smith. He walked the mile north to Christensen's field and began working.

The valley, known then as the Teton Basin, sparkled in the early morning. Dave was taking water that flowed out of Darby canyon, one of the many drainages that slide down into the valley from the divide created by the Teton Range, which separates the north and south forks of the Snake River. By early July the spring torrents had subsided, beginning to fade like the lilac blooms that had scented the air a few weeks before. It was a glorious morning, windless and the air fresh from the night's cooling.

By 9 a.m. the day's heat had begun and Neal was diverting water into the field.

The basin was dotted with small farms, nearly all of them owned by pioneering Mormons. As Neal managed the water, he could see that Octavus "Tave" Smith, Ellington's nephew, had started on his morning chores in his own farmyard across the road.

Tave had left his sleeping family in the house and saw Neal as he walked to his barn. His chores took time. Tave milked his cows, turned his horses out of the barn, then returned to his house and joined his wife Ellen. She placed bowls of oatmeal before her young sisters Ida and Essie, and her two young children. Tave offered a short blessing over the breakfast. They agreed that Essie would help Tave weed the garden behind the house, but first he had to tend to an irrigation stream running in his own field. Tave and Essie walked outside. Essie, just 13, went to the vegetable garden, and kneeled to pull weeds from the rows of carrots.

A mile south, sometime just before 10 o'clock, Ellington Smith mounted his bay horse in his yard across the county road from Neal's place. He brought his rifle, a Winchester Model 86, a repeater. The hills surrounding the valley were full of wildlife, not in the same numbers seen by the earliest settlers and the natives who preceded them, but there just the same. The gun chambered a .40-82 cartridge used to kill large game animals like elk. The black powder cartridge imparted higher velocity to the large, 260 grain bullet than others of its day, making it easier to shoot accurately. Smith had no plans to shoot elk.

Smith rode the mile north to the road's end at its intersection with the Darby Canyon Road, which runs west from the mouth of Darby canyon. The Darby Canyon Road separated Christensen's field on the north, where Neal was irrigating, from the homes of Smith and Harvey Loveland to the south. Tave's house, garden, and fruit trees were planted along the southwest corner of the intersection. Harvey and his brother Oscar lived in a house fifty yards east of Tave's place.

When his uncle rode up, Tave was hoeing carrots in his garden. Essie weeded, working on her knees. Ellington greeted him.

"Good morning."

"Morning, Ton." He stopped hoeing.

"Lot of weeds."

"Well, it's that time of year."

Ellington slid down from his saddle and tied the horse to the corner of Tave's pole fence. Taking his rifle with him, Smith crossed the Darby Canyon Road, climbed a fence and stepped into Christensen's field. Octave watched him. Must have seen a coyote, Tave thought. He'll shoot it.

His uncle had not seen a coyote. Ellington strode out into the field and walked within shouting distance of Neal. It was a still day but Neal, intent on his irrigation, had not seen or heard him.

"Neal, you son-of-a-bitch. Why'd you steal my water?"

Neal turned to him. "I never stole any water. I took my own water."

Smith raised the rifle, sighted down the barrel, and pulled the trigger. The sound of the blast reached Neal with the bullet. It smashed into his left shoulder, dropping him.

In his vegetable garden, Tave stepped toward Essie. "He shot Mr. Neal."

Essie began crying and started for the house. Tave stopped her.

Tave stood with his hoe in hand. He watched as his uncle, unsure or unsatisfied, walked closer to Neal, raised the gun and fired a second time, putting the bullet into Neal's head. Tave looked away.

Now certain that he had killed his neighbor, Ton Smith walked back to the fence, crossed it, then crossed the Darby Canyon Road and untied his horse from his nephew's fence. He said nothing to Tave and nothing to Essie but swung up into the saddle and turned his horse west, riding slowly away from his nephew and past the dead man down in the ditch.

Octave's wife came rushing around the house.

"Tave! Essie, come in with me and Ida." Essie ran to her and they went into the house. Tave instead turned away. Getting his horses into the barn somehow made sense in the moment. He grabbed their halters, put them in, and only then returned to the house and the women huddled inside.

Oscar Loveland appeared at their door. He knocked and pushed it open. Oscar and his brother Harvey had heard the shots and stepped out on their own porch to see Ton leave the field and ride away. "He wasn't in no hurry," Oscar observed.

They agreed that the constable must be informed. Someone had to tell May Neal. Oscar walked back to his own place and conferred with Harvey. A few moments later Tave saw Oscar set off down the road the killer had ridden up. He had a mile-long walk to figure out how to deliver the news to a woman who did not know she was a widow.

Harvey went the other way, crossing into Christensen's field and walking toward Neal. He pulled the dead man out of the ditch – it seemed the right thing to do – and slowly walked back to his porch. Time slowed. Octave waited a few minutes, then called from his porch to his neighbor. They should go cover the body. Tave went to his barn and found a canvas, met Harvey in the road and they walked to the dead man. They saw that the wounds bled and the blood slowly seeped into the dirt. Tave straightened Neal's arms and Harvey helped spread the canvas over him. No wind. It would stay in place. They walked back to their houses. One of them had to go find Constable Eddington.

After shooting Neal, Smith rode on west, walking his horse. He was not done with his killing. He expected to find A.C. Larsen, another Darby ward member, a good friend of Neal. Andrew Larsen, Smith believed, had conspired with Neal to harass him into selling his farm. The water theft, the threats Neal shouted at him, and other unmentionable, unthinkable insults were part of their twisted strategy. He knew Andrew Larsen used the Darby Canyon Road when he returned home from his trips to Driggs. He would run into him there or down on the main road connecting Driggs to Victor.

But Larsen got lucky that day. He chose a different route home and Smith did not find him.

Ellington turned the bay. He knew his fate. Deputy Pickett or the constable would find him and take him to St. Anthony and the county jail. Confident in his justification, he did not fear arrest.

He rode to Ezra Plummer's place. Plummer stepped out as Smith reached his porch.

"Neal is layin' up dead in the ditch in Charley Christensen's field,"

Smith said, looking down from his horse.

Plummer could not turn his eyes from Smith's strange, piercing gaze. He saw the rifle lying across the saddle below the horn.

"I guess he won't steal any more water," Smith muttered.

Plummer pondered the description of the school teacher dead on the ground. Murdered.

"Can I cut across your fields there to get back to my place?"

"No, Ton. I can't let you do that," Plummer paused. "I can't help you now."

Smith looked at Plummer. They had known each other a long time. He turned his horse and walked it back to the road. Then he rode the old horse home. He found a way around to avoid going back past Christensen's field and the people he knew would be gathering there, waiting for a wagon to carry the dead man's body into Driggs. He reached his house and looked across the road to the Neal place. No one was in their yard and no one was at his own house. He remembered that his daughter Mabel, young, lovely Mabel, was with friends in Victor. He put the horse away and walked back to his porch. He propped the rifle near the door. He went into the house and waited for the constable.

He did not wait long.

CHAPTER TWO

First accounts of the murder

News of Neal's murder by Smith spread quickly through the upper Snake River Valley and the region. Water, and disputes over its use and development, deeply interest the people of the arid West. A shooting and murder blamed on a water fight gives the region's journalists a story they know their readers will devour.

The initial reports that appeared in the weekly and daily newspapers were brief, reporting that Ellington Smith shot and killed D.S. Neal, a fellow farmer, in a dispute over water. The stories do not note that Neal was the principal of the Darby school nor that both men were faithful members of the Mormon congregation in Darby.

The day after the shooting, the *Rigby Star*, located some sixty road miles west of Driggs, ran a one-paragraph story, squeezing it in at the bottom of Page One under the headline "One Farmer Killed Another in Teton Basin Wednesday." An afternoon paper, the *Star*'s editor must have held up printing to get the late-breaking news into his Thursday edition.

The paper reported that "Deputy Sheriff Taylor, at three o'clock this afternoon, informed the *Star* that a murder took place in Teton Basin Wednesday. Two farmers quarreled over water which resulted in Ellington Smith shooting and instantly killing David Neil. (This misspelling of Neal's name was repeated in many news reports.) Smith is now in the county jail, at St. Anthony."

Two days after the *Star*'s report, a report of the murder appeared in the *Rexburg Standard*, spreading the news further in the upper Snake River and Teton River valleys. The *Standard*'s short report included a few rich details, some of them dubious, others plainly wrong.

The *Standard* ran a headline declaring "David S. Neal Killed at Bates." Although the headline wrongly placed the shooting at Bates, the story itself, datelined Driggs, July 5, correctly located the shooting at Darby. It asserted that the shooting "was over a little water right controversy."

Rexburg is roughly forty-eight miles west of Driggs. How the *Standard* got its story is not clear, though the paper's editor no doubt had seen the Rigby paper's story. Some elements of the reporting are inaccurate. Whatever its genesis, the *Standard* included a dramatic recounting of the murder and Smith's arrest.

> *The quarrel is of short two years' standing over a little spring. It seems that Smith mounted his horse and rode about two miles with his rifle in hand, dismounted when he saw Mr. Neal in a field, just putting on his rubber boots to irrigate. Smith accused him of taking his water. Neal replied that he had not, when Smith raised his rifle and shot him through the shoulder, the ball passing through the body. Neal fell into the ditch; then Smith sent another ball through Neal's head, killing him instantly.*
>
> *Neal's wife soon after came onto the scene, and pointing to Smith said, 'You are the man that killed my husband.'*
>
> *Smith then began to use abusive language to her. Mr. Olmstead, who was then on the scene, forbade him speaking to her. She swooned and cannot be pacified in her grief.*
>
> *Neal's wife and five small children survive him. He was a school teacher and respectable citizen. He had lived at Darby but a few days.*
>
> *Smith is a pioneer here, having lived in the neighborhood for 22 years, and this the first wrong act known of him worthy of*

mention. He was at once arrested by Deputy Sheriff Pickett and taken to St. Anthony. Smith was about 50 years of age and Neal about 35.[1]

The *Standard* was the only paper to report that May Neal was at the scene and accosted Smith. The presumption of grief is fair; whether May would have swooned is uncertain. She was a strong woman who had moved with her husband to new teaching positions in rural Utah and Idaho, nursed her first daughter through whooping cough and had tended her father on his deathbed. She and Dave had filed a land claim together in Darby. Proving up the claim and developing a successful farm required years of hard, physical work.

May's confrontation of Ellington Smith must have occurred when Smith was arrested at his home across the road from the Neal house the afternoon following the morning shooting.

Other newspapers spread the story quickly throughout the Rocky Mountain region via a shared news service. A three-paragraph story was published July 10 by the *East Oregonian* in Pendleton, Oregon headlined "Water Dispute Leads to Killing". It was one report among several in a shared column of Idaho news briefs that the Oregon paper and many Idaho papers published in July.

"The shooting was a severe shock to the community as both men were of a quiet and retiring nature, neither showing anything of a quarrelsome disposition and both held the confidence and respect of their neighbors," it said.

The report suggested there was more behind the killing than a simple water dispute. Upon arriving in St. Anthony, the county seat of Idaho's Fremont County, the story said Smith told Deputy Sheriff Pickett, "When it is time for me to speak I will show that I had just provocation for what I have done. Further than that I have nothing to say at present."

News of the shooting shocked people in the Neals' old home country, the Weber River Valley in northern Utah. The *Kamas Courant* circulated in Summit County where the dead man and his wife grew up. The *Courant* published a one-page extra edition on Wednesday, July

12, basing its report on information delivered by May's brother Dan Lewis and his wife. The Lewis's had hurried to Darby to be at May's side after learning of the murder. (The *Courant* misspelled Neal's name throughout its extra.)

"DAVID NEIL SHOT" the supplement declares in an all-capital-letters headline. "Particulars Just Received". Relatives and friends in the valley "have waited anxiously for a week for the particulars, searching the Salt Lake dailies in vain."

The *Courant* reported that a dispute over water was the underlying cause. Using a familiar tone that reflected Neal's deep roots in the rural community of Summit County, the report said, "Mr. Smith, Dave and another man had used water from the same spring. Fearing the spring might be taken up by someone else, Dave had filed on it. Probably Mr. Smith thought this would deprive him of the water, but Dave expected them all to use it as they had done."

The story includes details that surfaced officially when eyewitness Octavus Smith testified during a preliminary hearing in the Fremont County Probate Court on July 25 in St. Anthony. Dan Lewis must have spoken with Smith or someone else who had. There was some confusion in the *Courant*'s retelling.

> *Between ten and eleven o'clock on the morning of July 5 Dave started out to water a place he had rented. Mr. Smith got on a horse and followed him, overtaking him close to the house of a neighbor. Mr. Smith called out Your garden is pretty weedy.*
>
> *Dave said Yes, it is. Then Mr. Smith said why are you stealing my water?*
>
> *Dave replied that he was only taking his share and began digging to turn the water.*
>
> *Mr. Smith then took up his rifle and shot Mr. Neil through the arm, the ball passing directly through the heart and through the body. He dropped, killed instantly, probably without knowing the man intended to shoot. Smith then went up to where the dead*

> *man lay and shot him through the head, not leaving a whole bone in his head.*
>
> *The neighbor and his wife saw and heard it all. Smith went into his house where the officers found him. They put him in jail at St. Anthony to await his trial.*

The extra closed with a reminder to the Neals' old Kamas neighbors that he left a wife and five children. "The family has the deepest sympathy of a wide circle of friends."[2]

Over the following weeks, regional newspapers continued to track the murder story. On Aug. 3, the *Evening Standard* of Ogden reported that Smith had appeared at a preliminary hearing in St. Anthony and was ordered held on a first-degree murder charge. It added a few more details about the shooting and the dispute that had riven the neighbors.

"The case is attracting much attention in this district. Smith was apparently a quiet and unassuming man, who has lived with his daughter for a number of years past, his wife having died ten years ago." Smith, it said, "associated but little with his neighbors."

Then the report raised an odd aspect of Smith's relationships in the community. Though Smith's farm was a fine one with good animals, he "has had bad luck in colts and at times accused his neighbors of poisoning them." The story added that Smith "claimed that he had had trouble with people regarding his water rights, but no one supposed it was of a serious nature until the morning of the shooting."

After killing Neal, "Smith went to his neighbor, Mr. Plummer, and told him what he had done." Smith made no resistance when officers came to arrest him. "He told Constable Eddington that he had been driven to the deed by the aggravation of Neal, and added there were two more he was after, one of them by the name of A.C. Larson."

Larsen would have met Smith that morning "but for some unaccountable reason he took a different road to his home from one he usually traveled.

"The general impression in the neighborhood is that Smith had brooded so much over his troubles that the deed was committed in a fit of despondency which he was unable to withstand."³

The newspaper reporting in the days and weeks following the murder leaves several significant questions unanswered. Where, exactly, was May when she learned of her husband's death? Who told her? One can speculate. She likely was at home with her children tending to her own daily chores. The sound of the shots might have reached her. No trains served the valley then and cars were still a rarity. Its farms were quiet except for the squeak of a wagon or a complaint from a cow. The blasts from Smith's gun would have resounded on a windless day.

Most likely, May received the news of the killing from Oscar Loveland after his mile-long walk to her home. Did she rush to the field to see her husband's body? If she did, Smith already had ridden away, searching for A.C. Larsen. She could not have challenged Smith there as the *Rexburg Standard* reported.

May must have witnessed Smith's arrest at his home that afternoon by Constable Eddington. She could have accosted Smith when the constable arrived with others, rushing up to accuse her neighbor of being the man who killed her husband. Then Smith responded, threatening her with such abusive language that the man identified only as "Mr. Olmstead" intervened. Unfortunately, no reporter was on the scene and no editor asked a reporter to interview her after the shooting and Ellington Smith's arrest.

CHAPTER THREE

Smith Arrested

After leaving his neighbor dead in Christensen's field, Smith rode his horse west from Octave Smith's house. He would say later that he intended to find Andrew Larsen, whom he believed had plotted with Neal to conduct a campaign of harassment to drive him to sell his farm.

Smith's second intended target, Larsen was one of thousands of Danes who crossed the Atlantic to join the Saints in Utah. He arrived in 1895 and moved to the Teton Basin where many Mormon families were making land claims, hoping to secure their futures.

When Neal was murdered, Larsen was in his early forties and married to Amelia, also a Danish immigrant. They had a son, Henry, 18, and three daughters, Mary, 20, Martha, 7 and Dora, 4.[4]

Perhaps Ellington had heard that Larsen and Neal hoped to take advantage of the extension of rail service into the Teton Basin. They were farmers and farmers take risks, speculating in crops and the vagaries of weather. They were game to speculate further. They had discussed various land deals, and tried to determine where the Oregon Short Line would lay its railroad tracks through the Basin to Driggs and, eight miles south, Victor, according to my father David Lewis Neal.

Ellington Smith believed that his neighbor and Larsen were devious land grabbers rather than honest yeoman farmers, even though he had joined Larsen in a successful water development project fifteen years earlier. The project involved eleven other farmers with fields and homes north of Darby Canyon. They planned a diversion from Darby Creek just a few hundred yards east of the Idaho-Wyoming border line. The location required authorization from Wyoming water regulators in Cheyenne.

The farmers designed a project to irrigate 2,100 acres and laid the plan before Wyoming State Engineer Elwood Mead. The Wyoming and Darby Bench Canal project was expensive. The proponents estimated total costs of $3,500.[5] Mead authorized the project, but the farmers failed to meet a completion deadline in 1899. Wyoming granted a one-year extension; the project's head gates and ditches were completed in 1900.

A legal problem surfaced six years later. The farmers learned that Wyoming's state engineer had not received paperwork documenting completion of the project and beneficial use of the water. Without certification from the State of Wyoming, the farmers involved in the project who held Desert Land Entries could not prove they held water rights necessary to acquire title to their acreages.

In April 1906, Andrew Larsen and two others submitted affidavits to Wyoming to explain how the project's reporting obligations had been mishandled. They assured the state engineer that the project had been completed and maintained in tiptop shape, and its works were delivering the water to irrigate their farms.[6] The engineer's office certified the water rights. The farmers who needed official certification could breathe easier.

This worrisome period in which Smith faced the prospect of losing his water from the irrigation project and Larsen's involvement in securing them may have somehow turned Smith against Larsen. He later claimed that Larsen induced Neal "to annoy me systematically in many petty ways." Larsen, Smith wrote six years after the shooting, "desired to purchase my property for less than it was worth."[7]

So after shooting Neal, Smith went hunting for Larsen, believing that his fellow irrigator had gone to Driggs that morning. He did not rush. Witnesses described Ellington's departure from the murder scene as "leisurely," riding his horse in a walk west on the Darby Canyon Road. A quarter mile on, he turned north, riding in a walk about an eighth of mile. When he did not encounter Larsen, Smith turned around returned to the Darby Canyon Road and rode on to Ezra Plummer's place.

He knew he would soon be arrested and asked Plummer if he

would handle Smith's farm chores until he could contact his own sons. Plummer testified later that Smith told him Neal was dead and would never steal any more water.

Ellington "looked strange out of his eyes" as he talked and asked if he could cross Plummer's property. Plummer refused. Smith found his way home and changed his clothes.[8]

While Smith hunted Larsen, his nephew Tave or one of Tave's neighbors got word of Neal's murder to Constable Elijah Eddington in Driggs. The constable went to Smith's home opposite the Neal residence and found his suspect there about 2 p.m. Smith came out of his house, met Eddington and shook his hand.

"I was expecting you," he said, looking Eddington straight in the eye. "I won't resist."

The farmer calmly conceded that he had murdered his neighbor. "I had to kill him," Smith told the officer. Neal had tormented him over the water they shared. Then he told the constable that Andrew Larsen was the bottom of the entire trouble. He asked Eddington to allow him to go into his house to get his hat and coat. They went in together. Smith said he wanted to take some of his papers with him, fumbled around in a trunk for a few minutes, then scooped up some papers that were in plain sight.

Others had followed Eddington to see him make the arrest. Smith asked one of the bystanders to clean his rifle. He pulled a pistol from his pocket and left it.

May Neal lived just across the way. Was she watching the arrest? Did she confront Smith as the murderer of her husband, then weather his abuse and threats? She later wrote a letter to Idaho's governor pleading against a pardon sought by Smith. She warned the governor that Smith had threatened to destroy her and her children.

Constable Eddington took Smith to the home of Ed Holden, a neighbor who lived north of the Darby Canyon Road. On their way, they would have passed close to the site of the murder. At Holden's place, the constable turned the suspect over to Deputy Sheriff John Pickett. Smith spoke with several people standing in front of Holden's home. Pickett eventually put Smith in his wagon, and started for St. Anthony, the county seat about forty-five miles away where Smith would be jailed. They drove through Driggs, where Don Carlos Driggs, a prominent local church official, politician, and businessman, saw and spoke with Smith. Many of these people later testified at Smith's trial.

At a decent pace on horseback, the trip from Driggs would have taken at least six or seven hours. It's not clear when they departed Driggs. In a slower wagon, the deputy apparently intended to drive through the night. On the way, however, Smith complained of faintness and stomach pain. Pickett decided stop about midnight at Canyon Creek to take shelter. They left the stopover before dawn.[9]

Pickett delivered Smith to the Fremont County Jail about 10 in the morning. Smith was convivial and talked with several people at the jail. He asked a couple of men to recommend an attorney to defend him.

Later that afternoon, Deputy Pickett appeared in court before Fremont County Probate Judge Oliver C. Dalby. He told the judge the basic facts of Smith's crime. The judge signed a criminal complaint, a chilling statement.

"Ellington Smith did commit the crime of Murder," in Darby on July 5th, the complaint says, "... as follows: did then and there willfully, unlawfully, feloniously, and with premeditation and malice aforethought, kill and murder one David S. Neal, a human being." The judge also issued an arrest warrant that was served on Smith in the county jail by Sheriff John T. Fisher.[10]

Ellington Smith's home on his second Teton Basin farm stood on the west side of the county road separating Smith's place from the Neal homestead. This 1961 aerial photograph depicts the Smith farmyard. The Neal home is just visible among the trees opposite Smith's old house. (Photo courtesy of Susan Smith Foster.)

CHAPTER FOUR

He looked very natural

May quickly put together the arrangements for her husband's funeral with help from local church officials. They scheduled the service on Saturday in the Darby schoolhouse, four days after the murder. The plan gave David's mother and four of his brothers time to make their way to the Teton Basin from northern Utah. May's brother Daniel Lewis and his wife Laura also made the trip from their Utah farm. The train could take them from Salt Lake City or Ogden to Rexburg, then all had to make their way by horse or wagon to Darby.

"The funeral was a very large one, everything possible being done to show respect for the dead and give comfort to the living," the *Kamas Courant*'s extra reported.

During their stay, the Neal brothers and their mother made their way to a photographer's studio for a photograph of the five of them with their sister-in-law Carrie May. It is a somber family portrait. May, then 32 years old, sits next to her husband's mother, Ellen Christiana Stevens Neel. The widow wore a black mourning dress for the photograph, with a pleated bodice, long sleeves, its neck tightly clasped with a brooch. She looks directly into the camera, her eyes shaded and lips closed in a thin, straight line, a sad woman.

The eyes of her mother-in-law, a 60-year-old matron, drop slightly below the camera lens, looking through glasses in thin wire frames, her lips turned down in a frown. The grief seems ready to break out of her with the wisp of hair lifting from her head. A wide-collared coat covers her mourning dress. It is unbuttoned and reveals a watch and chain hanging from her neck.

Four of David's five brothers, William Austin, James Monroe, Charles, and Samuel Frank, stand behind the women. Each wears a suit with a vest, white shirts beneath, and thin ties tied tightly at their necks. Like May, the four brothers neither frown nor smile, but look into the distance. Charles' left hand rests lightly against his jacket.

There is no record of how long Dave's family stayed with May to help her through the initial trauma and loss of her husband. Dan and Laura Lewis returned to the farm at Marion, Utah, a day or two after the funeral, in time to provide the *Courant* with its story.

Local church leaders conducted the funeral. Following Mormon custom, David's body was displayed at the service.

"Strange as it may seem his face was unmarred and he looked very natural," the Courant reported.

D.S. Neal's mother and four of his brothers traveled to the Teton Basin to attend his funeral. The group posed with Neal's widow May, whose grief is plain. Front from left, Ellen Christiana Neel and May Neal. Rear from left, William Austin Neal, James Neal, S. Frank Neal, and Charles Hugh Neal. Unlike her children, Ellen Neel never changed the spelling of her surname. (Photo courtesy of the Neal family)

The bishop of the Darby ward, C.A. Larsen, and other elders of the church prayed and spoke during the service at the school and later at the cemetery. May did not. Her influence on the funeral can be felt in the songs performed by a quartet from the Pratt ward. The songs offered succor to the bereaved and the promise of redemption in the afterlife. The quartet, Genevieve Morgan, Angus Greene, and Charles and Birdie Christensen sang "Dear to the Heart of the Shepherd," a hymn that was and remains a favorite among Mormon congregations. The song appears in the LDS hymnal with a notation that it should be sung calmly. Its lyrics portray a caring shepherd searching for his sheep that have strayed or are lost.[11]

Dear to the heart of the Shepherd,
Dear are the lambs of his fold;
Some from the pastures are straying,
Hungry and helpless and cold.
See, the good Shepherd is seeking,
Seeking the lambs that are lost;
Bringing them in with rejoicing,
Saved at such infinite cost.

The second hymn offered by the quartet was "My Future Home," from the Deseret Sunday School Songbook. The lyrics promise the living a reunion with a lost mate and redemption by the savior.

There's a place of bliss supernal,
Where no angry billows roar;
There's a landscape ever vernal,
Just beyond the sunny shore;
There my loved ones wait to greet me,
And to bid me welcome home,
My Redeemer there will meet me
Bid me to His bosom come.[12]

The funeral service followed a pattern commonly used at contemporary LDS funerals. After the second hymn, friends and church officials remember the dead and offer condolences to the survivors. The Darby ward secretary recorded only the names of those who talked; no notes were made of the speeches. Among the speakers was Alma Hansen, whose family just days before had enjoyed the Fourth of July celebration with Neal and his family. Elders Alex P. Hamilton and Harold D. Winger also addressed the mourners. Their talks were followed by a quartet performance of a Mormon standard often sung at funerals, "I Know that My Redeemer Lives." Two more speakers followed, including Teton Stake President Don Carlos Driggs.

The closing hymn was "Sometime We'll Understand," written by Maxwell Cornelius. The hymn was an appropriate one for May Neal to hear as she confronted the sudden, confusing loss of her husband. Perhaps the second verse provided her some comfort.

We'll catch the broken threads again
And finish what we here began.
Heaven will the mysteries explain;
And then, ah, then, we'll understand.

Then trust in God through all thy days.
Fear not, for he doth hold thy hand;
Though dark the way, still sing and praise;
Sometime, sometime we'll understand.[13]

What did May think as she sat through the service among her family, her four girls and toddler son at her side? Her mother, a sister, two brothers, and her brothers-in-law and Dave's mother sat close by. Her church community surrounded her and sang and talked to her. Reminded by the speakers of the Mormon gospel and hearing hymns meant to assuage her grief, she also knew that a member of her own ward fired the shots that ripped her husband away.

D.S. Neal's body was carried to his grave in the Darby Cemetery by six pallbearers. Harvey Loveland was among them. As the grave was dedicated, the devout May wondered what her Heavenly Father had planned for her.

Why hopes are crushed and castles fall,
Up there, sometime, we'll understand.

CHAPTER FIVE

Roots in Mormon Zionism

The story of D.S. Neal and May Lewis, my grandparents, has its beginnings in Denmark and Wales and the early Mormon Church. Their parents' faith in the church motivated decisions that brought them from Europe to the Rocky Mountain West to raise their families. Both sets of parents were ardent Mormon converts who heeded the church's call to gather Zion — God's select people who devoted themselves to the Mormon prophet Joseph Smith and his restored gospel — in anticipation of the Second Coming of Christ. They left homes in the British Isles and in Denmark for new lives in America.

God had told church founder Joseph Smith that the gathering would be in Missouri. The announcement of the consecrated place came in a revelation Smith recorded in July 1831. God spoke with striking specificity when he announced the location of the temple that would be Zion's centerpiece.

"Behold, the place which is now called Independence is the center place; and a spot for the temple is lying westward, upon a lot not far from the court-house," the Lord told Smith. A month later, the Lord instructed church members to "... open their hearts, even to purchase this whole region of country, as soon as time will permit."[14]

Such frank declarations of the Mormons' intent to take control of the region got the attention of other Missourians. Devout Protestant Americans found Smith's theology bewildering. Some thought it blasphemous. They questioned the Saints' claims that no true church could exist where there was no speaking in tongues, no miracles, and no healings.[15]

But those claims brought others attracted to the early Mormon church's assertions that God was close to all his people, not just to the magnetic Smith. They were pulled by his theology with its promises of equality on earth and, after death, salvation and, for the most faithful, godhood.

Smith's charm for some was considered charlatanism by others. He made many enemies with his claims that his theology represented the one true course to heavenly salvation.

"Wherever Joseph Smith went he roused a storm," Fawn Brodie wrote in her biography of the Mormon prophet. "During his short, tumultuous career Joseph was hauled into court more than a score of times on charges varying from disturbing the peace to treason."[16]

The church had run into opposition and internal strife as it moved from New York and Ohio, but nothing like that encountered in Missouri. The Missourians feared the political power the church exerted when it moved hundreds of people into sparsely populated rural areas. The anti-Mormons organized vigilante groups and militias that attacked Mormon settlements, finally driving them out of Independence. The Mormons fought back. When the violence escalated in 1838, Missouri's governor declared that the Mormons had made war upon the people of his state and said they "must be treated as enemies, and must be exterminated, or driven from the State if necessary for the public peace."[17]

Smith surrendered and was briefly imprisoned. The church's Quorum of the Twelve Apostles organized a move out of northwest Missouri to Illinois. The prophet encouraged the establishment of a new Mormon settlement at Nauvoo on the Mississippi in southern Illinois. The place flourished and grew rapidly to a community of about 20,000.

Though Illinois first welcomed the Mormons, the old concerns and fears followed them. Questions about church doctrines continued to swirl, particularly spurred by rumors of polygamy among the church leaders.[18] Some of the insiders who learned the facts behind the rumors objected. They started a newspaper, the *Nauvoo Expositor*, and published one edition in which they revealed Smith's secret doctrine of plural marriage and the multiple marriages of several leaders including Smith. The prophet denied the doctrine and engineered an order from the Nauvoo city council to destroy the *Expositor* for libeling Smith and the church.

It was a step too far by Smith. Surrounding communities demanded action by the state. Promised protection by the governor, Smith and his brother Hyrum surrendered to authorities. Both were jailed in Carthage, Illinois, fifteen miles east of Nauvoo. The governor failed to provide protection. Mobs stormed the jail and assassinated Smith and his brother on June 27, 1844.

The prophet's death and the threat of further mob violence staggered the church. A contest for succession ensued, further dividing a membership already fractured over the rumors of polygamy. The prophet's first wife Emma and many of his followers believed the presidency of the church belonged to Smith's family. Others broke away after deciding that polygamy was a revealed doctrine they could not abide.

Brigham Young, for years a powerful presence in the church leadership, was serving a mission in New England when he learned of Smith's death. He returned to Nauvoo, arriving on Aug. 6. His timing was fortuitous. The president of the Nauvoo High Council had scheduled a church conference to name a new leader two days later.

At the conference, Sidney Rigdon, the only surviving member of the church's presidency, made his case to succeed the dead prophet. But Young countered Rigdon's oration. With "one of the more remarkable speeches in Mormon history, using emotion, derision, and the promise of temple ritual to brush aside Rigdon's claims," Young argued that the keys to the Mormon priesthood lay with the Quorum of the Twelve Apostles, which he led as president. He promised to build the Nauvoo Temple and said that if their enemies drove them out of Illinois, he would lead the church and its holy endowment in the wilderness. His claims to leadership were buttressed by many of the people in attendance who said that when Young spoke, they saw and heard Joseph Smith.[19] To many church members, it was another example of God embracing his Saints in miraculous ways.

Young had joined Smith's Church of Christ in April 1832. Like the Christian savior, he was a carpenter. Absolutely loyal to his faith, Young built and lost five homes as Smith moved the church from upstate New York to Kirtland, Ohio, Far West, Missouri, Montrose, Iowa, and Nauvoo. He gave up another home at Winter Quarters in Nebraska, where he and other church leaders made their final plans to take the Saints to the remote Great Basin in the West.[20]

Brigham motivated the faithful with reminders that they were building a new Zion under a divine plan with a divine purpose. He masterminded the exodus of thousands of faithful church members to the Salt Lake valley in 1847 and succeeded.

The exodus became one of the great mythic stories of Mormonism. It became deeply ingrained in the world view of the Mormon settlers of Utah and southeastern Idaho and remains ingrained in their descendants.

May Lewis and David Neal grew up with that story. So did I in the middle of the 20th century. During my childhood, the myth was drilled into the minds of the children attending the 18th ward Sunday School in north Idaho Falls, Idaho. This was my ward. We learned about the persecution of our forebears by the Gentiles. Our ancestors, the pioneers, simply sought to practice the true Gospel revealed by Joseph Smith. They escaped to the great Utah desert, which they made blossom like the rose through faith, hard work, and ingenious irrigation projects.

During my high school years, students like me left campus to walk to the Mormon seminary school built nearby. There the people who walked the Mormon Trail were set apart for us, the church's fifth generation, as both heroic, brave pioneers and persecuted refugees seeking safety and religious freedom in the "mountain fastness" of the empty West. There they could practice their religion freely.

We celebrated the anniversary of the day in 1847 when Brigham Young and his party reached the Salt Lake Valley. Pioneer Day was a big celebration in Idaho Falls. Each church ward poured creative energy into parade floats that carried covered wagons, hand carts, and kids costumed in ragged clothing, calico bonnets, and fake beards. A pageant was staged at the city's Civic Auditorium. It was a grand time.

The mythic exodus was part of daily life, too. My family's neighbors in Idaho Falls hung a copy of the Pioneer's Creed on a kitchen wall. It was a piece of craft work featuring a pressed metal outline of a covered wagon with a row of hooks beneath it for hanging keys. I read the creed every time my mother sent me next door to borrow a cup of sugar or an egg.

The coward never started
The weak died along the way
Only the strong made it through

We were the children of the strong and resolute. David S. Neal's grandparents had been swept up in these early Mormon struggles. John Neel and his wife Clemency Casper Neel had been among the group that fled Missouri for Nauvoo. David's father John Austin Neel was born in Carthage just seven months after the death of the prophet. When the Saints departed for Nebraska and the Mormon Trail, the Neel family returned to Missouri where they lived in the vicinity of Independence for several years. In 1855, they joined the gathering of Zion when they left Missouri and made the trek west to the church's haven in the Salt Lake Valley.[21]

May's father Daniel Lewis reached Utah a few years later and settled in the Weber River Valley. Her mother, traveling from Denmark, arrived in Salt Lake City with her parents in 1864.

CHAPTER SIX

Doctrine and Confrontation

The fertile valley of Utah's Weber River lies northeast of Salt Lake City. The river begins its run in the High Uintas, a mountain range that contradicts the generally southeast to northwest line of the great Rocky Mountains from Colorado through Utah, Wyoming, and on through Canada. Contrary like the Mormons, the Uinta peaks stretch east to west. They stand 11,000 to more than 13,500 feet in elevation capturing the winter snows, then pouring melt water into the Weber and many other streams, including the Bear River, Blacks Fork, and the Duchesne.

The first emigrant parties traveling with Brigham Young in 1847 got a look at the Weber Valley after they left the route of the Oregon Trail at Fort Bridger to follow the Hastings Cutoff through Echo Canyon. At the bottom of the canyon, the Mormons reached the Weber River, then turned south and walked up-river until they could turn west to take their wagons and livestock down canyons cutting through the Wasatch range to the Salt Lake Valley. There they founded their Zion.

Brother Brigham had big plans for the region he hoped eventually would become the state of Deseret. Known as "The old Boss,"[22] Young directed the church's colonization of the region. He sent church members far from the Salt Lake Valley, south to St. George and to the deserts of Nevada and southern California to the coast at San Diego, envisioning an ocean port there. He sent his saints to southern Idaho and Wyoming. Many left established homes and businesses in Salt Lake

City in obedience to their president, just as Brigham had left homes to follow Joseph Smith. New emigrants arriving in Salt Lake were welcomed by Young, who informed them where they would settle. Many were moved quickly out of the city to one of Brigham's outposts.

The first fifteen years of Mormon settlement preceded the Homestead Act. When the Mormons arrived, they simply squatted on what was Mexican land until the 1848 Treaty of Guadalupe Hidalgo, then the settlers took up federal land and assumed they eventually would be granted possession. There was no worry about the rights of the native inhabitants who had lived in the region for perhaps hundreds of generations. The Mormons considered them Lamanites, cursed descendants of the dark-skinned tribes that wiped out the Nephites, whose history Smith's Book of Mormon revealed to believers.

Young's gathering of Zion intersected the history of May Lewis's family in Wales and Denmark. Church missionaries made converts of her parents and grandparents in the 1850s. The church missionaries first proselytized in the British Isles in the 1830s as Smith moved his church to Missouri then Nauvoo. Missionaries went off to Denmark after the relocation to Salt Lake City.[23]

Brigham Young was among the first elders sent to Britain. They relied on evangelism infused with a compelling socioeconomic analysis. They had no ties to the British ruling and business classes nor its rampaging capitalism that left so many people poor, sick, and with little hope for improving their lives.

The missionaries "unflinchingly lamented the poverty of the laboring classes, denounced the monarchy's conspicuous consumption, and promised their converts land and employment in Illinois," noted historian John Turner. While on a mission to Herefordshire, Brigham Young reported to his colleagues in America that "[a]lmost without exception it is the poor that receive the gospel."[24]

Morgan Lewis, May's uncle, was the first member of the family to join the faith. He was a young man, 24 years old, and working in an iron foundry when the missionaries found him. Daniel Lewis, my great grandfather, joined the church several years later. He was baptized in October 1854. By then the Lewis brothers were coal miners; Morgan an expert blaster.[25] Their mining experience made it easier to find employment when they emigrated to America.

Morgan, his wife Mary, and two other Lewis brothers left Wales with their children in February 1856. Their party joined nearly 460 faithful Mormons who sailed from Liverpool on a clipper ship, the *Caravan*. They reached New York a month later.[26] Rather than joining the emigration to Utah immediately, Morgan's party made its way to Scranton, Pennsylvania to work in the coal mines there. Most of the rest of the *Caravan* saints traveled on to Iowa City and eventually walked to the Salt Lake Valley pushing and pulling handcarts.

Daniel Lewis left Liverpool later in the spring of 1856. He sailed on the *Samuel Curling* to Boston along with more than 700 other saints. By late May he had reached Scranton, where he almost immediately contracted small pox. He recovered and joined his brothers in the mines. The Lewis brothers spoke only Welsh, but Morgan's wife Mary Jane had some formal education and could translate for them well enough when needed.

It took Daniel and Morgan nearly six years to put together the nest egg they wanted to make the trek to Zion. They left Pennsylvania after a year to move to the mines in Coal Valley, Illinois. There Daniel met and courted a Welsh woman, Mary Elizabeth Davis. They were married in May 1860. Daniel was 26 years old. She was his first wife, but not his last.[27]

Two years later, they were ready to make the move to Utah. With the American Civil War raging, Daniel and Mary and Morgan and his small family departed Rock Island, Illinois by steamboat. They traveled down the Mississippi to St. Louis. On the way, the boat docked to pick up more cargo at Montrose on the Iowa side of the river. From there, they could see Nauvoo and the remains of the Mormon temple still standing in the community abandoned by Brigham Young and the majority of Joseph Smith's Mormons. Joseph's widow Emma still lived there.[28]

They arrived in St. Louis a few days later. A slave state, Missouri had remained in the Union, barely. The war forced open the divisions among the Missourians and their politicians. Shortly after it started, these divisions had erupted in skirmishes and riots in St. Louis involving unionists and secessionists. A few months later, a majority of unionist legislators impeached the newly elected governor, Claiborne Jackson, after Jackson laid plans for Missouri to secede. The unionists voted him out of office and forced him into exile.

The Confederacy controlled the river further south, but federal armies had secured control of the region that spring after a battle at Pea Ridge. General Grant had begun his campaign to capture Vicksburg and secure full federal control of the Mississippi River.

Given the circumstances, the traveling Mormons must have kept their heads down. They needed to change boats in St. Louis to travel up the Missouri River and they were uncertain how the divided city might perceive them. The church leadership in Utah had not chosen sides, though Young saw God's justice in the war. President Buchanan had sent troops to Utah in 1857 to force compliance with federal law. Though this "Mormon War" ended with few casualties, Buchanan took steps to end the Mormon theocracy by replacing Young as governor and establishing a garrison in the heights above Salt Lake City.[29]

After seven states seceded following the election of Abraham Lincoln, Young had spoken out from the Tabernacle in Utah, claiming, "There is no more a United States." He predicted the secessionists would not be able to sustain a government and referred to Lincoln as "King Abraham" weeks before his inauguration.[30] The failure to wholeheartedly support either side made Young and the church members suspect by both sides.

The Lewises must have been aware of these suspicions. They certainly knew the history of Mormon persecution in Missouri. They boarded a second steamer in St. Louis that carried them up the Missouri River to St. Joseph, where they changed boats again to get to Omaha and Florence, Nebraska. Florence had served Mormons for years as the starting point for the long walk to Zion.

There the Lewis families joined a church-sponsored wagon train that took three months to reach the Utah Territory.[31] The church by then had given up the use of handcarts and had developed the Church Train system to move emigrants efficiently across the Plains and through the Rocky Mountains. With oxen and horses difficult to get during the war years, Young directed Mormon wards and settlements in Utah to supply drivers and teams and wagons to make the trip east to meet new emigrants in Nebraska. The church trains carried an average of 3,000 immigrants to Utah Territory each year in the 1860s.[32]

SALT LAKE CITY

When the Lewises and their wagon train reached Salt Lake City in July 1862, about 8,000 people lived in the growing Mormon capital. The train proceeded to the heart of the town, Temple Square. There the new arrivals were welcomed and heard instructions from Brigham Young. Around them, they saw that the great temple was under construction. The Endowment House stood nearby along with the Old Tabernacle and Young's family compound with its large house for his many wives and a schoolhouse for his children.

They reached Zion when the protective isolation of the church's "mountain fastness" was eroding. The Pacific Railway Act became law that July, authorizing construction of the transcontinental railroad. Telegraph wires already had supplanted the short-lived Pony Express.

"We have several times had in print here in the afternoon news of events transpired in Washington in the forenoon," Young told George Q. Cannon in a letter sent to the church apostle presiding over the European Mission.[33]

Young took advantage of the influx of emigrants to buttress the church's hold on the region, sending many to outlying settlements. He was deeply involved in immigration planning and made sure the new arrivals were immediately involved in their new communities.

"Brigham gave them a steady stream of practical advice, both by sermon and by letters of instruction. This had to do not only with the care of livestock and crops but how to keep house, cook meat, bake bread, train girls to be good wives, and how to wash and dress children," church historian Leonard Arrington wrote.

Welcoming committees provided places for the emigrants to stay. Morgan and Daniel Lewis were introduced to Samuel Hoyt, whom Young had directed to build a flour mill at Unionville in the Weber River

Valley. (The town later was renamed Hoytsville.) Hoyt told the Lewises that he could not afford to pay them cash for their labor but promised food for their families and livestock when they established their own farms.

The Lewis brothers agreed to the arrangement.[34] Before heading back up Parley's Canyon to Unionville, however, Daniel Lewis and his Illinois bride Mary Davis went to the Endowment House for the temple marriage that church doctrine assured them would keep their family together through their earthly lives and after death.[35]

The Weber River Valley offered Mormon settlers excellent land with plenty of water for livestock and irrigation, and timber for construction. It also brought them into the lives of two native tribes, the Shoshone and the Utes. Both tribes traveled through the valley in their annual migrations. They were a significant presence. One early local history said some of the Shoshone encampments included as many as 1,500 people.

"The Settlers were compelled to keep close watch on their cattle and horses but as a rule the Indians were very friendly," one early settler of the valley recalled.[36]

The Old Boss promoted a policy intended to avoid conflicts with the tribes. He urged settlers to keep food and other supplies on hand. " ... [I]t is better and cheaper to feed and clothe the Indians, than to fight them."[37]

David S. Neel's grandfather John Neel and his wife Clemency knew of the nomadic lives of the Utes and Shoshones, having moved their family to the Weber River Valley in 1860. They had been directed there by Brigham Young along with a group that included at least 17 other Mormon men and their families.[38] The Neels settled on a farm near Peoa.

It was another of many moves John Neel made for his church and for his family. He and his wife were early adherents to the church and had settled first in Missouri, then followed Smith to Nauvoo. They had a home in Carthage in 1844 when Joseph Smith and his brother Hyrum were killed. Clemency had worked in Hyrum's home.[39]

They abandoned Carthage and returned to Missouri. In 1855, when the call to gather in the new Mormon Zion proved irresistible, the Neels joined the Hindley company, a wagon train that followed the Mormon Trail to Salt Lake City over the summer. The company arrived in September.

John and Clemency Neel's own trail over the following six years can be traced by the births of three daughters: Romania Deseret born in Ogden in March 1857; Rachel Clemency born in Little Cottonwood in February 1860, and, finally, Mary Willmirth born in Peoa in June 1861.[40]

Many Mormon men were urged to enter into the covenant of plural marriage. Daniel Lewis and his wife Mary became polygamists in 1866 when he married a second wife who would become my great grandmother. John Neel never took an additional wife, but one of his sons did. John Austin Neel became a polygamist when he married my great grandmother in early 1870.

CHAPTER SEVEN

Exaltation? Or marriage overdone?

Frontier politics, financial crises, gun fights and violence drove the Mormon church's migration from New York to Ohio, Missouri, and Illinois. People already living in the frontier states feared the political clout of a sudden flood of Mormons into their sparsely populated counties. They believed the Mormons would vote in a block as directed by Smith and other leaders to take power. They weren't wrong.

Many couldn't abide Smith's visions and considered the Book of Mormon heresy. To them, the church was a cult, with its members following an authoritarian, charismatic leader promoting false religious ideas. Smith's advocacy of polygamy stretched Mormon doctrine far outside the American mainstream's ideas of marriage and society. Most Americans were Protestant Christians and many of them followed social mores inherited from the Puritans. Polygamy made the Mormons pariahs in America. It shaped their lives, including the lives of my grandparents.

God delivered "the new and everlasting covenant" of eternal marriage to Smith in a vision July 12, 1843. In the stilted language Smith used in his accounts of his visions, God explained why Old Testament figures like Moses and Abraham righteously lived with many wives and concubines. The covenant, Smith told his followers, ensured to Abraham that "his seed and the fruit of his loins" would live with him "both in the world and out of the world ... as innumerable as the stars; or if ye were to count the sand upon the seashore ye could not number."

This was the revelation that Smith publicly denied during his disastrous dispute in Nauvoo. It put Smith and his church at odds with the country but in some aspects reflected the 19th century cultural view of women in the U.S. and most of the rest of the world . A married woman lived under control of her husband with few legal rights. She nevertheless retained some agency. God said as much in the vision given Smith, saying women had to be willing participants in the covenant.

" ... if any man espouse a virgin, and desire to espouse another, and the first give her consent, and if he espouse the second, and they are virgins, and have vowed to no other man, then is he justified; he cannot commit adultery for they are given unto him; for he cannot commit adultery with that that belongeth unto him and to no one else."

So the first wife has to agree to add a second to the marriage. It's a marriage that requires consenting adults, but there's a kicker. A wife could oppose adding a particular woman to the marriage but she could not dismiss the principle without suffering the severest penalty. "... and if ye abide not that covenant, then are ye damned; for no one can reject this covenant and be permitted to enter my glory," Smith was told by God. Smith's wife Emma may have been the first woman to hear of the revealed covenant. In the revelation to her husband, God included a message for her.

"I command mine handmaid, Emma Smith, to abide and cleave unto my servant Joseph and to none else. But if she will not abide this commandment she shall be destroyed, saith the Lord."

The revelation promised "exaltation' and an afterlife in the presence of God. The covenant entered church doctrine as the "plurality of wives." Others called it polygamy and adultery, one of the "twin relics of barbarism" decried by the Republican Party platform in 1856.[41]

Though rumors and stories about the revelation and Mormons following their gospel swirled inside and outside Mormon circles, church leaders did not publicly acknowledge plural marriage until nearly 10 years after Smith received it. The announcement of the doctrine during a church conference in Salt Lake City thrilled some members. Hosea Stout, a former Danite who had served as one of Smith's bodyguards in Nauvoo, wrote after the conference that the Saints now could "publickly declare the true and greatest principle of our holy religion."[42]

Mormons knew this doctrine opened a chasm between them and other Christian faiths in the country. It produced much of the tension and conflict in its relations with non-Mormon America that lasted more than a half century.

The church, its socialistic communities, and especially polygamy fascinated Americans and people around the world. Unusual religious practices attract gawkers. Amish and Hutterite communities arouse curiosity but the tourists they attract generally do not see their practices as abhorrent and a threat to the rest of society.

National politicians, journalists, and foreign observers made their way to the Salt Lake valley in the 1850s to see Young's theocracy for themselves. In the late 1860s, travel writers rode the new continental railway to Ogden, then went by coach to Salt Lake City to see polygamy in practice. Images of Brigham Young's three-story Lion House, built in 1856 with a separate room for each wife, were widely circulated.[43]

Thomas Kane, long a political ally of the Mormons and a friend of Brigham Young, took his wife Sarah Wood Kane to see the church president in 1872. On their way to the prophet's winter home in St. George, they toured communities and stayed with local families. Sarah Kane kept notes of the visits. Two years later, her impressions were published as a book titled *Twelve Mormon Homes Visited in Succession on a Journey through Utah to Arizona*. The book was meant to show Mormon households more favorably than other depictions.

In a description of one household, Kane noted that young Mormon girls often worked as servants in other homes and sometimes married their masters, "A nice possibility for the wife hiring 'help' to keep before her eye!" Kane noted not so coyly.

"I met one woman who had claimed from her mistress the fulfillment of a jesting promise — that if she serve her faithfully for seven years, she would give her to her husband to wife. At the end of the seven years, she jilted a man to whom she was affianced, recalled the forgotten promise to her mistress's mind, and became her master's plural wife. There was no question of affection on either side. I believe she merely wished to share in his glory in heaven …."

The young woman, who "angled for a rich man quite as much as if she had not been a Saint," did not deserve sympathy, she wrote. Instead, Kane called for empathy for women who enter polygamy because of their commitment to their church and its doctrines. She related the story of Delia J., "the wife of a man double her age."

"Of her the first wife said to me, 'Delia is the blessing of my life. It is true that she has had trouble in polygamy. She could not bring her mind for a long time to see it to be her duty. But she is reconciled now. I thank the Lord every day that now that I am infirm, Brother Samuel and his health and comfort are attended to as he is growing old.'"

Sarah Kane thought Delia might find greater happiness with "a husband worthy of her," but she also saw more in Delia and her deep faith. The young plural wife spoke earnestly and described her belief "of polygamy as a divine institution, and [she] rejected with horror the solution of the Mormon difficulty which I advocated: that Congress should forbid any further polygamous marriages, but legalize those that already existed."

The doctrine had to be followed "to be assured of my position in God's estimation," Delia said. "If polygamy is the Lord's order, we must carry it out in spite of human laws and persecutions." Kane's proposal to resolve the "Mormon difficulty" would require Delia to "admit, as I should be admitting, that all I have sacrificed has not been for God's sake! I should feel as if I were agreeing to look upon my past life as a — as a worthless woman's — upon which I had never had His blessing. I'd rather die!"

"How I detested her husband as she spoke!" Kane wrote. Delia's husband had more than a half dozen wives. "I felt sure he could not believe that that was a divine ordinance which sacrificed those women's lives to his."[44]

In her effort to portray Mormon family life favorably, Kane could not suppress her view of polygamy's effect on women and society. In comparison to the voices of others who could not abide the practice, however, Kane's opinions sound almost accepting. Bill Nye, a Wyoming newspaperman who by the late 1880s had become one of the nation's more famous humorists, wrote scalding criticism of the church and its leaders that revealed other aspects of the debate of its religious practices. He described the difficulties facing non-Mormons — Gentiles in the eyes of church members — living in Utah, particularly federal appointees and journalists.

"Gov. Murray, the gritty Gentile governor of Utah, would be noticed in a crowd," Nye wrote of the heavily bearded Murray in his book *Remarks*. President Rutherford Hayes appointed Murray governor of the Utah territory in 1880.[45]

"He was called fine looking in Kentucky," Nye wrote, "but the narrow-chested apostle of the abnormally connubial creed does not see anything pretty about him ... only those who try to be Gentiles in a land of polygamous wives and anonymous white-eyed children, know how very unpopular it is."

The growing non-Mormon population in Utah regularly faced death threats, Nye claimed. "Judge Goodwin, of the *Tribune*, feels lonesome if he gets through the day without a poorly spelled, splattered, daubed and profane valentine threatening his life," Nye said of the editor of the Salt Lake newspaper.

"The last time I saw him he showed me a few of them. They generally referred to him as a blankety blank 'skunk,' and a 'hound of hell.'"[46]

Though he used humor to attack the polygamists, Nye made certain his readers did not miss what he saw as the forbidding side of the church.

"Matrimony is a good thing, but it can be overdone," is a funny line from *Remarks*. He sharpened his tone when he contended that wealthy polygamists like Young could provide separate homes or a suite of rooms for their wives, keeping their intimate lives private. Not so for those in poorer households. In the houses of poor Mormons, space had to be shared, he charged, leading to "the aggregation of vice and depravity ..."

Nye feared that the church's successful development of the territory would obscure the reality he saw. He dipped his pen into contemptuous ink to describe church leaders and the people who crossed the ocean to join them.

"With the wonderful music of the great organ at the tabernacle sounding in your ears, and the lofty temple nearby towering to the sky, you say to yourself, there is, after all, something solemn and impressive in all this; but when a greasy apostle in an alapaca duster, takes his place behind the elevated desk, and with bad grammar and slangy sentences, asks God in a businesslike way to bless this buzzing mass of unclean, low-browed barbarous scum of all foreign countries, and the white trash and criminals of our own, you find no reverence, and no religious awe.

"The same mercenary, heartless lunacy that runs through the sickly plagiarism of the Book of Mormon, pervades all this, and instead of the odor of sanctity you notice the flavor of bilge water, and the emigrant's own hailing sign, the all-pervading fragrance of the steerage."[47]

Poets and mystery writers took up the Mormon subject and considered the satisfactions and the abuses attributed to Mormon polygamy. In Rudyard Kipling's poem "The Betrothed," the narrator ponders his box of cigars and laments a potential bride who has demanded that he give up cigar smoking.

> *Open the old cigar-box — let me consider a while.*
> *Here is a mild Manila — there is a wifely smile.*
> *Which is the better portion — bondage bought with a ring,*
> *Or a harem of dusky beauties fifty tied in a string? ...*
> *I will scent 'em with best vanilla, with tea will I temper their hides,*
> *And the Moor and the Mormon shall envy,*
> *Who read of the tale of my brides.*

In 1887, a year before one of my great grandfathers was imprisoned for having two wives, Arthur Conan Doyle published *A Study in Scarlet*, the novel that introduced the world to the detective Sherlock Holmes and his partner Dr. Watson. It is a dark portrait of Mormon polygamy. Holmes investigates the murder in London of a Cleveland businessman and his male secretary. He ultimately deduces that the murder is a revenge killing by a forlorn Nevadan who lost his fiancé to the lustful polygamists of Utah. Doyle described a Mormon society in the 1860s as one that enjoyed prosperity because the industrious saints made the desert bloom. But he also portrayed a theocratic state that dominated the region. Those who questioned church doctrine did so at their peril.

The book casts Brigham Young as a leader who demanded obedience and enforced his will with violence carried out by the Danites, described as a secret vigilante society that spied on apostates and anyone else who dared question church directives.

First-hand accounts like Kane's and others far more critical, along with Doyle's and other fictional tales, buttressed enemies and critics of the church who demanded that Washington end polygamy. It took most of the last half of the 19th century to get it done.

The Mormons fought back in the press, in the halls of Congress, in the courts and by engaging with the women's rights movement. Young used the *Deseret News*, the church-owned newspaper, to massage the Mormons' public image in the minds of both members and Gentiles. Church women joined the national suffrage movement when Susan B. Anthony and Elizabeth Cady Stanton accepted polygamous wives as allies.[48] Through it all, Young and the prophets who succeeded him refused to abandon the practice of the most controversial doctrine of their faith, believing that the impending Second Coming would free them from all their critics and enemies.

Two short years after the Mormons' arrival in the Great Basin, Young launched a drive to convince Congress to recognize a State of Deseret. Church leaders organized elections in 1849 that tapped Young as governor, of course, and established a General Assembly. The Assembly organized the political and legal systems, and in 1851 incorporated the Church of Jesus Christ of Latter-day Saints, authorizing the church to solemnize marriage in accordance with its doctrine.[49] The move effectively legalized polygamy a year before the church publicly acknowledged the practice.

Young sent lobbyists to Washington to push for statehood. Unfortunately for Young and his representatives, the bitter national debate over slavery and whether it would be extended into the West overwhelmed their efforts. Deseret was lost forever in the Compromise of 1850.

Backed by President Millard Fillmore, the compromise postponed the Civil War for another 10 years. Under it, the national government accepted California as a free state, abolished slavery in the District of

Columbia, and created the Utah and New Mexico territories with no restrictions on slavery. In a concession to the Mormons, President Fillmore appointed Young to serve as governor of the Utah Territory. He could have named a supporter of his own Whig party.

Tension over polygamy and the church's domination of the territory's secular life continued through the 1850s. The Mormons chafed under federally appointed judges and other administrators sent to Salt Lake. They considered many of them corrupt — in certain cases with justification. In March 1857, the Utah territorial legislature sent a memorial to newly inaugurated President James Buchanan promising to force out territorial officials the legislature believed "corrupt demagogues."

The Buchanan administration took the memorial as a declaration of rebellion. In May, the President ordered an army of 2,500 soldiers to escort a new territorial governor to Utah to replace Young. The Old Boss said his people should prepare for conflict. The "Mormon War" lasted just under a year. It consisted mostly of guerrilla actions with Mormon militia leaders directing raids on army supply trains. There were relatively few casualties on either side but many Mormons were displaced. In the spring of 1858, Young ordered the abandonment of Salt Lake City and an evacuation to Provo, 45 miles south. When the army entered the territorial capital, the soldiers found an empty city.

Ultimately, peace was made. President Buchanan pardoned Young and others in return for their acceptance of federal sovereignty and the presence of federal troops in Utah. But the Mormons did not give up polygamy and Young remained the real power in Utah.[50]

European emigrants continued to make their way to Zion and built homes and communities for their growing families. Many, including my great grandfathers Daniel Lewis and John Austin Neel, added plural wives over the next three decades. They did so despite growing federal pressure to end polygamy.

In Washington, the newly empowered Republicans passed the first federal law aimed at dismantling Mormon polygamy in 1861. Lincoln signed the Morrill Anti-Bigamy Act in 1862. It threatened polygamists with imprisonment and undercut church economic power by declaring that no territorial religious corporation could own more than $50,000 in property. In what seemed a tacit agreement with Young to keep the Mormons out of the Civil War, Lincoln chose not to enforce the law. It instead became a template for other bills directed at the church and its marriage doctrine.

Church leaders argued that the U.S. Constitution's First Amendment guarantees of religious freedom protected their doctrine. The Supreme Court determined otherwise in 1879 when it ruled the Congress could not prohibit the belief in polygamy but could outlaw its practice.[51]

More restrictive laws followed. In March 1882, the Edmunds Anti-Polygamy Act made polygamy a felony in U.S. territories and declared unlawful cohabitation a misdemeanor. Enforcement was aimed at men, not women. Leading men of the church were targeted. Rudger Clawson, later a member of the Quorum of the Twelve Apostles, served more than three years in the territorial prison after being convicted of polygamy in 1882.

Not all the legal pressure came from Washington. In Idaho, the territorial legislature passed its own anti-polygamy law in 1884 that specifically targeted Mormons and their church. It required all voters to take a Test Oath that would "disfranchise all voters who believed in plural marriage, practice it, or belong to an organization teaching this doctrine." Anti-Mormon juries assured convictions. The law forced some men to abandon the church to maintain their right to vote.[52]

The same year, Congress passed the most far-reaching of its anti-polygamy laws, the Edmunds-Tucker Act. Its sweeping provisions disincorporated the church, ended the Perpetual Emigration Fund, took the vote away from Utah women, and required men registering to vote to swear an oath in which they, if married, named their legal wife and promised to obey federal anti-bigamy laws. The act also restructured the territorial system of education. It abolished the office of the territorial superintendent of schools, required the territorial supreme court to appoint a commissioner of schools, prohibited school use of sectarian books, and required filing an annual report that listed the number of Mormon and non-Mormon students attending the schools, and the number of teachers who were Mormon or non-Mormon.

Federal officials struck at the heart of the church six years later when they threatened to confiscate its temples by declaring them private, not public places of worship because the temples were open only to Mormons that church officials judged worthy to enter them.[53]

Facing the loss of its holy temples, the church finally caved. Church President Wilford Woodruff wrote a manifesto on Sept. 24, 1890, and publicized it the next day. It announced his intention to submit to federal anti-polygamy laws. Woodruff promised "to use my influence with the members of the Church over which I preside to have them do likewise." The manifesto was read to attendees of the church's General Conference in October and was unanimously sustained by them, sanctioning the manifesto as official policy.[54]

It was a bitter pill for the church and for Woodruff personally. He had joined the church in 1833 and had worked directly with Joseph Smith as one of his most trusted men. Woodruff practiced plural marriage for decades and was one of numerous church leaders who went underground in the 1880s to avoid prosecution. He married 10 women. Five of those marriages ended in divorce.[55]

CHAPTER EIGHT

Faith and polygamy in the Lewis and Neel families

Woodruff issued his manifesto as David Stevens Neel and Carrie May Lewis were growing into adolescence in polygamous families in neighboring communities in the Weber Valley. May would have been 11 years old and David just nine.

The Edmunds-Tucker Act had had little personal effect on the Neel family. David's father died the year before it was passed. May's family did not escape its reach.

Both families knew the practice put them at odds with most Gentile Americans. As the national debate continued, they could track the latest swirls in the newspapers and hear the assessments of church leaders in their Sunday meetings. The debate moved into the center of their lives when they entered plural marriage.

Daniel Lewis married his second wife, my great grandmother, in late 1866. Karen Marie Sorensen was a Dane. She had joined the church three years earlier when missionaries preached to her family living in Denmark's Zealand region, west of Copenhagen. She grew up on the family's five-acre farm in Logtved where her father was a cabinet maker. They kept chickens, a few sheep, and three cows.

As a young girl, she attended a school several miles away, often carrying her younger brother Solon on her back. Her education ended at age 12 when she hired out as a farm hand. She milked cows, tended other animals, and helped in the farmer's home as a cook. The missionaries baptized her when she was about 20.

Her sister Christiane had married another Mormon convert, Lars Hansen. The two of them answered their faith's call to Zion in 1861. Karen Marie and the rest of her family decided to emigrate and departed in the spring of 1864. European politics may have spurred the timing of the decision. The Dano-Prussian War had erupted in February when German and Austrian armies invaded the Jutland peninsula.

Their father Jorgen Sorensen sold his small farm and other goods to finance their passage from Scandinavia to England and New York. They also had to pay for their rail and steamer travel from New York to the head of the Mormon Trail in Nebraska. Karen Marie gave up her savings from her work with the wealthy farmer to help cover the costs.[56]

Church elders chartered the vessels and made rail travel arrangements. "They fixed the price for each to pay for his or her passage and to them was the money paid and the people trusted all in their hands accepting such as they provided for them. If any should have asked for to know any of the particulars they would have been told it was not their business, and if any had complained they would have been considered in a spirit of apostacy," one of the emigrants, Hans Nielsen Hansen, wrote later.

The Mormon elders were in charge of hundreds of emigrants who sailed from Copenhagen to England on two ships that landed in Hull and Grimsby, both communities on the Humber estuary. (Fans of the novel Robinson Crusoe may recall that Crusoe embarked on his fictional journey from the Humber.) The Danes found themselves in a strange land among people whose language they could not understand. They were sheltered in a warehouse in Hull for a week or so, then traveled by rail to Liverpool. There they had no shelter and spent the night sleeping on stone pavement near the docks.

"It was poor accommodations for human beings, but then we were only Mormon emigrants and I did not hear of much complaints," Hansen wrote of the trip. "It was expected that the road to Zion would be a difficult one ...."

In Liverpool, they comprised nearly a thousand Saints emigrating from Scandinavia and Great Britain. All boarded the clipper ship

Monarch of the Sea April 23. Then they waited as the ship's owners put together a crew. Sailors were scarce in part because the U.S. Navy was paying bounties to induce them to join the service during the Civil War. The *Monarch's* departure was delayed until April 28, 1864.[57]

The Saints had high hopes, however. One of Karen Marie's fellow Danish passengers on the Monarch reveled in his prospects. Hans Nielsen Hansen was just 13 when he made the voyage.

"I was happy in what I considered the prospects before me, not only in the thoughts which my religion and hope in God now inspired, but the privilege of going to other parts (of) the world to see countries and people of who I had read in school studies I considered a great treat," Hansen wrote years later.

"I was looking on the bright side of all these things, not considering as I then could not conceive of the hardships and trials encountered upon a journey of over six thousand miles in those days, and especially with the accommodations furnished the Mormon emigration."

Hansen was convinced of the truth of the LDS gospel. Yet he knew that many of the new Mormons had questions about some aspects of the faith, particularly plural marriage.

"Polygamy at that time was not denied but was not mentioned by the elders unless brought up by others," he wrote, "when they had to try to defend it."

If any of the new converts said they could not believe in it, "they were told: do not trouble yourself about it, it is a holy principle if you can not see into it now, wait till you get to Zion, and all will come out right."[58]

They endured a rough voyage. The ship did not have the capacity to cook food for so many passengers. Families were told to bring their own pots to have the food cooked in turn. But the rule of taking turns "was not observed," Hansen wrote. "The stronger crowded their dish to the front, while that belonging to the weaker and more modest ones was behind."

Meat stored in barrels stunk and could be smelled from one end of the ship to the other. When sickness struck, the lack of palatable food "was very trying as nothing could be had such as would tempt the appetite of the afflicted one," he recalled.

Karen Marie remembered being seasick the entire voyage. Sickness killed many children. Hansen's eldest brother was among them. Hansen said measles or scarlet fever killed up to 60 children. Others attributed the deaths to scurvy.[59]

An infestation of lice plagued the ship. Passengers who tried to clean their clothing or bedding and dry them on deck risked losing goods. "[T]he sailors would without the least provocation throw the same overboard as soon as they came across it."

The difficulties tried everyone. Hansen noted that "all in our company were not Saint-like in their conduct one toward another" and some of the churchmen guiding them "who they had learned to look up to as the servants of Good ... were not such men they believed them to be."

A few of the emigrants who had left family members and friends behind in Scandinavia expressed regret at their decision, he remembered.

The ship battled strong headwinds for much of the voyage and passed "very large icebergs" off Newfoundland before reaching New York City after 40 days at sea. The *Monarch of the Sea* landed at The Battery on June 3. The emigrants were taken through Castle Garden, the American immigration station active then.[60]

The day after processing at the bustling Garden, the emigrants boarded a steamship that carried them up the Hudson River to Albany. There they boarded a series of trains that took them to St. Joseph on the Missouri River.

The first train had "cushioned seats and comfortable arrangements found in European railway car[s]," Hansen wrote. His family enjoyed the ride and scenery they passed but found space limited, making sleeping cramped and uncomfortable. The train often sidetracked for other trains, delays that could last for hours.

When the Saints were required to change to a second train, they found themselves loaded into box cars with hard seats in place. "Our condition was uncomfortable on the first train but it became tenfold worse in box cars," Hansen recalled.

They reached Chicago and changed to a third train, made up of passenger cars, that took them to Quincy, Illinois. There the company was offered another train of box cars. They refused and waited a day for a train of passenger cars to carry them on to St. Joseph. Altogether, the trains took about a week to reach St. Joseph, where they were "dumped off not at a depot but near the Missouri River."

Hansen realized later that the Civil War was the reason for the passenger trains made up of box cars. "I think now it may be that the railroad company had been furnishing cars for the transporting of soldiers to the battlefield and that the freight cars, fitted up with temporary board seats ... had been for such used transportation."

At St. Joseph, the emigrants had reached the end of the line for train travel. A river steamer carried them up the Missouri the last hundred miles to reach the newly established start of the Mormon Trail at Wyoming, Nebraska. Their swift travel in cars racing over rails and boats plodding up river had ended. The rest of the journey would be on foot or in wagons pulled by livestock.

In previous years, the Mormon emigrants had traveled about 40 miles further upriver to Florence, just four miles short of Omaha. Hansen believed the new starting point at Wyoming was made to prevent contact with apostate Mormons living around Florence and Omaha.

Church leaders feared "contact with these apostates, as they might bring them such information as would not be desirable for them to obtain, thus leading perhaps others to apostatize," Hansen speculated.

At last able to spread out, the emigrants stopped to wash their bodies and their clothes to rid themselves of the lice that troubled them in the crowded ships and trains.

The Saints separated into different types of traveling companies before beginning the trek across Nebraska. Emigrants with the means to buy teams and wagons left ahead of those without money. Karen Marie's family traveled with one of the companies that departed earlier. She walked the entire route, riding on a horse or climbing into a wagon only at stream crossings too deep to cross on foot. They arrived in Salt Lake City in early September.

Hans Hansen's group did not reach Utah until October. They

traveled with one of Brigham Young's church trains made of wagons pulled by oxen. Out of money, Hansen's family and others signed notes agreeing to pay $60 per person for transportation to Utah. These notes drew interest of 10 percent that was compounded. It was "an expensive privilege" and many did not understand what they had signed.

"The masses coming from foreign lands of course could not speak nor read English, but they asked no questions but did as they were told, and no one explained what their signature meant," he wrote.[61]

Once in Utah, Karen Marie's father and mother decided to put down roots in the Weber River Valley. Her sister Christiane and husband Lars already lived there along with many other Danish emigrants sent to the valley a few years earlier by the Old Boss. Karen Marie stayed there with her sister only until she found employment in Salt Lake City. She took a job as a servant in the home of John and Cynthia Clawson. As she had in Denmark, she cooked and handled other household tasks. Her life settled into a routine that included visits to her sister and her parents.

She also became a mother. At some point after leaving Copenhagen, Karen Marie gave birth to a son. Laura Lewis Stratton, a granddaughter who wrote a history of Daniel Lewis, concluded the pregnancy and birth occurred in Salt Lake City.[62] As an unwed mother with a very young child, her prospects in Utah were dimmed. "As a single mother ... she needed the support of a husband, but it was difficult finding a worthy man that she liked," according to Gary Young, another family historian.

In the summer of 1866, Karen Marie made a trip to see her parents, who worked a farm near her sister's place. Someone introduced her to Daniel Lewis and his wife Mary Elizabeth. The religious culture they embraced asserted itself. Church leaders had asked Lewis to consider taking a second wife. Childless after four years of marriage, Mary Elizabeth agreed to enter plural marriage.[63]

Daniel Lewis feared having no descendants, without which the greatest glories promised by his faith might be denied him. Karen Marie could provide them. Lewis asked her to become his second wife. She asked him to seek permission from her father Jorgen.

Lewis had a demand of his own. He either did not want the responsibility of her son or simply did not want another man's child. He told Karen Marie he would have her but not the baby boy.[64]

The young mother took the proposal to her family. Her sister Christiane and her husband said they would raise Karen Marie's son. The decision haunted her, a regret that her own grandchildren realized only years later when they learned of John's existence and understood that it explained her request that when she died, she should not be buried near Lewis.

Less than five months after their introduction that summer, Daniel Lewis and Karen Marie were married in the Endowment House in Salt Lake City. They returned to the Weber Valley, where they lived with their neighbors in a fort built near Peoa for protection during the early years of the Black Hawk War. People stayed in the fort at night and worked their farms during the day. Karen Marie gave birth to their first child there in May 1868. They named her Mary Elizabeth after Lewis's first wife, but her family called her Lizzie.

The two wives blended in the family as two Marys, Mary D and Mary K, and were known throughout the community by those names. Even the local newspaper referred to Karen Marie as Mary K.[65] After moving out of the fort, Daniel provided separate homes for his two wives. Daniel and Mary K lived on their farm near present-day Marion, Utah in a slab shanty with a sod roof and a dirt floor for another eight years. Mary D lived in a house about three miles away.

More children arrived every two years: Daniel in 1870. Sarah in 1872 and Morgan in July, 1874. But the risks of childhood overwhelmed the family. The infant Morgan perished in October. Their fifth child Clara had broken the two-year birthing pattern, arriving in the spring of 1875. Like Morgan, she did not live long, however; whooping cough killed Clara just five months later. Eleanor, their sixth child, survived infancy but not early childhood.

After Clara's death, Daniel had moved Mary K into a lean-to that wasn't much better than the shanty, but he expanded it, eventually, into a house built with milled lumber with floors and bedrooms upstairs. They needed the room. Over 15 years, Mary K gave birth to nine children, including Carrie May, my grandmother, on May 17, 1879. Her brother Eleazor was born one month after the death of four-year-old Eleanor on

May 18, 1881. Daniel and Mary K's last child, Edward, arrived two years later in May, 1883.

The six surviving children grew up in a household and community that spoke Welsh, Danish, and improving English. The two wives shared some of the responsibilities of motherhood, though with Mary D three miles away and Daniel working the farm, Mary K handled most of the child rearing. Lizzie recalled starting school at seven, after "I learned my ABC's on our Charter Oak stove." Polygamy was disguised if not denied. The children referred to Mary D as Aunt Mary. "I used to be with her quite a lot when I was a little girl," Lizzie recalled.

Mary D's house offered Lizzie respite from the crowding with her siblings during her teen years. "I think I was somewhat spoiled," Elizabeth said in the autobiographical sketch she wrote decades later. "Father was always so good to me, and Aunt Mary and Mother both used to give me my own way a lot as I can see now."

Her auntie's house provided an option after her school in Marion closed when she was 13. "I had to go to Kamas to go to school," she recalled. "Parents used to pay so much for each quarter and there were not enough students to keep it open. So I went to stay with Aunt Mary Davis and go to school at Kamas the rest of my school years until I was fifteen."[66]

A NEEL HOUSE FULL OF FEMALES

Like his future wife, my grandfather David S. Neel, was born into a polygamous household. His mother Ellen Christiana Stevens married his father John Austin Neel in February 1870. She was Neel's second wife and the daughter of William Stevens, a prosperous farmer and grist mill owner who lived in Oakley. The Neels farmed in Peoa, only a few miles from Oakley, Marion, and Kamas.

John Austin had married his first wife, Theresa Amelia Quarm, in 1866 on the same day that Daniel Lewis became a polygamist by marrying Karen Marie. Both marriages were made in the Endowment House in Salt Lake City. A year and a half after taking his second wife,

John Austin married Ellen's sister Emeline. Together, Neel's three wives bore at least nine children. Before my grandfather David was born in 1881, Ellen had five other boys: William, 1871; John, 1872; James, 1874; Charles, 1877; and Frank, 1879. Church records suggest there may have been a seventh child, T.E. Neel, who was born and died in 1876.[67]

Heaven — or Nature — was raining children on the family during the early 1870s. Emaline bore three daughters: Bertha, 1873; Eldora, 1874, and Theresa Emaline, 1875. (At least one church record shows that Theresa Quarm was the mother of Theresa Emeline.)[68]

These three wives, their children, and John Austin shared a home into the late 1870s. Then some issue, a personality conflict, a financial strain, a too-crowded house, became too much for the gospel gravity holding it together. Emeline decided to leave the family. She secured a temple divorce from Neel, severing their eternal bond. There was nothing unusual about Emeline's decision. No-fault divorce was easily available in the territory from the 1850s. After divorce, fathers were expected to support their children.[69]

Although she was finished with Neel, Emeline did not lose her faith in the doctrine of plural marriage. She joined another polygamous household when she married Daniel Bigelow in Salt Lake City in 1882. Together, they brought another seven children into the world. [70]

Bigelow had married his first wife, Permelia Meacham, in 1865. After marrying Emeline, he waited another 16 years before taking a third wife, Clara Ostensen, despite the intense federal pressure against polygamy. Bigelow and his wives ardently followed the gospel's directive to give more souls the opportunity for life on Earth. In addition to Emeline's seven children, Clara bore eight, and Permelia six.[71]

John Austin Neel died in Peoa in March 1883. Death took him before the federal authorities in Utah ramped up their pursuit of polygamists across the state. He was 38 years old. His eldest son was just 11 years old; the youngest, David, was still less than two. The remaining wives, Ellen and Theresa, carried on at the farm with their six boys. There must have been some help from their pioneer community and their church. Perhaps their deceased husband's two brothers, Joshua Wriley and John Marion, helped with the farming, though by the next decade both of them were living in poverty and struggling with serious legal problems.

The settlers worked hard to build Peoa and the other communities along the Weber River. They dug canals and ditches to irrigate their farms and built church houses to worship in. They made businesses, schools, cemeteries, and amusement halls. The Mormons made way for entertainment in remote Utah from the beginnings of their settlement there. They put up theaters and dance halls across the territory including in the Weber River Valley where local musicians played the tunes that delighted the dancing settlers.

"A crowd would often go to Rockport and Wanship by ox team for dancing," Jessie Stevens wrote for the Daughters of the Utah Pioneers 1947 history of Summit County. "It was necessary for them to leave [home] before sundown and the sun would be up when they returned, as the dances continued all through the night."

In the growing communities, homes and other buildings served multiple purposes. "Oscar Wilkins had a store in his home, which was the house where A. H. Marhant now lives," Stevens wrote. "A corner of the store was destroyed by an explosion of powder at one time. Afterwards, this was repaired and used as a saloon. It was later used as a Relief Society house and was commonly called the 'Gospel Shop.'"[72]

The mines in Park City became a source of cash for the early farmers after the discovery of silver there in 1869. The mining companies needed food for their miners and hay for their livestock. The settlers, including Daniel Lewis, logged the nearby forests to provide timbers that the miners used for building tunnels. Meanwhile, promise of steady freight shipments brought the railroad up the valley from Echo to Park City in 1880. A line to Salt Lake City was completed a decade later.[73]

The mines and the railroad brought social change. For years, the Old Boss discouraged church members from pursuing the quick riches promised by an ore strike. Conversely, federal officials, including army officers at Camp Douglas outside Salt Lake City, encouraged prospecting by soldiers and others and they discovered the territory's mineral wealth. The men who came to work the mines at Park City generally were Gentiles who worshipped in other faiths. The Catholic church and other Protestant denominations established parishes in the mining town, eroding the LDS Church's monopoly on faith.

DEATH AND GHOSTLY MYSTERIES

In those days before antibiotics and vaccinations, death was a constant fact of life, always near, shared by family and neighbors, explained by their spiritual beliefs as much as by science. Children under five years old were the most vulnerable. The Lewises were among those who experienced the losses of the very young. The six Lewis children who survived early childhood lived well into the 20th century.[74]

Some people coped with these losses through their faith in an afterlife that promised heavenly reunion with their loved ones. Infant deaths sometimes were explained away with assurances that the child was "too good for this life" and left the world to wait on "the other side" for their parents and brothers and sisters to join them. Others believed encounters with the dead could occur in this life. The spirit world was simply another aspect of reality. People reported sightings of loved ones after recent deaths, as if they maintained a presence in this world as they moved into the next.

For Mormons, there was another aspect of this spiritual reality. They believed — and still believe — in visitations by immortals. Smith had his visions. Angels helped the handcart companies on the arduous trek to Zion. Others reported mysterious visitations by the Three Nephites of the Book of Mormon. The Book of Mormon, one of the church's fundamental scriptures, was translated by Joseph Smith, according to LDS theological history. The story of the Three Nephites has penetrated deeply into church culture and lore. Many LDS families tell tales of encounters with strangers who appear suddenly, bring some spiritual comfort and maybe stay for a meal, then as suddenly depart, leaving those who see them to wonder if this stranger or that one might be one of the Three.

The Book of Mormon tells the world that after Jesus left his tomb in Judea, he did not immediately ascend to heaven. Instead, he went to the Americas and established his church there. The Three Nephites were among the twelve disciples that Jesus named when he ministered to their people. When Jesus asked the chosen twelve what they desired of him before he ascended to join his father, nine asked for and were granted a promise of a speedy reunion with Christ at the end of their lives.

But the remaining disciples, the Three Nephites, wanted to continue their ministries on earth until the Second Coming. Jesus blessed them as he did John the Beloved and told them they would "never taste death."[75]

The Three Nephites resumed their preaching after Jesus returned to heaven and many people received the gospel from them. Others turned against the immortal Three. They were subjected to the same social scorn and tribulation that plagued most of history's prophets. But the Three were protected by higher powers. They were imprisoned but "the prisons could not hold them, for they were rent in twain. And they were cast down into the earth; but they did smite the earth with the word of God, insomuch that by his power they were delivered out of the depths of the earth; and therefore they could not dig pits sufficient to hold them."

Other nonbelievers threw the Three into furnaces and into dens of wild beasts, but they survived unharmed. They went on preaching the gospel until all the people of the Americas accepted and joined "the church of Christ, and thus the people of that generation were blessed, according to the word of Jesus."

The account of Jesus's sojourn in the Americas and his promise to the three Nephites was written by Mormon, according to Joseph Smith. Mormon wrote his account long after that blessed generation, but Mormon said he had seen the Three Nephites himself and they had ministered to him. God forbade Mormon to name the immortals "for they are hid from the world." But he declared that the Three would continue their work among the Jews and the Gentiles, though both "shall know them not." Their preaching, Mormon said, would save many souls.

"And they are as the angels of God, and ... they can show themselves unto whatsoever man it seemeth them good."[76]

That last line lies behind the stories that Mormons tell of strangers appearing out of nowhere with assurances of good will and peace, offering a helping hand or a word of encouragement before disappearing at the edge of the yard or melting into the sagebrush, vanishing into an empty horizon.

Individual Mormon settlers may or may not have believed in ghosts or the immortal disciples, but they reported what they had seen to others and those tales were and are woven into the larger culture. The Lewis and Neal families have a few of these tales. Most are long on mystery but often short on detail.

One Lewis family story is told by Laura Stratton in her history of Daniel Lewis and his two wives. It opens with the teen-aged Mary Elizabeth waking in the middle of one night in 1884 to find Auntie Mary D's father standing at the side of her bed, looking at her. She knew he should not have been there as he was ill. She and her Auntie had stayed at his bedside that day. When Lizzie returned home, she thought he would not recover. She was correct.

"Later that morning Mary Elizabeth told her father about seeing Father Davis. He asked her what time that happened. When she told him, he said, 'Father Davis died last night just about that time.'"[77]

CHAPTER NINE

Daniel Lewis flees Utah

By 1885, the federal government, through its marshals and courts, was pressing the polygamists hard. Rudger Clawson, a future church apostle, was in the territorial prison after being convicted and sentenced to serve 42 months for polygamy and six more months for cohabitation. Church President John Taylor, Apostle George Q. Cannon, and other leaders went into hiding, relying upon a Mormon underground, a network of safe houses and spies that tracked federal marshals and warned church leaders of their approach, enabling them to escape capture.

Taylor had been severely wounded in the 1844 mob attack that martyred Joseph and Hyrum Smith in the Carthage jail. He assumed leadership of the church after Brigham Young died in August 1877. Taylor was sustained officially as the church's prophet and president three years after Young's death. [78]

After the death of the Old Boss, Cannon stood out as the most well-known Mormon in the country. He had been elected six times to serve as Utah's territorial representative in Washington. Before his political service, he filled many prominent roles for the church. He translated the Book of Mormon into the Hawaiian language while serving as the head of the Church's Hawaii mission in the early 1850s. In 1856, Young posted him in San Francisco where he edited a church newspaper set up to defend the church from the vigorous attacks of the California papers. Cannon later edited the *Deseret News*, and in 1860, Young made him a member of the Quorum of the Twelve Apostles, the elite leadership of the church. He later was elevated to serve as a counselor in the First Presidency, a select group that includes the church president and two apostles.[79]

In the Weber Valley, Daniel Lewis and others were also feeling the federal pressure. The church helped him escape it, at least temporarily. In May 1885, Lewis was called on a two-year mission to his native Wales. There he told people that he left his home just before the law closed in. His story inspired Isaac Evans to write "The Escape," a poem that the Welshman Evans dedicated to "Elder Daniel Lewis Morallsville North Kamas City, Sumit County, Utah at the time of the prosicution On the Saints for keeping the 'Celestial Law of Marriage' 1885." [*Spelling and punctuation in original.*]

> The "warning came," — while danger crept around;
>   Against the law" of God" "the rule of men"
> Came to its signee — and marshals would have bound
>   Another trusty father in the pen: —
> But at the dawn-of-day while baby sleeps, —
>   The Sainted — honest parent bids farewell
> To wife and daughter that with sorrow weeps,
>   The weight of grief — and love — no man can tell.
>
> From "Kamas" town behold the youthful Son
>   Uphold his faithful father in the flight
> From tyrants-clutches both are riding on
>   Until they pant in tears at morning light.
> The care of home is left to him, — brave boy,
>   A greater hero than a chief of war
> Of nobler aim than him — that would destroy
>   His fellow-man, — and Heaven's Peace debar.
>
> Angels was watching o'er the faithful two —
>   Those persecuted ones that shook the hands
> To separate — and brave the unjust woe

> Created by vile laws of tyrant bands;
> The Youth, — (age fifteen years) — returned home
> To care and guard the Stock — and till the land
> The father — On his "Mission" Cross'd the foam
> To far-off countries, — this was "God's Command."
>
> And they do prosper! — the noble youth that Stay
> To Labour-temporal — on that land sublime!
> And the good father — many miles away, —
> Make's sure "Great Blessings of the Coming Time!
> "The Pay"! That waits the "Faithful" that is blest
> With "power to Preach" — and also to "Baptize" —
> And "lay the hands" to bring the "Mighty Test"
> On Sinners that repent with honest guise!
>
> — *Isaac Evans (Perolau)*
> *Penrhiwceiber Glanmonganahine South Wales*
> *Great Britain*
> *(Composed, 1886)*
>
> A Supliment:
>
> A portion of notion, — and motion, — not strife;
> And a portion of wisdom is wanted through life;
> A portion of "Power" while growing in grace,
> And a portion of mercy at the end of the race.[80]

Lewis was ready for the mission. He had been very active in his church. He served in a priesthood office as a member of the twenty-second Quorum of Seventies, which required him to attend stake conferences, where he often spoke. As Evans' poem noted, he left his teen-aged son Dan in charge of the farm. It was not an easy time for the family in Utah. Daughter Lizzie, who was 16 when her father left, remembered those years as "quite hard times. We [had] very little to do with."

The "trusty father" made the journey by rail to New York and sailed from there to Liverpool. He brought little money. Missionaries of the time were expected to go into the field "without purse or scrip," depending instead on local members of the church for room and board.[81]

In Wales, the missionaries mostly walked as they carried the Gospel from community to community. Lewis kept a diary of his mission. It records arduous treks through rough country in rain and snow to meet both members and potential converts.

He also took the opportunity to look up old friends and his surviving relatives, people he had not seen for nearly 30 years. He once stopped proselytizing for a few days to stay with his stepmother and help her with her farm harvest and also to make a visit to his wife Mary D's family. Mindful of his church's precepts that place important religious responsibilities on the living to care spiritually for their ancestors, he went to his family's old church in Caio in July 1886. There Vicar Charles Chidlow provided baptismal records that Daniel intended to use after his return to Utah to conduct temple work for long-deceased members of his family.

His family and a few friends kept in touch with Daniel via letters. He depended on them for news of the family and the farm but he recorded little about this correspondence in his diary. He did, however, mention in it his worry over a letter from home in December that informed him "of sickness and hard weather at home which is quite a Sad News to me here so fare away and Wife Mary D Lewis had give her [self] to the care of a Doctor. I don't know what the consequence would be …"[82]

Lewis was appointed president of the church's Welsh Conference Mission in October 1886. The administrative work was demanding. The former coal miner, who once spoke only his native tongue, three decades later was reading and writing both Welsh and English, managing missionaries, collecting tithing and getting the revenues to British Mission headquarters in Liverpool.

His mission ended the following June. He left Wales with five other returning missionaries and a contingent of 105 emigrating Saints. Getting home took much less time than his original emigration in 1856.

No Forgiveness

The days of the Old Boss's train system were long gone. Crossing the Atlantic by steamship then traveling the rest of the way by rail from New York got Lewis to Salt Lake City on July 7, less than three weeks after boarding the *S.S. Wisconsin* in Liverpool.

There Lewis could see the progress made on the construction of the new temple and found people talking about a fire ignited by Fourth of July fireworks that damaged the Tabernacle. The returned mission director made his official report to church authorities in Salt Lake, then boarded a stage to Wanship, where his son Dan met him and took him home to the farm.[83]

The returning missionary brought home gifts for his children that included memorabilia from Queen Victoria's Golden Jubilee. "Father brought me a silver watch and chain that was the pride of my heart," Lizzie recalled. "I was the first girl to own a watch in that valley."[84]

CHAPTER TEN

It caused a breeze

The church officials who greeted Lewis on his return from Wales must have taken time to discuss the threats of federal prosecution hanging over Daniel's head as he resumed his life of plural marriage. In the Weber Valley, he would have asked local church leaders and other friends in Marion and Kamas about the continuing government pressure on them that followed passage that spring of the Edmunds-Tucker Act. Facing the inevitability of a confrontation with the territorial court, Daniel decided to prepare the family and its affairs.

Just a few days after returning to Marion, he sold chunks of his property to his two wives. Mary K bought 60 acres of his 160-acre farm for one dollar, the same price he charged for 34 acres sold to Mary D.[85] He hoped the sales would limit the cost of a conviction for cohabitation or, worse, polygamy. Newspaper articles of the time reported that many of the men who appeared in federal court attempted to avoid paying fines by pleading poverty. With little or no property, they could avoid the fine, if not the penitentiary.

Lewis decided to work his farm for a year, then turn himself over to the authorities in late summer, after the harvest. He was delaying the inevitable. His family waited along with him, knowing he would be imprisoned but uncertain of the sentence he would receive.

On Sunday, Sept. 16, 1888, he left his wives and children and traveled the fifty miles to Salt Lake City. He hoped to face the court's justice, take his punishment, and return well before spring, when he and

No Forgiveness

his son Dan would again plant the farm's crops. Carrie May was nine years old when her father left to face the federal judge. Her eldest sister Lizzie was 20; her youngest brother Ed was five.

Lewis expected a quiet court hearing when he appeared Monday morning along with other church elders charged with unlawful cohabitation. He was wrong. As Daniel Lewis and a neighbor from the valley waited in the courtroom, Apostle George Q. Cannon pulled up in front of the federal courthouse in a grand, four-horse carriage and surrendered to the marshal.

The apostle's dramatic surfacing from the Mormon underground spurred the *Salt Lake Herald* to rush an extra edition into the streets to blast the news throughout the city. The extra, the *Herald* proclaimed the next day, "probably created the greatest sensation ever produced by any similar document."[86]

"It Caused A Breeze" the headline in the *Herald* asserted. "It was but a few moments ere the whole city was astir with the news and it was eagerly discussed on all hands, those who received copies of the extra going from store to store and stating the news."

The *Deseret News* reported Cannon's unexpected surrender more formally in a sympathetic editorial church leaders hoped would assure members of their resolve by analyzing Cannon's decision and its implications for the church. The editorial was published in the *News'* evening editions on the 17th and again on the 19th.

"In surrendering to the law he has made no sacrifice of principle," the editorial asserted. "This should be distinctly understood."

The sudden appearance of Cannon, famous as the leading public defender of the church and its belief in plural marriage, was shocking because the Mormons knew that he had successfully hidden from a federal search to find him for more than two years. Cannon first had gone "underground" in February 1885, along with LDS President Taylor and other top leaders, a few months before the church sent Daniel Lewis to safety in Wales. A year later, on February 8, 1886, U.S. Marshal Edwin Ireland made Cannon the government's prime target when he put up wanted posters offering a $500 reward for information leading to the polygamist's arrest. The reward offered for information about the whereabouts of Taylor, the church prophet, pointedly was lower: $300.

The pressure pushed Taylor to move ahead with plans for another exodus of the Saints. Their first exodus from the United States gave them reprieve from the mobs and militia of Missouri and Illinois. They now looked to Mexico to put themselves beyond the reach of the marshals. Just a few days after the wanted posters went up, Cannon and others in the underground attempted to slip out of the territory. They hoped to go to Mexico to buy land for the future relocation of the church.

It was not to be. The plan was foiled after a brakeman spotted Cannon and others entering their sleeping car on the Central Pacific train carrying them out of Utah. Lawmen in Nevada were alerted and Cannon was arrested at Humboldt House, a famous eatery on the Central Pacific line some forty miles west of Winnemucca, Nevada.

A federal marshal took custody of the apostle three days later to transport him back to Salt Lake City, another rail journey during which Cannon either jumped or fell from the train. Cannon claimed he fell. He was found, dazed and his nose bleeding, and re-arrested. A company of soldiers was mustered to take him back to Salt Lake. The imposing military escort was unnecessary, his supporters claimed, and proved the extent of the government's animus against him and the Mormon Church.

Once in the territorial courtroom, Judge Charles Zane set bail at $45,000, an extraordinary sum for the time. The bail was raised, however, and Cannon was freed.[87] The money did not matter more than the church's leading spokesman. His friends feared severe punishment at the hands of Judge Zane and advised Cannon not to appear for trial.[88] Cannon jumped bail and returned to the underground. A fugitive, he avoided recapture until he presented himself in the courtroom 30 months later, surprising the judge, the community, and other elders who came to plead guilty, Daniel Lewis among them.

Cannon left the Mormon underground largely because national politics brought changes to the federal judiciary in Utah. In July 1888, President Grover Cleveland replaced Judge Zane, long known for imposing punitive sentences on polygamists, with Elliott Sanford.[89] Judge Sanford was hearing his first cohabitation cases in the Third

District Court the day that Cannon and Daniel Lewis turned themselves over to the justice system.

"In stepping forward today Brother Cannon took considerable risk. But results show his judgment was sound," the *Deseret News* observed. The self-sacrificing leader wanted to be the first "to test whether fair treatment of offenders against the anti-polygamy laws would be accorded under the new judicial regime, he has demonstrated that his expectations were correct."

The *Salt Lake Herald* extra reported that the apostle entered guilty pleas to two counts of unlawful cohabitation. Cannon first pleaded guilty to having "lived with Martha Tully Cannon and Emily Little Cannon" as his wives from July 2, 1885 to Dec. 31, 1885. Defense attorney F.S. Richards told the court that his client wanted to have his sentence pronounced immediately.

Prosecutor George Peters asked that the second indictment be considered before sentencing. Cannon then pleaded guilty to living with five wives from March 21, 1886 to Sept. 15, 1888.

"Your plea of guilty has saved the government the expense and labor of a trial, and your submission is an acknowledgment — a tacit admission that you submit yourself to the authority of the law, and to the supremacy of the law, which every man must obey," Sanford said.

The judge sentenced Cannon to serve 75 days in the penitentiary and fined him $200 on the first count.

The apostle "slightly bowed" when he heard this sentence. The judge noted the initial conviction was Cannon's first-ever offense. Sanford then imposed the sentence on the second indictment, ordering the apostle to an additional 100 days behind bars and to pay a second fine of $250.

"Mr. Cannon again bowed in acquiescence, and, accompanied by Marshal Dyer, went to the Marshal's office. A few minutes later, after bidding goodbye to a number of friends who had followed him from the courtroom, Mr. Cannon was taken down stairs and out to the penitentiary," the Herald reported.[90]

A subsequent Herald editorial praised Cannon, saying, "... he has shown the courage of his conviction, and his readiness to endure for his religion what he has encouraged others to endure for the same thing."[91]

The *Deseret News* — the public voice of church leadership — accepted Sanford's handling of the case but found a victory for the church in it. "His sentence, severe as it is, indicates that the laws of Congress applicable to this Territory are to be administered as other laws are in the different States and Territories of the Union. This is all we have asked for since this anti-polygamy crusade commenced."

The last sentence is not true. The church for years had demanded that the nation recognize its practice of plural marriage as a matter of freedom of religion deserving protection under the First Amendment. The Supreme Court found otherwise in the Rudger Clawson case.

After the sensation of Cannon's surrender and sentencing, Judge Sanford took up the first case on his docket. It was a murder case, not the cohabitation cases of Daniel Lewis and others. It did not take long. The judge sifted through the testimony of several witnesses and discharged others. He then summarily declared there was not sufficient evidence to warrant a conviction and ordered the jury to render a verdict of not guilty.

The *Herald* reported the details of Cannon's conviction and explained the disposition of the murder case. Those cases diminished the interest in the cases of Daniel Lewis and others accused of cohabitation. Their cases were reported under a headline of "Other Business." It was not such a small matter for the six polygamists and their families. All of them were ready to admit they supported plural families.

Archibald Hill was the first to plead guilty. He requested a suspended sentence because of his age, 72, his large family, and the claim that he possessed "but little property."

Prosecutor Peters objected to the idea. He told the judge that Hill had escaped police when first arrested and "had distributed his property to various members of his family." Sanford quickly sentenced Hill to 50 days in prison and fined him $50. A second cohab, O.H. Hill, "against whom," the *Herald* reported, "there was a 'relic of barbarism' in the shape of a two-count indictment, next stepped forward."

Hill's attorney asked for leniency from the court because the defendant had surrendered voluntarily. Peters sniffed at this. He told Sanford that Hill had evaded officers for two years, prompting the judge

No Forgiveness

to ask if Hill had been released on bail.

"He was out on leg bail," Peters replied.

"The court does not recognize such bail," the judge retorted. He slapped a fine of $75 on Hill and imprisoned him for 60 days.

Lewis and his Summit County neighbor James Woolstenholme were among the last three men charged with misdemeanor cohabitation that day. All pleaded guilty. Sanford postponed sentencing until the next day. On Sept. 18, 1888, Lewis again appeared before the court. The *Herald* editor played its report of the proceedings in the regular daily, not a dramatic Extra. The account ran under the headline "Five Mormons Sent to the Pen Yesterday." The report of Lewis's sentencing was succinct:

Lewis came forward for sentence on the going charge.

The Court: Your age?

Lewis: Fifty-four.

The Court: What is your business?

Lewis: Farmer.

The Court: How old is your youngest child?

Lewis: Five years last May.

The Court: Is this your first offense?

Lewis: Yes, sir.

The Court: By your plea of guilty you have saved the government the expense of a trial, and have admitted the supremacy of the law of the land, to which all must yield obedience. In consideration of your plea and your circumstances, you will be fined $60 and imprisoned sixty days.[92]

Daniel Neal

COHABS IN PRISON

Lewis and the others convicted of cohabitation were taken by local authorities to the territorial penitentiary located in Salt Lake's Sugar House neighborhood. They did not enjoy the same transportation that carried Apostle Cannon the previous day. The famous Mormon had made the trip to the courtroom and to the prison in a splendid carriage.

"The carriage which Bro. C. H. Wilcken had provided (one of the finest barouches of Grant Bro's. & Co.) and driven by Chariton Jacobs, and which had carried Bro's. F.S. Richards, Legrand Young, C.H. Wilcken and myself from the Gardo House to the Court Room, was accepted by Marshal Dyer to carry me to the Penitentiary," Cannon wrote in a prison diary. "Brothers H. B. Clawson and Jas. Jack followed in a buggy."

Daniel Lewis stands third from left in this photograph of Mormon men imprisoned in the Utah Territorial Penitentiary in November 1888. Apostle George Q. Cannon sits at center. (Photo: Charles Savage. Courtesy BYU Digital Collections).

The next day, Cannon noted that "Brothers A. N. Hill and his son Samuel and Bro. W.J. Parkin" had been sentenced and transported to the penitentiary. The apostle's prison diary does not mention the arrival at the pen of Daniel Lewis, James Turner, nor the other cohabs sentenced on September 19.[93] He did describe the prison welcome the new prisoners received when they entered the pen.

"When these brethren arrived there were loud yells of 'fresh fish' heard all over the yard; this being the mode of salutation with which all new arrivals at the penitentiary are received," Cannon wrote.[94] "I escaped this reception, a fact that was commented upon by the brethren."

At the pen, Lewis joined dozens of Mormon elders then serving terms for cohabitation. They were among more than 1,000 men ultimately incarcerated for polygamy and unlawful cohabitation in Utah's prison. All believed that the federal anti-polygamy laws violated their constitutional rights. In their view, the only crime they had committed was living with their wives and providing for their children.[95]

New inmates were put in prison stripes and sent to the barber where their hair was cut. Beards and mustaches might be shaved, though not in every instance. The rules regarding facial hair seemed arbitrary. Daniel Lewis did not lose his beard, as a photograph taken of him there reveals. Loss of facial hair, according to Rudger Clawson, "was a real humiliation to these Mormon patriarchs, a visible symbol that they had lost their freedom."[96]

The prison was crowded. Inmates ate in groups of 100 in a dining room "with lice sometimes crawling on the tables." Meals were simple. Breakfast usually consisted of a tough piece of meat, potatoes, and bread; lunch brought soup and bread; supper, more of the same.

Rules governing visitation, access to newspapers, and the pleasure of receiving food brought by family and friends from outside the prison changed at the whim of the prison administration. Abraham Cannon, a son of the apostle, served time in 1886. He found himself able to conduct his work for the Cannon family's magazine *The Juvenile Instructor* from the penitentiary and enjoyed a nearly "endless stream of visitors" that included his wives and his business associates.[97]

Daniel Lewis's family may have managed to make the trip from

Kamas to see him, though there's no family record of one. Lewis did not keep a prison journal.

In early November, Salt Lake City photographer Charles R. Savage made at least two trips to the pen to photograph Cannon and other cohabs there. Prison authorities accommodated the photographer and allowed prisoners to gather outside their cells in front of a dark prison door. One of Savage's photographs depicts Daniel Lewis and Cannon among 13 cohabs in prison stripes. Lewis, Cannon and three others in the photo have beards. The rest do not.

Cannon kept his prison diary from the time of his imprisonment until early December. He thought his presence had a good effect on his church brethren there. "My coming here ... proves that the leading men [of the church] are willing to suffer but not to concede" for the church's plural marriage doctrine.

Like his son two years before, he also recorded many visits from his family, including on Oct. 8, "a wagon load of my children."

A former New Jersey congressman, George Halsey, visited Cannon in the prison that November. When Halsey asked what the future held for him, Cannon told his friend "... how necessary it was that we should have clearly defined what we could do with our families and what we could not do without violating law." The apostle wanted to determine how to prevent future charges for cohabitation against those who served time.

During the fall, Cannon recorded the names of many of the cohabs released from the pen. But his journal abruptly ended on Dec. 12, too soon for him to mention Lewis's release. The *Deseret News* reported the end of Lewis's imprisonment in a short note in its Dec. 17 edition.

"On the 18th of September last Daniel Lewis, of Kamas, Summit County, was sentenced in the Third District Court for unlawful cohabitation, the judgment being sixty days' imprisonment and a fine of $60. Not being able to pay the fine, he was held for thirty days, and was released this morning."

The questions Cannon asked of Congressman Halsey now confronted Lewis. What was he going to do about his polygamous household? How could he avoid future criminal charges?

No Forgiveness

Freed from the penitentiary, Lewis returned to his farm at Marion and joined Mary K and his six children in their enlarged house, now with six rooms. Mary D continued to live in her separate house at Kamas. These separate living arrangements with regular visits between homes lasted about two years after Daniel's return from prison. They did not outlast the church's decision to end its practice of polygamy.

CHAPTER ELEVEN

Cornering the church while it awaits Jesus

Passage of the Edmunds-Tucker Act in 1887 gave federal prosecutors and marshals new weapons to attack polygamy, including the power to confiscate all church assets over $50,000. The authorities did not wait long to put them to use. After John Taylor's funeral in July, 1887, the prosecutors moved to "escheat" church property, including confiscation of the temple block in Salt Lake City.[98]

The moves pushed church leaders into a corner. They found creatively practical ways to resist, such as transferring church property to individuals. Their belief that the Second Coming of Jesus was imminent inspired the effort to delay any doctrinal surrender to the Gentiles.

Unsurprisingly, their thinking relied on the man who had inspired the aging leaders to join the faith, Joseph Smith. The prophet had promised as early as 1835 that the Second Coming would occur within the next 56 years. God had assured Smith that, if he lived, he would witness the return of Jesus when he was 85.[99]

In the minds of the Saints, both the Bible as well as Mormon scripture had predicted the suffering they had endured in Missouri and Illinois. The oppression of the church and its Saints continued with the California Compromise that cut Young's state of Deseret to pieces. The legal assault on plural marriage and the jailing of men who practiced the doctrine extended that oppression. They were convinced that the relentless attacks on their church and their beliefs were proof that the time of Christ's return was near.

In January 1880, Wilford Woodruff, a beloved church apostle and a polygamist, had a vision while hiding in the San Francisco mountains in northern Arizona Territory. In the vision, the voice of God warned that he would burn up the nation or people that interfered with the Saints who lived in obedience to the Patriarchal Law of Abraham, the holy doctrine of plural marriage. The church's millennial prognostications promised that a council of Mormon leaders would form a theocracy that would rule the world by revelation once Jesus returned.[100]

Church leaders believed their religious laws were superior to temporal laws including the U.S. Constitution. They saw the Constitution as a divinely inspired but transitional document that established the form of government necessary to prepare for the ultimate imposition of God's rule through the Mormon men ordained to his priesthood.

Woodruff became the church's fourth president on April 7, 1889, just under two years after the death of his predecessor, John Taylor. Woodruff believed the signs of the millennium were piling up. That fall, he reported a revelation telling him that the church should not deny God's law. Anticipating the return of Jesus in 1890 or 1891, Woodruff declared that the judgment of the nation persecuting the Saints was "at the door."[101]

Events in 1890 seemed to confirm Woodruff's prediction that the whole nation was about to make war upon the church. Early in the year, the U.S. Supreme Court upheld an Idaho state law that disenfranchised any voter who was part of an organization that advocated the practice of polygamy. On February 10, the church's Peoples Party was turned out of office in Salt Lake City's municipal elections and the Liberal party took power.

In Washington, legislation modeled upon Idaho's law targeting Mormon voters was introduced in both the House and Senate. In May, the Supreme Court upheld the Edmunds-Tucker Act, affirming the power of the federal government to confiscate church property.

New federal officials indicated to church leaders that they planned to abandon an earlier agreement that church property used exclusively for worship would not be escheated. The agreement had meant that LDS temples remained in church hands. But the new officials argued that "... temples in Logan, St. George, and Manti did not qualify because they were not places of public worship." Unlike its ward houses that were built for regular Sunday meetings and other ward gatherings, admittance to the consecrated temples is offered only to church members determined by local leaders to meet the church's highest moral standards, including payment of tithes.

The new federal policy threatened the church's holiest places, the temples where Mormons perform their most sacred ordinances, marriage and baptism of the dead. It was this crisis, this threat that drove Woodruff to issue a manifesto ending the church practice of plural marriage. Still awaiting Jesus's arrival, Woodruff found himself "under the necessity of acting for the Temporal Salvation of the Church," according to historian David Bigler.

Woodruff took action on Sept. 24, when he issued a statement denying recent press dispatches that said forty or more plural marriages had been conducted by the church over the summer. He also denied claims that church leaders continued to teach and encourage the practice of polygamy.

Woodruff's announcement of the end of officially sanctioned plural marriage is titled "OFFICIAL DECLARATION" in church scripture and addressed simply *"To Whom it may Concern."* There is no thundering voice of God behind it. It was a human decision. Woodruff simply declared to the world that the church had stopped solemnizing plural marriages.

"We are not teaching polygamy or plural marriage, nor permitting any person to enter into its practice ... in our Temples or in any other place in the Territory," Woodruff wrote.

"And I now publicly declare that my advice to the Latter-day Saints is to refrain from contracting any marriage forbidden by the law of the land."[102]

The Woodruff "Manifesto" was unanimously sustained by Mormons attending the church's general conference on Oct. 6, 1890. This final step meant the end of officially sanctioned plural marriages; however, it did not finish its practice. Some members continued to marry into polygamous families in ceremonies conducted in Juarez, Mexico and more secretly in Utah. Many Mormon men, including general authorities, continued to cohabit with polygamous wives and at least 250 polygamous marriages were approved by the church through 1904.[103]

LEWIS STAYS CLEAR OF THE LAW

Like other polygamous Mormon men with sufficient resources, Daniel Lewis had provided separate houses for his wives. After his release from prison, he spent most of his time working his farm with Mary K and their children. He and his children continued to make extended visits with Aunt Mary. Lewis stopped the visits to Mary D after Woodruff's manifesto.

Lewis did not leave any notes discussing this break with Mary D and its emotional effects on him, his wives, and their children.

A few years later, the toll on Mary D became apparent, at least the toll on her spiritual life. In April 1893, Lewis attended the dedication of the temple in Salt Lake City, the best known of all the church's holy places. Brigham Young had laid the cornerstone for the granite building forty years before. Mary D wanted to go there to conduct rites for her ancestors and wanted her husband to go with her.

She made her desires known in June. Lewis stopped in Morrell to see his daughter Lizzie and her husband of 15 months, Peter Sorensen. His eldest child, always independent, had resumed contact with her Auntie Mary after leaving her childhood home. Lizzie gave her father a letter dictated to her by Lewis's shunned wife.

"As the Salt Lake Temple is completed, and I am very desirous to go there, and do my work for my dead. I write to you to ask what you want me to do in regard to it," Mary D wrote. "Are you going with me there, to do that work, or will it be necessary for me to have someone else.

"Of course my wish is to go with you, but if that does not meet your approval, it must be otherwise. I feel that time is precious, none of us have a lease on life, and you have the genealogy of my folks, I write to ask you what we can do. If you do not feel to go with me there, of course

I must do the best I can. I do not know, Bro. Lewis that I have ever done anything to forfeit my right to go to that house with you, but am willing to abide by your decision. But please let me have the genealogy of my mother, and my friend as soon as you can.

"I hope you will excuse my writing, but you know it is my only way of coming to an understanding with you, not having the privilege of going to your house, or of your coming to mine. Hoping you will give this your earliest consideration."[104]

Lewis's response to Mary D's plaintive request is not known. His great granddaughter Stratton wrote that he read the letter with "a tear in his eye." Gary Young, another Lewis family historian, said that Lewis cried when he read it. Young speculated that Daniel Lewis arranged for his brother Morgan to go with Mary D to the new temple since several names of family members who had died in Wales were submitted at the Salt Lake Temple at that time.[105]

May Lewis was 14 years old when her father received the letter from Mary D. She knew that Daniel Lewis had provided Mary D with both real property and some livestock when he put her aside. She might not have known that her father no longer provided cash to Mary D, leaving his first wife to manage her own financial affairs. Auntie Mary failed to handle them, however, and sank into poverty. She sued Lewis for divorce and more financial assistance a few years later.[106]

CHAPTER TWELVE

The education of May Lewis

The early Mormon theocracy monopolized the education of the territory's children for a dozen years or more after Brigham Young claimed the Salt Lake valley. Schools were run by Mormon wards or stakes and financed privately: parents paid for their students' attendance. The schools did not provide books. Families supplied them and passed them on as children advanced to higher levels.

This monopoly eroded as more settlers migrated to the West and cracked after the discovery of silver at Park City (about 1868) and the completion of the continental railroad in 1869. Both developments brought more non-Mormons to the territory with children who needed education. Catholic and other churches began setting up their own schools in the 1860s. Many accepted Mormon children as students.[107]

Responding to this competition, the church launched its own effort to avoid the evangelization of its children by the missionaries running the non-Mormon schools. In Summit County, the community leaders found ways to support education publicly. In 1863, the schools were financed in part by a toll levied on people crossing the Weber River via the Brizzee Bridge. Staffing costs for the schools were not high. In 1865, the county agreed to pay the county superintendent of schools $50 annually for four years. Usually, each town had a school district of its own, such as Heneferville, No. 1, Coalville, No. 2, Peoa, No. 4, and Kamas, No. 5.

When the Catholics and Protestants began opening secondary

schools, the Old Boss established Brigham Young Academy in Provo in 1875. More than 30 other academies were opened across Mormon Country over the next two decades, including one in Rexburg, Idaho, the Bannock Stake Academy.

The Utah territory itself finally took steps to provide free public education in 1890, when the legislature established tax-supported free elementary schools. It was the last U.S. territory in the West to do so.[108]

The church continued to provide secondary education. In 1892, President Woodruff approved a charter for the Summit Stake Academy in Coalville. The church contributed $500 to launch the academy. The first year did not go smoothly. The school opened in the upper floor of the Coalville Co-op store, where students and teachers found the facilities uncomfortable and inconvenient. The site was given up. At the end of the summer of 1893, stake leaders informed members that "now we are unable to find any place that is suitable to hold the school this winter."

They decided to build. Summit Stake President W. W. Cluff announced the decision in a letter to the stake's members pegging the cost at $2,000. Cluff laid out a financing plan that apportioned the construction cost among "leading Elders" of the stake. The stake presidency, the letter noted, was expected to contribute $185. The Presidency of the 22nd Quorum of Seventies was asked for $105. Similar amounts were requested from the presidencies of elders quorums, members of the stake high council, the priests quorum, and others.

The requests came on a typed form letter that had space to write in the name of a particular church organization by hand. It also reserved a line for writing in the name of the individual elder to whom it was delivered. The copy sent to Daniel Lewis, a member of the 2nd Elders Quorum, on August 30 set his "individual apportionment" at $15.

Cluff was confident. His letter notified recipients that, "As the season is advancing, the building committee will proceed at once, in good faith that sufficient funds will be received as the work progresses to meet their obligations."[109]

The two-story, frame building was erected in Coalville. It had eight rooms to house the academy classes.

"The school offered two courses: a preparatory course for students who had not yet finished the eighth grade but who were older than the average students in their grade, and a high school course open to graduates of the eighth grade. Students took classes in mechanical arts and domestic economy and participated in debate groups, glee clubs, and literary societies. The school also sponsored a lecture series for the community at large," a centennial history of Summit County reported.[110]

This rosy description of education at the academy differs from official reports on the quality of education in state schools in the county. In a report submitted to the Utah Superintendent of Public Instruction, D. S. L. McCorkle described a struggling school system. Few of the county's districts made any attempt to enforce the compulsory education law in 1896 and 1897, McCorkle wrote. Teacher quality was uneven with many teachers lacking professional qualifications.

"Teachers generally have too little information on the subject of nature and ordinary duties of life. Another common defect is the lack of culture. This makes the discipline of such schools assume a low order."

The teachers needed better education themselves. "The average ability in methods of instruction and psychology is only mediocre. Among many, there is a very deplorable lack of knowledge along the lines of Natural History and the sciences and make up of the things of ordinary life. Through this lack of knowledge, there is of course the corresponding lack of ability to interest pupils in these subjects."

Some of the county's teachers were professionally trained, others not. In a further acknowledgment of the difficulty of improving education in the rural county, McCorkle conceded that the trained teachers delivered only a "somewhat higher" percentage of success than those without training.[111]

By the late 1890s, public schools were providing books for students. McCorkle said the Summit County schools used titles newly adopted by the state but had issues "… getting the books fast enough."

The superintendent closed his frank report with a bright assessment.

"While there is much in the school system of this county that needs improvement, it is gratifying to note that there are many substantial improvements. The tone of the schools is better, [and] the scholarship of the teachers is constantly improving … we shall hope for constantly increasing progress."[112]

Like her sister Lizzie, May Lewis no doubt began her education at home around the family stove before attending grade school. Unlike her sister Lizzie, she did not compile a personal autobiography later in life, as many of the sons and daughters of the pioneers were urged to do by the church. She did tell her grandchildren a few anecdotes about her childhood.

Diana Black, a granddaughter, recalled one miraculous tale. In her early childhood, May struggled with a birth defect or birth injury that made it impossible to extend her right leg. The impairment meant May had to be carried upstairs to her bed each night. She lived with the limitation until she was eight or nine. While her brother was carrying

Carrie May Lewis, circa 1898. (Photo courtesy of the Neal family)

her upstairs to bed one night, he tripped and dropped her. Her leg "broke loose," May told Diana, and she suddenly could extend the leg.

Her father believed a bicycle would aid her recovery and strengthen the leg. He bought her one. May used bicycles for the rest of her life as her preferred mode of transportation.[113]

After elementary school, May attended the Summit Stake Academy in its program for older students. She was one of 59 pupils enrolled at the beginning of the 1897-98 school year. Tuition cost each student $3.50 per ten-week term.

A constant booster of Coalville and other communities in the valley, the *Coalville Times* rarely missed an opportunity to promote and celebrate the school. A story about a March field trip by Summit Academy students and their teachers to Upton, a small community just east of Coalville, reported that the students displayed their musical and writing talents and celebrated their progress. The "great improvement and advancement made in education under such efficient teachers was flattering."[114]

May graduated in June. She was 19 years old and one of eight students who successfully completed the 8th grade that year. At the graduation ceremonies, May was one of five students who spoke. The first speaker's address was a description of the life of Christ. May's essay described the school's language classes. The graduation marked the end of her formal education.

CHAPTER THIRTEEN

College Days and a new way to spell Neel

My father loved his family name and often repeated a story about his young son L.G. assessing it. Dad said that one day he overheard the nine-year-old talking to himself. "Neal, Neal," L.G. said. "Hell that's a good name."

A family myth lies behind that story. In the early 1900s, the Neel family, at least the sons of John Austin and Ellen Christiana Neel, changed the spelling of their surname to Neal. In my childhood, I wanted to know why and asked my father to explain.

Dad believed that the change stemmed from an improper relationship that his uncle Frank Neel had with a student while teaching in Springville, Utah. Dad said the ensuing scandal prompted Frank to pull up stakes in Utah and emigrate to Canada. The scandal, Dad thought, pushed the brothers Neel to become the Neal brothers.

Though the story seems believable, there is no evidence confirming a school-teaching scandal involving Frank Neel. Frank did give up teaching, but it was for a career in business. In March 1905, the *Ogden Morning Examiner* reported that Frank Neal, a former Springville school teacher, was in the city representing "an eastern grocery house."[115] Frank later left Utah and moved to Winnipeg. There he and two of his brothers launched a successful grocery wholesaling business and eventually opened a chain of grocery stores.

But all of that followed a different sex scandal, one that involved an uncle of my grandfather and his brothers. The uncle, Joshua Wriley Neel, was convicted of sex crimes in two widely publicized cases that dragged on for years in the local press.

Well before his uncle's legal problems, Frank had decided that the higher education opportunities offered by the state promised a better future than farming in northern Utah. He decided to pursue a teaching certificate at the Normal School, Utah's teacher training college at the University of Utah in Salt Lake City. Utah's new state government was anxious to educate and train new teachers and get them out into the state. It opened enrollment in the Normal School to men and women age 15 and up. State law said teachers must be 18 years old, a requirement the students would meet after completing the four-year program.

Applicants qualified via examinations given each September — or if their grammar school principal signed a certificate affirming they had completed the eighth grade. The Normal School did not charge tuition, though each student paid $10 in fees.

Frank was 17 when he started his first semester. He and his fellow students studied courses ranging from drawing and music to botany and chemistry, zoology, physics, English, civics, and history. Education classes included pedagogy, history of education, educational psychology, and physical education.

The university had no dormitories. Students were directed to find housing in the community, where they could expect a family to provide room and board for around $10 a month. They could sometimes reduce expenses by forming clubs or simply renting a room and feeding themselves.[116]

Frank first enrolled in the fall of 1896. When David entered the Normal School two years later, they kept expenses down by sharing a home on Quince Street, three blocks south of the Utah Capitol. The arrangement lasted until Frank graduated in the spring of 1900.[117]

When fall rolled around, Frank moved on to a teaching position at Park School in Springville, south of Provo. David took a room with a family, the Fraziers, at 36 P Street in the Avenues neighborhood northeast of Temple Square. From the Fraziers' home, he had a short walk to South Temple Street where he could board a streetcar to ride to the campus. University students paid discounted fares, just half that charged to others. It was a good set-up for a student trying to live as cheaply as possible.[118]

David had more than school on his mind, however. He had begun courting May Lewis. Given the 50 miles of mostly mountainous terrain separating Salt Lake City from Marion, pursuing this love interest was a challenge. He couldn't pick up a phone. Though telephones arrived in the territory in 1883, expansion of service had been slow. By 1900, only about 1,200 people subscribed to the Salt Lake City exchange.[119] Letter-writing remained the common method of staying in touch with absent family members and sweethearts.

The Neels and Lewises wrote plenty of letters but few remain. I have just two letters that David wrote to May in the fall of 1900. Both are sweet and playful. There are misspellings and references to church-taught ethics in both of them.

David started one letter to May on Saturday, Oct. 13. He addressed it to "Miss Mamie Lewis" in Marion.

Dear Little Large May,
Your letter was a welcome visitor last Tuesday.

He described his student life at the still-new University of Utah, where major construction had just been completed, then turned to his family news.

I have written several letters to the folks home, and two or three to Frank the last few days. Frank says in his note to me that he does not think school teaching as bad as he anticipated. On Saturday and Sunday he goes hunting with his school boys. He is also reading 'The Life of Joseph Smith.'

Although my brother likes his school pretty well, I believe I like mine the better. The coarse I am taking this year is simply grand. All the studies are entirely new, and to a certain extent advanced. The work is all scientific and consequently makes one work energeticly. But, none are so happy as he who worketh.

His university had been launched by the Old Boss in 1850 as the University of Deseret. It languished throughout the early years of the territory, "having but a nominal existence" until the late 1860s, when Brigham Young and the church took more interest when competition to educate the territory's youth began to build.

In 1892, the territorial legislature granted a new charter that re-christened the school as the University of Utah. Two years later, the federal government granted a site encompassing about 60 acres for the university on the U.S. Army's old Fort Douglas, its permanent home at the base of the Wasatch mountains.

When David started his fall semester in 1900, the university was in the process of moving into newly constructed facilities, including a new building for the Normal School, a physical science building, and a new library, described as "the largest and best equipped in the state." The library held a collection of 20,000 books, 10,000 pamphlets, and served as the federal documents repository for Utah.[120]

> *The University may be seen from almost any point in the city ... I tell the students that although we shall not ever enjoy the future splendor of our school, probably our children will. Of coarse, it will be some time before it will reach the extent of its beauty.*

In his letter, David reported his social news, too, noting that he joined Ed Sorensen and two friends, Len and Mida, for an evening at the home of other friends, Della and Mrs. Jensen.

> *By some means we managed to do something so as to have a pretty good time before it ended.*

May no doubt knew the friends whose names he listed so familiarly. He finished the letter on Sunday with a confession.

> *I came nearly going to Sunday school this morning, and should have gone had my clothes been brushed, too bad. You may think I am gassing but I am not. Jonah went. Jonah Birch is boarding here and has been all the time. He is a very nice boy, sure.*

I know of nothing more to tell you. Only I am sick a bed. I weigh 5 pounds more than I did when I came in. Hoping not to hear from you sooner that it is possible for you to answer, I remain as ever your good friend.

He signed with a lover's signature:
X
X
X
XXX David.

When he wrote that letter, my grandfather was just 19 years old. He was working hard at his studies, but, as college students always do, found time for fun, or "hijinks," as they said at the time. He told May about

D.S. Neal, circa 1900. (Photo courtesy of the Neal family)

both in a letter written at the end of November.

> *I have a whole pile of news to tell you but I am afraid time will forbade at present. I have just finished my lessons for this evening, that is, they will do, I guess; still, I might study hours yet if I would. It is eleven o'clock and thereby passing my bedtime.*

Then he told May about his social recreation, at length.

> *Other things have taken my time also. Austin* [his eldest brother] *and intended were going to Christensen's to a dance last Saturday, and invited me to go with them.* [Christensen's hall was a popular local events venue that hosted many dances.]

> *I decided this way — Well I've been studying very hard the past week and have stayed entirely at home; I reasoned that I thought it the right thing to partake of the fresh air and also take some exercise as a help to do good work in school. Another thing is, I said to myself, that I may not get a chance to go another time for a long time. Of coarse this side over balanced the other by far, in fact, I could not produce any argument whatever against this stand. So, I went to the dance.*

> *I got 'fixed up' about so, too, and like a good old self-comforting bachelor found my way to the hall. I didn't go with Austin, because he had to go after his girl. To cut the matter short, the dance was a grand occasion. I found the floor slick, but the girls were quite accommodating and assisted me whenever I should make a slip, this way I got along fairly well. We had a very good time, yes, I called it a 'swell time.'*

With no letters written by May surviving from these early months of their courtship, her feelings about these tales of her beau's social life in the city must remain unknown. A woman of 21, she had her own society in Marion and the valley. Community dances were held regularly. Did she tell him about slick floors and accommodating boys who held her up when she made a slip?

David's letter mentions a second dance, a university dance that "was not inferior to Christensen's."

> *I didn't catch a cold neither did the tramps 'hold me up.' I never thought of such a thing as tramps; it never entered my mind in the least. I soon got home; I didn't have very far to go. I think I was not longer* [than] *20 minutes walking all the way.*

He teased her about his Christmas vacation plans as he closed the letter.

> *I have not decided to stay in here for Xmas, neither have I decided to go away. I am on the fence you see. There are a few, however, out there, I am quite satisfied, that would not break hearts about my not coming.*

Along with his schoolwork and budding love life, David had other worrying concerns. There was a cloud hanging over the Neels of Peoa. An uncle's sex scandal two years prior had stained the family name. John Austin Neel's brother, Joshua Wriley Neel, was accused of raping a Peoa woman in November 1898. The case played out over David's three years at the Normal School with broad publicity in the local and regional newspapers.

Joshua Wriley Neel was one of the Weber Valley's struggling farmers. He had been married and was the father of three children when, in June 1899, a district court jury convicted him of raping Jeanette Lyons, a married woman.[121] Neel and his attorneys immediately filed the first of a long series of legal challenges to the conviction with a motion requesting a new trial. The newspapers followed each filing in the case, each report deepening the stain for the rest of the Neel family.

The court dismissed the request for a new trial, and instead set sentencing on July 17, 1899. When J.W. Neel appeared before Judge A. N. Cherry, the judge asked Neel why sentence should not be rendered.

"I am an innocent man," he declared without hesitation.

Judge Cherry reminded him that a jury had found him guilty and sentenced him to serve five years in the Utah penitentiary. Neel and his attorneys quickly appealed to the Utah Supreme Court, challenging the admissibility of evidence given at trial by Lyon's husband.[122]

The steady drip of news continued. A hearing before the state supreme court was scheduled in October, then delayed until February 1900. Then Neel's case worsened.

In late December 1899, a second woman, quite young, came forward to accuse Neel. She was Ella Jorgenson, a teen-ager. Jorgenson told County Attorney Charles A. Callis that Joshua Wriley had sex with her in December 1898, about a month after the rape of Lyons. Jorgenson was just 16 at the time. She became pregnant and delivered a baby in September.

"She is but 17 years of age while Neel is 50," the *Salt Lake Tribune* reported.

Jorgenson told the county attorney that Neel had threatened to harm her if she made a complaint to the authorities. "It was while he was on trial for rape that he intimidated the girl by threats and thus prevailed on her to keep silent. Neel would have been arrested when the girl first made complaint, which was about two months ago, but her condition has been precarious since her confinement, and she requested the County Attorney to defer action in the matter until she was stronger."[123]

The *Park Record*, Park City's newspaper, piled on. "He offered to marry his victim," the paper asserted, "but she indignantly declined to accept the proposal of the old seducer."[124]

Neel was arrested again and charged with a misdemeanor: having carnal knowledge of a female under the age of consent.

In February 1900, the state supreme court heard Neel's appeal of his felony rape conviction. His attorneys argued that Third District Court Judge Norrell should not have allowed presentation to the jury of certain evidence, including the testimony of Jeanette Lyons's husband. The court agreed the husband's testimony should not have been admitted.

" ... the court, upon being requested to withdraw the matter from the jury, answered that it would 'instruct them generally in the charge,' and then failed to do so, thus permitting irrelevant testimony, prejudicial to the defendant, to be considered by the jury," Chief Justice C. J. Bartch wrote. "The judgment is reversed and the case remanded, with directions to the court below to grant a new trial."[125]

The reversal freed Neel from prison and he returned to the Weber Valley. Local authorities took the supreme court at its word, however, and filed new charges. The filing launched another round of news stories about the case and its renewed progress through the court system. Each report put the Neel name before the public.

In late April, as David looked forward to his brother's graduation from the Normal School, Joshua Wriley was arraigned again in Judge Norrell's court. This time the prosecutor charged him with both a felony rape and a misdemeanor crime of carnal knowledge of a female under the age of consent. A trial was set for the June term of the court.[126]

The slow drip of news about the case continued through the summer and into fall. In June, the defense won a postponement. In August, the *Coalville Times* reported that a witness in the rape case would be deposed before trial because the man planned a trip to Europe and might not be available when the trial opened. In September the rape trial was scheduled to open Oct. 1, with the misdemeanor trial the following day.

Judge Norrell's court quickly convicted Neel on Oct. 1 and sentenced him again to the state pen. A jury could not be seated in the misdemeanor trial, however, and it was rescheduled for February 1901. The Salt Lake papers reported Norrell's Oct. 15 rejection of a motion for a new trial on the felony case and his order sending Joshua Wriley back to a penitentiary cell. Neel was convicted in the misdemeanor case the following year and sentenced to five years behind bars.

Still refusing to concede, Neel's attorneys appealed the misdemeanor conviction to the Utah Supreme Court. They argued that one juror was improperly challenged and that the district court erred when it allowed Ella Jorgensen's child to be brought into the courtroom for Ms. Jorgensen to identify. The court refused the appeal.

"The supreme court held the challenge of the juror was properly sustained and that the defendant was not prejudiced by the child being brought into court as long as it was not introduced in evidence for the purpose of comparing its features with those of the accused to show a resemblance," the *Salt Lake Tribune* reported.[127]

Intent on distancing themselves from their uncle's sex crimes and public notoriety, the brothers responded by changing the spelling of their family name. That spring, David started using the new spelling when he realized his name might appear in the papers. The spelling showed up in reports about the 1901 Normal School graduation activities, including a Salt Lake Herald story headlined "High Jinks Session at the University." The story listed "D.S. Neal" among the performers in a "very lively burlesque on the fourth year normal graduates" given June 17 at the university by the third year normal students.

"Instructor R. L. McGhie, the godfather of the fourth years; their class color, green; their leading students and their efforts to raise funds with which to secure the Grand theatre for their class day exercises, were the chief points of attack," the story reported. Neal acted in "Come Up Some Time," a parody of a faculty meeting evaluating the fourth-year students. The skit "was the biggest hit of the performance…. The oddities and personalities of many of the professors were strikingly brought out."

David spent his last summer vacation from his college studies in the Weber Valley, where he could find work, help his mother Ellen with the family farm, and continue his courtship of May. He returned for his final year of classes and the collegiate social swirl that fall. He was a member of the Zeta Gamma Society, a campus club that sponsored debates, balls, and other events. The debaters delved into questions such as Chinese exclusion laws, instituting a federal income tax, and raising the salaries of state officials. David participated in one debate that November in which his team argued against U.S. intervention in the Second Boer War, known to the debaters as the British South African trouble."[128]

He continued to be as interested in performance as in the debates themselves. He tested his acting skills in more parodies, including a Zeta Gamma "burlesque" of a Current History class debate that had explored the issues expected to drive the 1904 U.S. presidential campaign.

His heart remained with the girl back home. He stayed with friends in Marion, May's hometown, over the Christmas holidays, not with his mother in Peoa. Community news reports say that he attended a dance in Coalville with May and a mutual friend in early January.

After the Christmas vacation, David returned to Salt Lake City for his final semester at the Normal School. Letters substituted for being together. They did have a chance to connect in person in April, when May and a friend from Marion attended the annual church conference at the Tabernacle in Temple Square.

David graduated that spring. He was among 91 students who received certificates from the Normal School, proving them ready to teach in Utah's growing system of public schools. The name change had not taken hold completely. While the *Salt Lake Herald* listed him as D. S. Neel, the *Deseret News* reported David Stevens Neal of Oakley was among the graduates. The *Salt Lake Tribune* found its own spelling: David Stevens Neil.[129]

CHAPTER FOURTEEN

A plural wife complains

Daniel Lewis's decision to end any regular association with his first wife suggests the split was painful but accepted by all concerned, according to Lewis family histories. Daniel gave Mary Davis Lewis both property and livestock. He avoided further prosecution for cohabitation by living on his farm with just one wife, Karen Marie (Mary K), and their children. Mary D moved on, lived alone and sought to fulfill her religious responsibilities to her ancestors. The family histories hint that Daniel and Mary D may have taken some heart from the church's assurances that husbands and wives will be reunited in heaven.

The facade of acceptance of the split maintained before their friends and neighbors lasted until June 1899. Then Mary Lewis filed for divorce.

The filing must have shocked their extended family and surprised the community that surrounded them. The divorce suit declared that Daniel Lewis had abandoned his wife. Mary D told the court that her husband was living in an "adulterous state with Carrie Marie Sorenson." The complaint charged that her husband "has utterly failed, for nine years last past to provide her with the common necessaries of life" despite having the ability to do so and knowing his wife was "feeble and infirm" at age 60. The adultery with his second wife continued during that period at "divers times," it said.

"And plaintiff further alleges that she has not forgiven, consented to, nor condoned said acts of adultery nor any of them." She told the court that her husband had "wickedly and wrongfully deeded his homestead to Carrie Marie Sorenson," then duped her, Mary D, "to relinquish her dower right therein by promising to provide for her, which said promise was wickedly and falsely made, was never intended to be kept or performed, and was never in fact performed by said defendant in whole or in part."

She asked the court to dissolve their marriage and demanded that Daniel Lewis give her $50 for support pending resolution of the case and ultimately award her monthly alimony "as to the court shall seem just."

Daniel Lewis, her complaint asserted, had the necessary resources to do all that and to pay her attorney fees and other court expenses, a cost estimated to reach $175. She assured the court that her husband owned personal property including horses and cattle and held at least $3,000 in cash.

Mary D signed the complaint with an X. A local notary public witnessed her mark.

District Judge A.G. Norrell responded in her favor just three days later. He found "good cause" for issuing the temporary order she requested. Daniel was ordered to deposit $50 with the clerk of court to pay Mary D's attorney fees and $25 for her support. The court also restrained Daniel from selling or encumbering any of his property.[130]

It took Daniel Lewis a few weeks to compose his official response to the complaint and to the court order. The response is handwritten and does not list any legal representative. He may have had legal help, or perhaps his service as president of the church mission in Wales provided him the confidence to take up the legal arguments without an attorney.

Lewis called the claims of adultery false and malicious. Likewise, he said, his wife's claims of abandonment were not true. In fact, he said Mary D had told him "nine (9) years since at Kamas ... that she was competent to manage her own affairs and did not want any more of his assistance, company, nor his association."

He denied the allegation that he failed to provide Mary "with the common necessaries of life" and called the claim false and misleading. He recalled the division of land between his wives in July 1887, a year before he turned himself over to federal authorities for prosecution for cohabitation. He wrote that "he did in the year A.D. 1887 deed to the plaintiff, Mary Lewis, one piece of land suited to cultivation consisting of thirty acres ... and thirty-three acres of Meadow land ... along with five milk cows and a calf all of which was done at the request of said plaintiff and by and with her consent and approval...."

The response adds that on April 7, 1890, Lewis transferred to Mary D an equitable division of personal property, thirteen (13) head of cattle consisting of one, twos, and three years old cattle," all of which she managed for herself since the transfer, "without let or hindrance of this defendant."

He confirmed deeding his homestead to Karen Marie for her support and the support of his children by her, "including the youngest [Edward Lewis] of whom is just sixteen years old."

He denied swindling Mary D out of her dower right in the property. The arrangement was made, he asserted "with the full and free consent, good will, and unreserved approval of the plaintiff Mary Lewis...."

He suggested that the divorce filing had more to do with finance than the pain of adultery. Shortly after transferring the two parcels of land to Mary D, his wife sold both acreages to two different buyers for a total of about $1,000 on terms that guaranteed payment to her until the year of the divorce filing.

He asked the court to reject Mary's claim that she was destitute and deny her request that he should subsidize her legal costs and support her in the future.

The filing and Daniel Lewis's response comprise the surviving legal record of the divorce case. Local newspapers tracked the case as it appeared on the dockets of the Third Judicial District Court from July 1899 to January 1901. Judge Norrell called witnesses for Daniel Lewis in September, then laid the case over to his court's following term. The legal wrangling finally ended when it was settled on Jan. 15, 1901, according to the *Coalville Times*.[131]

No divorce was declared and there are no records in the court documenting terms of the settlement. Nearly two years of legal struggle and local and regional publicity of family discord produced unknown results. They apparently battled to a draw. Both had years more living to do. Perhaps Daniel promised further material support. In any event, the Lewis divorce case illuminates how the federal pursuit of the polygamists continued to reach into Mormon lives long after Woodruff's manifesto.

CHAPTER FIFTEEN

David and May together

After his graduation from the Normal School, David left Salt Lake City with his life spread wide before him. The West was tamed, mostly, but still offered land that could be claimed with a legal filing and held with hard work. His teaching degree promised a steady income. Raising his eyes to that promising horizon immediately was not possible, however. He needed to assess his financial situation after borrowing money from his family to pay for his studies in Salt Lake. He returned to the Weber Valley to consider his prospects, especially his future with May Lewis, and to help his mother work the family farm.

He found a teaching position that fall and rented a room in Oakley, roughly midway between the farm at Peoa and the Lewis home in Marion. He discussed the pay in a late October letter to his brother James, and described his circumstances, both financial and romantic. James had announced his engagement to marry Lillian Sharp in Idaho. James invited him to attend their wedding at St. Anthony, Idaho.

"From the way you write you must have a lovely girl," David replied. Then he suggested that he was not far behind James in anticipating wedlock.

"May and I are still getting along well. Some day we may live happily together. The way things are turning now it may happen next spring. I am telling you in time so that you can make arrangements to be here."

He reluctantly informed his brother that he could not afford to attend his Idaho wedding. "If I did not owe any one it would be different," he wrote.

> "I had to buy a little team because I had no other way of getting anywhere. I expect to run mothers place next summer and maybe for two or three years. So I bought a pair of colts. I have to pay $75 on them between now and next spring."

He was struggling to repay loans from both his mother and James. He told his brother that he had promised to pay their mother $70 over the winter, "and she needs it very badly, I think." The obligations worried him.

> "Now I don't blame you for wanting your money and you may depend on it that you get it as soon as I can possibly get it for you. I am working hard and intend to do the right thing.

> "I am afraid I will not be able to pay mother all. $10 will be all she can get before Xmas. I clear about $40 after paying my board and so on. ... I have saved $36.50 out of this my first month's wages. You see how I am fixed."

It was a message he knew his brother would not appreciate. He closed the letter as positively as he could.

> "James the only thing I dislike about you getting married is that I shall not be there, I'm afraid. The best wish I can make you is, that you as like always have a pleasant home and live happily with your dear little wife."

If he was earning $40 to $50 per month, the wage did keep a light in his debt tunnel. It was not enough for him to thrive. In 2024 dollars, $40 would have been worth somewhere near $1,300.[132] Assuming the salary was paid for eight or nine months, his annual teaching wages would be considered poverty-level pay in the 21st century. At the time, the pay likely put teachers on par with many of their neighbors. A few farmers, merchants, and mill owners in the valley likely fared better.

Other information about David's and May's lives in the months after his graduation in June is scant. The church and the rural communities they lived in remained central to their personal activities. Dances offered a chance to get out at night and see friends. That autumn, May was named an assistant to the leaders of the Marion Sunday School. All of the leaders, of course, were men.[133] She would not have expected otherwise.

David's prediction to James that he and Carrie May Lewis would have a spring wedding came true. He married May in Coalville on June 1, 1903 at the Summit County Courthouse. It wasn't a church wedding but the president of the Summit Stake presided.

"Mr. David Neal of Oakley and Miss May Lewis of Marion this county, were married at the courthouse yesterday afternoon by President George W. Young," the *Salt Lake Tribune* reported. "The young couple are well and favorably known in the southern end of the county, where they were born and raised, and have many friends who join in the wish that happiness, prosperity and peace be theirs during their married life."

The newspaper noted that the couple planned to move to Box Elder County. David had secured a teaching post in Honeyville, a small farming community at the north end of the Salt Lake valley, not far from the Idaho border.

The newly wedded couple sat for their wedding portrait, a large black and white photograph from which my grandfather and grandmother gazed out over my childhood in Idaho Falls a half-century later. In the picture, May exudes the blush of youth, her hair in curls and wearing a high-collared blouse beneath a jacket decorated with embroidered flowers and vines. David, handsome in his starched collar and white tie, parted his hair just about down the middle, revealing his high forehead. His dark suit coat is unbuttoned. May tucked her right shoulder tightly next to his left shoulder. Neither of them smiles but light glints in their eyes as they stare straight ahead. They are ready to take on the future together.

By the end of June, May was pregnant. They moved to Honeyville in time for David to take his post as the school principal in mid-September. The village, which today remains a small farming community tucked at the base of the Wasatch range, lies about 100 miles from David's home town of Oakley. The waters of Crystal Hot Springs rise just outside the town, a natural spa used first by indigenous people, then by the early settlers and workers building the transcontinental railroad. David and May must have taken a plunge there themselves.

The Honeyville school was a challenging assignment. The school's teachers worked to educate scores of students ranging in age from six to eighteen in a small building on the eastern edge of town. Both teachers from the 1902-03 academic year had resigned, creating the opening that David Neal filled.

The previous winter, David's predecessor as principal, "Mrs. Carlson of Corinne," decided to raise funds for a new school organ. Rose Wheatley, the teacher of the primary grade students, joined the effort. "The two teachers are working hard to raise sufficient means to buy an organ to be used in the school house. They have already given a couple of dances, an entertainment and a fair, the proceeds of which are to be used for that purpose," the Brigham City paper reported.

Raising money in addition to handling their teaching duties must

This portrait of David Stevens Neal and Carrie May Lewis Neal was made at the time of their wedding on June 1, 1903, at the Summit County Courthouse in Coalville, Utah.
(Photo courtesy of the Neal family)

have worn them out.

Box Elder County's schools did not open until October, timing that enabled the students to help bring in the summer's crops. With harvest complete, the Honeyville school's doors opened and the community settled in for autumn and winter.

"Our town is very quiet but for the noise of the school children," the Honeyville correspondent for the *Box Elder News-Journal* reported in late October. "School started on the 5th with Mr. Neal and Miss Ella Hunsaker as teachers. The enrollment has reached 70 already."[134]

The state continued its drive to improve its public schools. Utah school leaders brought the effort to Box Elder County in November. William Stewart, the professor of pedagogy who taught David and other teachers-to-be at the Normal School, and Rosalie Pollock, the supervisor of the primary schools in Salt Lake City, conducted a teachers institute in Brigham City. Pollock spoke to the primary grade teachers about reading. The new Honeyville principal had the chance to participate in a discussion with Stewart of the entire course of study provided to older students.

A few months later, May delivered their first child, Melba. She was born in Honeyville on Feb. 15, 1904. Her arrival pushed the young parents to reconsider life in Honeyville versus other options. The federal government still offered land for homesteading, but they had not found available land in Box Elder County. They decided to move back home. When the school's spring term ended, they left Honeyville and took Melba to Marion to be among family and old friends in the Weber Valley. David helped his mother with the farm over the summer before taking a new teaching position in Woodland, south of Kamas, for the fall term. Life was good. In mid-July, May wrote a letter to her brother Elie. The letter brimmed with domestic news and family gossip. She held her baby as she wrote.

> *"I hope you will excuse me for writing with pencil but I must write this way or not at all for I have babe on my lap and it is impossible for me to write with pen and ink with babe in my arms."*

Elie had moved to Driggs in eastern Idaho's Teton Basin. Despite having both plenty of work and a developing love interest, he had complained to May that he suffered from melancholy.

> *"I am so glad you are getting along so well and now don't work to hard ... and do take good care yourself now. What in the world makes you feel so blue? ...It gave me the blues to read your last letter you silly kid you."*

The valley's farmers were cutting the first hay crop of the summer and its communities planned to celebrate Pioneer Day on July 24, the date of Brigham Young's 1847 arrival in the Salt Lake valley.

> *"Everybody are so awfully busy haying now that they can't say how do you do at a body even. ...We have lots of trade now. I am so busy I hardly know what to do first."*

She did not resist relaying gossipy news of the latest shifts in their young brother Ed's love life.

> *"I am feeling bad for Ermina Lennon. She wrote Ed yesterday and told him she'd be home for the 24 and now [he] is going to write and give her the bounce. He says he don't want her. ...Now don't you tell any one I told you. Ed just told me last night in confidence. Belle is coming home to stay too, so Ed says."*

May could not have been happier.

> *"Write soon and tell us how you are. Babe is on my lap just kicking and talking and I expect a howl any time. She says hello uncle Elie and a XX for you from her. Write soon to your loving sister May."*[135]

Elie and May maintained a constant correspondence. Unfortunately, she burned most of the letters sent to her. Only a few that she wrote remain. Those reveal a woman of confidence and humor who loved social news and gossip about her friends and family. They also give a sense of the tightly knit relationships that bound the community and its families together.

> *I received your most welcome letter yesterday and was surely glad to hear you are well and so happy. ...I was awfully worried for fear you were so long about ans* [answering] *my letter and the folks kept telling me they heard from you and you wanted to know where in the world I was until I decided you hadn't received my letter at all.*

She told Elie that "Grandma Sorensen," their brother-in-law Pete Sorensen's grandmother, had died of consumption on Thanksgiving Day and had been buried two days later.

> *She was living up to Lizzies in the North bedroom for quite a while before she died. Pete felt pretty bad I tell you.*

Elie had a fiancé in Idaho, Roxie Jean Jackson. He planned to take her to Utah to meet the family a few days after their late-December wedding. May was anxious to know her.

> *Tell Miss Jackson hello and give her my love. I am very glad you are going to bring her out so we can get acquainted with her. Not be like we are with Sarah's husband. Not know her at all and I am going to come up there to visit you and I want to know her before I come.*

> *Now be sure and leave so you can be here on the 24th of Dec. The folks will be so surprised they will all faint so you must have Miss Jackson prepared for the worse. They were all over to see me just the day after I rec'd your other letter.*

Her parents asked May to share that letter but she refused. She did not want her parents to see her personal exchanges with her brother.

> *I told them it was burnt up. I burn all my letters as soon as I read them so they won't pile up to make trash when we have to move, I told them, and they believed it all.*

She ended the letter with a few proud lines about her daughter.

Babe is so sweet and cute, she is the nicest girl in the U.S. indeed is she. Here are some kisses from her XXXX. I got up at 5 o'clock this morning and she had to get up with me. So you see she is very bright.

The letter doesn't quite end there. May prevailed upon her husband to suggest arrangements to pick up Elie and his new wife when they made their Christmas trip to Utah by rail. Depending upon the route they chose, Elie and Roxie could ride the train to Ogden and on to Wanship south of Coalville or go to Salt Lake City, then travel on to Park City. David added a few sentences at the end of May's letter.

Friend Elie,
You may write to me the place [to rendezvous] *Wanship or Park City and I will meet you. No difference to me at all. If it's good roads I will bring May along. So long until I see you.*
Yours truly D.S. Neal [136]

A few weeks later, Elie married Roxie Jackson, just 16 years old, in Driggs. The marriage deepened David and May's interest in Idaho and the Teton Basin. There was land to be had there under the Homestead Act and it harbored a growing Mormon community. Mormon settlers had been moving north into southeastern Idaho for decades. The first new settlements there served Brigham Young's vision of an expansive desert kingdom. The Mormon moves into Idaho started with the establishment of Franklin in the early 1860s and had pushed on to Rexburg and Teton City by 1883.

Five years later, Salt Lake attorney B.W. Driggs happened to attend a meeting of the Sugar House ward in Salt Lake, where he heard others talking about the opportunities in the Teton Basin. A couple of Driggs's friends decided to have a look for themselves and found the valley lush with good soil, abundant wildlife, and "grass like a waving lawn" that would feed livestock. Their report enticed the attorney to make a trip to see the area himself and it convinced him to make the move.

B. W. Driggs and his fellow "young prospective 'cattle kings'" talked up the Teton Basin around Salt Lake City and attracted "quite a colony" to make the move to Idaho in mid-March 1889. They formed a wagon train in front of the Salt Lake Temple on March 18 to make the journey. Driggs's brother Don Carlos Driggs joined them. Unmarried and unemployed, B.W. enlisted young Don Carlos "to come up with his team, haul logs, and start log cabins on the different locations that were to be selected."[137]

Don Carlos Driggs drove his own wagon, staked out a homestead and built the first house in the Teton Basin, a two-room log cabin. He married a young school teacher later that summer. She insisted on bringing her organ, the first purchase she had made with her teacher's pay. Good Mormons that they were, they considered music and entertainment among life's necessities.

When the post office was established in 1891, the settlement was named after the Driggs family and Don Carlos was appointed postmaster. He became a prominent business and political figure in the Teton Basin and served the LDS Church in many roles. In September 1901, he was appointed president of the newly formed Teton Stake. Nearly two decades later, it was as stake president that Driggs became involved in the struggles between May Neal, her family and friends, and those who advocated for the release of her husband's murderer from prison.

All of that was years away. David and May enjoyed Woodland where their life as a young married couple continued to bloom. Elie and Roxie made their holiday trip to Utah so Elie could introduce his young bride to his parents and family.

The winter was hard on May's aging father. Seventy years of a life as a miner, pioneering farmer, and incarcerated polygamist had worn him down. She worried about him in a letter sent to Elie and Roxie a few weeks after the holidays.

"Ma and Lizzie and Daphne and Naomi and Ruth have all been over here all day today we had a real nice visit. They are all well now but pa," she wrote, *"and he doesn't seem to get along very well. Ma said he is real miserable yet. I am sure I don't know what to think about him he looks so bad. We are going down Saturday to*

try to get him to come over and live with us for a week or so to see if the little change won't do him good. We won't let him work anyway.

"I do hope he will come. I'm sure he could enjoy his self very well reading and walking around in the sun. It is quite a little warmer here to than it is over home and that is what he needs."

Their return to Marion was complicated by a January thaw that meant "the sleighing is all gone." Most group travel meant hitching a horse or a team of horses to a buggy or, in winter, a sleigh. Because of the thaw, her mother, sister, and nieces had made the trip from Marion to Woodland in her mother's apple cart pulled by a single horse they called Frank.

"They all came over in it with just poor old Frank hitched up and there wasn't hardly a grease spot left of him when they got here so they decided that Belle and him could better pull them home in a sleigh on bare ground than he could alone in the buggy," she wrote. *"... away they went and I guess they are home by now. I hope so anyway."*

She lamented that "news is scarce as hens teeth out here," but still told some social news of her own. She and David had attended a Calico Ball in Kamas on a Monday night in late January. "We have a dance once in a while that is all the excitement there is."

Calico Balls originated as East coast charity events. A Calico Ball in New York City in 1855 specified that no woman participating could "wear a dress which costs more than 12½ cents per yard." After the ball the women donated their dresses, sending them to a local minister for distribution among the city's poor women.[138] By the time of the Kamas dance attended by May and David and their friends, the balls of the early 20th century were no longer dedicated to charity, though dress requirements remained.

"The ladies wore calico dresses while the men had to have on a calico bow tie before mingling with the dancers," the *Salt Lake Tribune* said of a Calico Ball staged by the city's 19th Ward.[139]

The idea was to have some fun. "Get you calico ready for a good time," the *Park City Record* directed readers of a story about an "Old Time Calico Ball" planned by the Modern Woodmen of America, Park City Camp No. 10637. "Elaborate preparations are being made for the event which will be a novel one." Tickets cost $1.[140]

At the Kamas Calico Ball, May, Dave, and their friends danced through the night and well into the next morning. When the ball ended, they decided to extend the party, despite having to work the next day.

"It was real good," May told Elie and Roxie in her letter.

> *"Ed S, Cay Mitchell, Jim Snapp and May Snapp, Leone Stevens and Miss Conley the Oakley primary teacher were all out to it and they all came over here and had supper before they went home. We didn't get to bed until 4 o'clock a.m. and had to get up to get Dave off to school by 8:30 a.m. so we didn't sleep much and I'll bet they just got to Oakley in time for Miss Conley to eat her breakfast and go to school."*

The demands of teaching kept her husband busy, she noted, especially when he turned to the theater to educate his students.

> *"Dave and his school are going to give a swell entertainment on the 22 inst, and he's got his head and soul all in that and books so I can't get a word from him once in 24 hours."*

May closed her letter to Elie and his new wife with an appreciation of domesticity.

> *"I am please to hear you are well and happy and so comfortably settled, continue to be so for all we get out of this life is the comfort at home. We are well at present. Here is a xxxx from babe for both of you she is so sweet and cute now she tries so hard to talk."*

She did not mention what she by then must have suspected: she was pregnant again. Their second daughter Ilah Aleene did not arrive until summer's end. Though her pregnancy went well, other health problems plagued the family. Whooping cough struck the valley later that spring, infecting all of sister Lizzie's children and nearly killing her brother Dan's baby. Melba suffered, too.[141]

Potentially mortal childhood diseases were a fact of life before vaccines and antibiotics. The flu, scarlet fever, pertussis (whooping cough), tuberculosis, enteritis with diarrhea, and measles sickened and killed thousands of them in the late 19th and early 20th centuries. In the first decade of the 20th century, one in 10 babies born in the United States did not reach their first birthday. Clara, a sister of May's, had died from whooping cough a few months after her birth in 1875. Mortality rates were higher among the rural poor and other segments of the population, including immigrants and African Americans.[142]

Once past their first birthday, a child's prospects improved, but not enough to eliminate parental worry. At the turn of the century, children under five years old comprised 30 percent of all deaths in the U.S.[143]

Home alone with her baby while Dave worked, May fretted over her young daughter for weeks. "Melba has got the whooping cough," she wrote to Elie and Roxie. She described the frightening symptoms.

> "[S]he is some better still she coughs very hard two weeks ago she was very bad she would choke six or more times in a day and night until I was afraid she was dead so I sent for Dave for I was all alone here."

Dave finished the short letter. "She and Melba have gone to the land of nod and I am going. Good night."[144]

May's second pregnancy ended successfully with Ilah's birth in mid-September. With Melba recovered and a second daughter in the cradle, the family again looked ahead. In his correspondence and visits to Marion, May's brother Elie painted an appealing picture of the prospects for a life in the Teton Basin. Dave and Lizzie's husband Pete Sorensen decided to see the place themselves. They traveled to Idaho and stayed with Elie while they looked for land. They found parcels they liked south of Darby and "returned to Kamas Valley that fall enthused about their land purchase."[145]

They planned their departure from the Weber Valley over the fall and winter. Dave had to determine how to obtain a teaching certificate from the state of Idaho. They needed heavier wagons to haul both their household goods and the provisions the families would need on the long trip.

As they prepared for the move, a major family loss unfolded. A November horse wreck left May's father Daniel sickened and finally killed him. Details of the accident were not documented at the time. Daniel's biographer Laura Lewis Stratton turned to a sort of magical realism to describe what might have happened.

"One miserably cold November morning in 1905, Daniel saddled his horse for the two mile trip to the post office," Stratton wrote. She imagined him thinking of his 19 grandchildren, three of them still in the womb, and his church as his horse plowed through the drifted snow.

"'My family is increasing and so is Zion,' Daniel said to himself ... Daniel chilled, bringing him back to the present. He pulled the collar of his coat tighter to his neck as he shuddered." In Stratton's creative description, the horse spooks, shies, and bucks Lewis into a snow drift. The horse runs off, leaving Daniel dazed and freezing. Fortuitously, a brother in the church finds him and takes him home. There Mary K "quickly put a large tub of water on the cook stove." She removes his boots from his frozen feet, puts him in the hot bath, then into bed covered with extra quilts. As he drifts to sleep, she goes to the chicken house, slaughters a hen, and makes chicken soup that will be ready when he awakens.[146]

Lewis contracted pneumonia. The local paper followed his decline and death, noting visits by his brother Morgan and others. Sarah Delaney and family came home to see him.[147] (Sarah and her husband Joe were planning a permanent move from Iowa to Utah, according to Stratton. They did move, but to the Teton Basin, not Utah.)

Daniel Lewis, Sr., the former polygamist, died Dec. 11 at home. Stratton imagined a scene of grief suffused with Mormon ritual.

"Mary K washed his body and dressed him in home made white temple clothing. She placed coins on his eye lids to keep them closed and set weights on his body to prevent it from retracting. The body was packed with ice to slow the deterioration process. A wooden casket was built by neighboring brethren.

"... The four days between his death and burial the family had reminisced of his life experiences. The love he had for his church was strong. He had dedicated his life to serve and follow the teachings of his leaders."[148]

May Lewis filled out and signed the death certificate. It notes that Mary K Lewis served as acting undertaker. Perhaps she did put coins on his eyelids.

CHAPTER SIXTEEN

Interstate immigrants

In June, Dave Neal and Pete Sorensen made a final scouting trip to Idaho. They traveled by train. Rail service then extended to St. Anthony, the seat of Idaho's Fremont County. Brother Elie or Sarah's husband Joe Delaney likely met them there or in Rexburg with horses or a wagon to take them on to Darby, a few miles south of Driggs.

The place purchased by Pete and Lizzie Sorensen had a cabin. There's no record indicating whether the few acres Dave and May purchased had any housing in place. The scouting trip enabled them to make the last arrangements necessary in Idaho before their families made the long journey by wagon.

The families made the move in September. The last summer hay harvest at the old Neal farm near Peoa would have been cut and stacked, the completion of Dave's last work duties for his mother. As for the Lewis farm, with Daniel Lewis buried in the Marion cemetery, May's brother Dan now had full responsibility. Mary K stayed on the farm with her son and his family and continued her work as one of the valley's active midwives.

Uprooting both the Sorensen and Neal families meant leaving established lives for prospects, just as their emigrant parents and grandparents had done. David left behind a teaching job and land he might inherit. May's sister Lizzie served Marion as postmistress. She and Pete had lived in the same house there for 14 years. The home, like their family, had grown over the years.

"It was a nice two room house that Peter had built and paid for. We had a good well on the place, too," she remembered in her autobiographical life sketch. "We had a cow, a team of horses and our house furnished comfortably. In that house Arnold, Douglas, Leland, Daniel, Daphne, Naomi, Ruth and Gordon were born."[149]

She did not want to give up the community and their full lives in it, but agreed to pursue the Idaho prospects with her husband. She deputized her cousin Christine Sorensen as Marion's postmaster just before they departed on Sept. 2. Nearly four decades later, she described the two families' journey to the Teton Valley in a long conversation with her granddaughter Margaret Hansen. Margaret wrote down Lizzie's memories for a high school theme she had been assigned. Her essay has feeling. She deserved a good grade.[150]

"Terror filled my heart as I sat on the large box filled with clothes. Looking around me, I saw boxes, blankets, and everything that could be used to pack was being used," Lizzie said of their preparations to leave. "My sister, her husband, and their two small children were going with us. I had been a postmistress and didn't want to go. Neither did the children, in a way, but it would be an adventure."

The Sorensen family filled four wagons with their goods and children. Teams of four horses pulled each wagon. Lizzie drove one team and kept her baby Gordon and nine-year-old Daphne with her. Pete handled a second wagon. Arnold, just 14, drove the third wagon and the fourth was assigned to brothers Douglas, 12, and Lee, 11. Dave and May crammed their belongings into a single wagon with their two young girls.

"Of course, we didn't always travel in this order," Lizzie told Margaret.

Leaving in the early morning, their wagon train made good time, quickly covering the first 20 miles or so by mid-day.

"The first day we had lunch near Coalville," she recalled. "That night when we made camp, the children slept in the wagons because of the chilly September nights." The parents slept under the stars.

They rose early to prepare the livestock and the children for each day's haul. The route took them through the Cache Valley to Logan, Utah, then to Pocatello, Idaho.

"It was in Cache Valley where we ran into the first bad weather."

Rain drenched everyone. "We stopped at a farmhouse and were greeted by a friendly man. He told us that his family would be very happy to have us spend the night, but they had scarlet fever and were quarantined."

The farmer set them up in his granary, a dry haven. This Samaritan treated the waggoners very well.

"As we were getting supper, the man brought us a large pan full of steaming hot biscuits that his kind wife had fixed for us. They were eaten with gratitude because the rain had soaked nearly everything."

The days in the wagon wore Lizzie down, leaving her exhausted. Eight days into the trip, while climbing a steep hill with the horses at a "very slow walk" she fainted and fell from the wagon seat.

"… everything went black … Daphne, who was tending the baby, screamed at her father. Why I wasn't kicked by the horses when I fell is something I will never understand."

Daily chores that had been simple at home became demanding tasks on the road. They stopped each day to wash diapers for the babies and clothes for the older children. "It became everyday routine. We watched the colored hills vivid in their autumn foliage."

As they followed the Portneuf River and neared the outskirts of Pocatello, "I glanced back into the wagon. I could see Daphne, who didn't want to miss anything and was hanging out the back, but I couldn't see the baby, Gordon.

"I asked her where he was. She turned very unconcerned to me and said she didn't know. For a moment I was paralyzed with fear. I couldn't stop the team just then because of the traffic. The first possible moment, I stopped the team and began searching the wagon for the baby. I moved boxes wondering if he had fallen out of the wagon. I finally found him under the pillows."

She was certain she had saved Gordon from smothering. "Thanking God, I started on my way again."

From Pocatello, they continued north to Idaho Falls, Rexburg, and Salem, where they could turn east and make their way to Teton City, then skirted the northern end of the Big Hole Mountains, the range that stands as the western boundary of the Teton Basin. They reached Driggs and Darby after 20 days on the road. It was not a cheerful arrival.

"The valley greeted us with a dismal slow drizzle," Lizzie recalled. They stopped at the Delaney home where sister Sarah "insisted on having my sister and her family stay there for the night but my family had to go on home.

"When I saw that cabin with the dirt roof and weather-beaten logs, my heart sank. When I went inside and saw the pole standing in the middle of the room supporting the roof, my whole soul ached with homesickness. I wanted my family and friends, but most of all I wanted the little white, five room, frame house I had left in Utah."

She found the place more welcoming the next day when a neighbor stopped to offer assistance. She must have said something to the man about the home she had abandoned in Utah, because he told her she had better return there quickly "... because after we had been here a while we would never go back."

The next day, Sunday, Sept. 23, presented the Teton Basin in its autumn glory. "Never before had I seen such a beautiful valley. At the church house my family filled two rows of seats. The people turned and stared at us, and I felt like crying right then and there."

Ten years later, Lizzie returned to Marion to visit her relatives and friends. She discovered that, just as that first friendly neighbor at Darby had predicted, she had given her heart to her new home.

"It was wonderful to see old friends and places. But I would not want to go back to Utah to live because I have fallen in love with this lovely valley."

CHAPTER SEVENTEEN

Settled and teaching in Darby

After their stay with May's sister Sarah and her husband Joe, Dave took his wife and daughters to their place two miles or so south of the Darby School. Pete's and Lizzie's farm lay just to the north with the make-do cabin that had disappointed Lizzie.

The Neals improved their place quickly, building a home that faced the county road marking the farm's west boundary. They built a chicken coop, corrals, and planted apple trees. A spring just uphill on their land produced a stream of good water. It ran through the Neal yard, then through a culvert under the road to the neighbor's place on the west side of the road. Ellington Smith had purchased that farm in 1903, but continued to live in a house on his farm north of Darby canyon. Smith had used the stream as he wanted before the Neals located at their place. Neal apparently took the same approach when he moved in and used the water however he needed it.

Dave had to secure his Idaho teaching credentials. In Utah, his diploma from the Normal School had served; however, the State of Idaho required candidate teachers to pass an examination given by the local county's superintendent of public instruction. Dave arranged to take the test from Fremont County Superintendent Grace Taylor. She issued him a "Teacher's Second Grade Certificate" just after Thanksgiving. The certificate lists his examination scores. His best was in "Orthography," the art of spelling and writing words correctly. He scored well in U.S. History, Penmanship, and Grammar; not so well in State Constitution,

School Laws, Civics of U.S. and Reading. Physiology and Hygiene, Arithmetic, Geography, and the Theory of Art of Education completed the list of exam subjects. The certificate deemed him "qualified to teach in any Public School in the State for three years from this date," Nov. 26, 1906.

Darby's teachers first had taught students in a log building that served the little community as a ward house as well as a school. By the time D.S. Neal began teaching classes there, the log building had been replaced with a red-roofed, frame schoolhouse with two rooms. The new building featured a belfry holding a big bell that summoned Darby's students. Outhouses provided toilets. The fenced grounds were spacious enough for baseball games. The school served eight grades and more than three dozen students. Ellington Smith's daughter Mabel was among them.

At home, Dave and May kept cows and chickens to provide milk, butter, eggs, and meat. They opened a checking account at the new Driggs State Bank. Their family continued to grow. Carmen arrived in May 1907. The last sister, Lelia Ellen, was born 18 months later.

They filed their legal claim to their new farm just a few months after Carmen was born. Brothers-in-law Joe Delaney and Pete Sorensen traveled with Dave to the Fremont County courthouse in St. Anthony to serve as witnesses to his "Possessory Claim."

Homesteaders filed their claims under state law, which laid out the rules for taking public lands for farming and grazing. Anyone could file a claim so long as they were a citizen or had made a legal declaration of their intention to become a citizen. Homesteading had been one of the keys to incentivize the settlement of the vast American West for 40 years. Congress passed the original Homestead Act in 1862. Territorial and subsequent state law governed the initial process; final patents conferring ownership came from Washington and were signed by the sitting president.

Ultimately, roughly 270 million acres of public land were transferred to homesteaders. In Idaho, settlers claimed more than 9.7 million acres.[151]

Neal made his filing under oath to Justice of the Peace J. P. Clark.

The oath attests to compliance with the law.

"First, That the said claim does not embrace more than 160 acres of a land. Second, That he [the claimant] holds no other claim under the provision of the Chapter and Title aforesaid. Third, That to the best of his information and belief no part of said land is claimed under any existing adverse title."[152]

Once filed, the claim secured the acreage, prohibiting claims by others. The law required improvements of at least $200 within 90 days "unless the same has been previously improved ..." Improvements could be fencing of the entire claim or construction of a home. The Neals already had met that requirement.[153]

Their social lives revolved around the church. Dave and May regularly made the ride north to attend Sunday meetings of the Darby ward along with Lizzie and Pete. With his love of the stage still strong, Dave was named to the ward's Amusement Committee to help organize plays and other shows. His beliefs were strong and noticed. He was ordained as a priest in March 1909.[154]

The following summer, Ellington Smith moved into a house on the farm across the road from the Neal home. Smith had purchased the farm six years previously from homesteader Thomas Cox.[155] The Neals knew Smith reasonably well. He had farmed in the Darby area for many years and had children who attended the Darby school.

Experience made Neal a better educator. His first teaching certificate expired that fall and he again had to take the state examination to obtain another. Harriet Wood, the new superintendent of Fremont County's schools, found him better prepared than he had been three years earlier. He raised his scores in nearly every segment of the test, including a perfect score in Geography, and again was determined by Wood to be a "person of good moral character." Wood certified him to teach for another three years.[156]

They needed the teaching salary. May was pregnant again. She delivered her son, my father David Lewis Neal, on April 1, 1910. Dave proudly reported on his prospering farm and growing family in a letter to his brother Charles. Since Charles had sent Dave a photograph of his own first son, Dave replied by addressing his letter to "Dear Nephew and your Papa and Mama." He spoke for his new baby boy.

> "*David Lewis is so sorry he cannot send you his* [photo] *in return, because he hasn't had his taken yet ... He is a fine youth I tell you. His mama thinks an awful lot of him. She wants his papa to give him a dandy fine colt that is now three weeks old, but da-da simply says 'hem, hem.'*

Charles and Frank Neal had made a trip to the Teton Basin the previous summer to check on the Idahoans and their new farm. Dave was clearing a field behind his house when they arrived.

> "*That piece of ground on the hill that I was breaking when your papa and uncle Frank came to see me a year ago is raising the finest crop of Fall wheat in the country* [and] ... *stands as high as the bottom of my trousers pockets and is in the boot. Everyone is admiring it.*"

The farm continued to increase its livestock. "Your uncle is milking 5 cows now and expects more in the future. You ought to be here and help Lewis tend a calf. Only one sucks we feed the rest, one," he wrote. "Aunt May has 37 little chickens and a hen is hatching today."

He pressed his brother Charles to join them in Idaho. According to "the papers," Dave wrote, "... the Basin is destined to have a railroad in the near future. Your papa is missing it in not securing some land...."[157]

The young father believed his future was bright. His teaching career was on track. He had a thriving family and a good farm. He earned additional cash working for other farmers, helping with irrigation and other tasks. He considered himself a knowledgeable father, too. In a letter to his mother the previous February, Dave confidently offered parenting advice for his mother to relay to Charles, whose son had been born two months before his own.

> "*Now tell him to let the baby have the nipple of nature and not the artificial nipple of rubber. Let it have regular hours for nursing and do not bounce and jolt it on his knee,*" he advised. "*Practice the 'leave it alone' method and he will be able to sleep all night and not*

have to walk the floor."

Despite his confidence in the future, in the present he needed cash. His mother had offered to sell him some cattle, but he instead saw the potential for a maternal loan.

"What I need is <u>money</u>," he told his mother. He suggested that she sell her cows, then make a loan to him from the proceeds. "Now if you wish to sell the cows I will pay you good interest. I am paying twelve per cent now. I am trying to do better than this. If you can do better I will pay the interest promptly.

"Mrs. Lewis sent us $200.00 at 4 per cent," he said of May's mother. He did not expect such a low rate from his own mother. "Of course you could not do so well, but some better than 12%."[158]

He did not say why he needed the loan.

The Darby school trustees extended his contract again that spring and raised his pay. "We are getting along pretty well now days. An insurance agent called a couple of days ago and wrote me for a 1,000.00 [life policy]" he wrote. "Aunt May complained a little not much."[159] It was a prescient purchase.

TEACHING IN DARBY

Like most teachers, he touched many lives. A 1908 photo at the Darby school depicts Neal with his school class of 40 students. The students' clothing reflected their rural lives. Most of the boys hold hats. Some wear coats. The girls, including Ellington Smith's daughter Mabel, posed in dresses or skirts and blouses. Some of the clothes fit well. Others appear to be hand-me-downs. D.S. Neal wears a suit and a tie, which mostly is hidden behind a vest.

He made a lasting impression on his nephew Paul Delaney, the son of Sarah and Joe Delaney. Paul started school at Darby in the fall of 1910.

"David Neal, my uncle, was the principal at the school when I started the first grade," Paul recalled decades later. "He was a large man, and because of his size and strength was able to demand the respect from the big kids."[160]

Maintaining student attendance was difficult, especially at harvest time and during the planting of fields in the spring. In April 1910, Dave sent out report cards announcing student promotions for the following school year. Each card listed the student's grades in examinations given in the third and sixth months of the school year. The cards carefully tracked attendance and absenteeism.

Student Leona Pascoe's card noted that in the first exam she had excelled in reading and arithmetic, but struggled with history. She made headway over the winter and registered better scores on the second exam. She missed just three days of school. Her teacher promoted her to the sixth grade along with her brother Willie.

Seventh grader Arland Davidson had problems just getting to school. Despite missing nearly all of the first two months of the term, he performed reasonably well on the first examination. He missed the second set of exams. Principal Neal promoted him to the 8th grade, though "on condition of more sufficient attendance."[161]

When Ellington Smith moved to his second farm opposite the Neal home, only two of his children, Mabel and his eldest son Joseph remained in Darby. His sons Earl and Bill and daughter Zora had

D.S. Neal poses with his students outside the Darby School on April 3, 1908. Neal stands just right of the three women in back. Mabel Smith, her hair parted down the middle, is in the fourth row, fourth from left. (Photo courtesy of Church of Jesus Christ of Latter-day Saints, FamilySearch)

left home.

The Neal and Smith families must have seen each other regularly. Perhaps Neal occasionally gave Mabel a ride to school on a horse or in a sleigh. No existing family letters written from Darby mention problems with Smith. But the small stream that flowed through the Neal barnyard and under the road to Smith's place became a serious point of contention between the neighbors.

After Smith relocated to his new farm, the stream provided his culinary water. Neal took his domestic water from it, too. Neal must have drawn or piped water to the house from above his barnyard and its livestock, avoiding pollution from animal waste that inevitably found its way into the stream before it flowed under the road. The pollution angered Smith. The two neighbors failed to work out a solution that satisfied both of them.

Among Neal's friends in the valley was another teacher, Alma Hanson. Hanson taught at Bates and Cedron, across the Teton River a few miles west of Darby. It was a close friendship. The families became related years later when my father David Lewis Neal married Alma's daughter Gladys. Their first son Lewis Grant helped Alma with field work when he was a young boy in the early 1940s. Alma and his grandson shared many lunches in the field and Alma once told L.G. what he remembered about the day before Neal was killed on July 5, 1911.

Alma said that he and his family bumped into the Neals and their five children in Driggs after the July 4 parade. They spent the rest of the day together. The families enjoyed a picnic lunch during which the two men discussed teaching and the challenges of controlling classes with some students physically as big as them.

"They also discussed politics, church events and the trouble Grandpa Neal was having with his crazy neighbor, Ellington Smith," L.G. Neal wrote later. "Mr. Smith accused Grandfather Neal of stealing water that was his for many years."[162]

CHAPTER EIGHTEEN

Ellington Smith and Nick Wilson

The Neals' neighbor across the road was, like them, an emigrant from Utah. But Ellington Smith was two decades older. Like David and May, he was born into a polygamous Utah family. He grew up on a farm near Hyrum, south of Logan, and attended school there. He matured into a man of average stature, about five feet seven inches tall and weighing just over 150 pounds. He sported a red mustache when he grew it out.

Ellington liked to hunt and shoot. It did not always go well. Just before his 23rd birthday, he narrowly avoided serious injury in a gun accident. While hunting near Hyrum on a cold day in late January 1883, he dropped his loaded rifle. It discharged at his feet.

"The muzzle was close to his legs but fortunately in a slanting position," the local newspaper reported. "The ball tore his pants, boot leg and sock, and inflicted a very slight flesh wound."[163]

The injury left one or more of the scars on Ellington's legs and feet that were listed when he was registered as Inmate 1884 at the Idaho State Penitentiary in 1912. Those intake documents state that he had lived in Idaho for 31 years.

Ellington married a young girl, Hannah Louise Wilson, in Utah about a year after the incident with the gun. Hannah was the daughter of Nick Wilson, famously known for leaving his own Mormon family as a young boy to run off with Chief Washakie's band of Shoshones. Wilson, also known as Uncle Nick, lived a romantic life in the Wild West, and left behind a memoir describing it. His adventure with the Shoshones deserves a brief consideration here.

Washakie's band was one of the native groups that roamed into the Salt Lake valley in the 1850s. In the summer of 1856, his band was camped in the vicinity of Grantsville, Utah, a few miles from the southern tip of the Great Salt Lake. The camp was set up near a pasture where young Nick Wilson, about 12 years old, shepherded his father's sheep. He had taken up this duty two years before after trouble with the Goshute Indians there had quieted. Nick watched the sheep along with Pantsuk, a young Goshute whose father worked on the Wilson farm.

"I had no other boy to play with, so Pantsuk, the little Indian boy, and myself became greatly attached to each other," Wilson wrote in his memoir. "I soon learned to talk his language and Pantsuk and I had great times together for two years, when the poor little fellow took sick. We did all we could for him but he kept getting worse until he died…. I loved him as much as if he had been my brother."

The ability to speak Goshute launched Wilson into one of the great individual tales of the settlement of the West. A couple of Shoshone men from Washakie's camp made friends with Nick. The men could speak Goshute and "liked to hear me talk Indian, for they never heard a white boy talk as well as I did."

One day, the Shoshones brought a pinto pony and taught Nick to ride "the prettiest thing I ever saw." They allowed Wilson to take the pinto for long rides. After one of those rides, one of the men asked if he wanted to keep it.

"I told him that I would sooner have the pony than anything I ever saw. He said I could have the horse, and I could ride him all the time, if I would go away with him."

A plan was hatched and Wilson ran away with the Shoshones. He found himself given to an old woman. She was Washakie's mother. Over the next two years, Wilson roamed with Washakie's band from Utah to Montana's Big Hole country, the Snake River plains of southeastern Idaho and the Wind River and Red Desert regions of western Wyoming. He returned finally to his white family, but Wilson and Washakie's band crossed paths many times over the following five decades.[164]

Nick continued to live an adventurous life. After returning to his Mormon family at age 14, he later rode for the Pony Express, worked as a freighter during the silver boom in Nevada, married a woman who bore him 15 children, took a plural wife who gave him two more sons, and was jailed for polygamy while farming the Bear River valley. He doctored children and parents during two major outbreaks of diphtheria, the first in 1880 in the Bear River valley, and the second in 1891-92 in the upper Snake River Valley. He moved on to Jackson Hole, where he established Wilson, a community at the base of Jackson Pass, and served for years as the bishop there.

Nick's daughter Hannah married Ellington Smith in 1886. She was 14 or 15 years old. Smith was 23.[165] Their first son Joseph was born in Idaho two years later. Ellington patented a homestead at Salem just north of Rexburg in September 1890, but it did not hold them. They sold or traded it to acquire land in Darby.

When Ellington and Hannah left for the Teton Basin, their timing was lucky. They dodged a deadly outbreak of diphtheria that swept through Rexburg and the upper Snake River Valley in the winter of 1891-92. The disease claimed the lives of 68 children and young women. There were no public health officers to coordinate a response to this plague, originally identified as "membranous croup" by local residents. Before they understood the risk of contagion, they held public funerals for the first victims, funerals that became what are now called "spreader events." When the plague reached Salem, Nick Wilson went to see and treat some of the sick. He recognized the symptoms from his battles with the illness years earlier in the Bear River valley and declared the disease "black diphtheria of the most deadly type."[166]

Wilson began treating anyone who asked him for help. He also asked for volunteers to serve as his assistants. He wanted people who were young, husky, unafraid of the disease, and willing to follow his orders. The ad hoc medical team he assembled treated the sick with a three-step remedy. They swabbed throats with a concoction of herbs, golden seal, and other ingredients that Uncle Nick's Shoshone mother taught him to use.[167] His treatments also included a gargle and plenty of olive oil. The applications were given 20 minutes apart. It was grueling work.

"Dear Uncle Nick never tired," volunteer Ralla Harris recalled. "He was always on the job day and night."

As community understanding of the disease improved, the handling of the dead changed. Public funerals were ended.

"The little bodies would be washed and dressed in a clean shirt of whatever could be found, put in a home-made box or coffin and passed out to men in the dead of the night, while the roads were free from [travelers], and taken to the cemetery where they were met by Brother Robert Archibald, the sexton, and with his assistance they were laid away," Harris recalled.

"During this time of trouble it fell to my lot to wash and prepare 28 little bodies for their last resting place. I went for three weeks one time without undressing and going to bed. I feel safe in saying that Uncle Nick and several others did the same."[168]

In the course of the outbreak, Nick's ministrations took him 25 miles north to the little community of Ashton. While he was trying to save lives there, the disease infected his own family in Salem. All but four of his ten living children died.[169]

"That summer he took my grief-stricken mother and family to Yellowstone Park to camp for the summer," daughter Nellie Wilson Ferrin wrote years later.

After a church mission in Anaconda, Montana, Nick moved his remaining family to Wyoming, traveling through Driggs and Victor to cross Jackson Pass. He likely stopped to visit his daughter Hannah and her family on the Smith farm north of Darby Creek on the Idaho-Wyoming border. Their family included three sons and their first daughter Zora.

The Smiths were active in the Darby Mormon community. When the Darby ward organized its Young Men's Mutual Improvement Association a few years later, Ellington Smith was its president. He remained in the ward post through the turn of the century.[170]

Ellington and other settlers in the Darby area had cleared their land for farming. They needed water for irrigation. A group of them led by

Emanuel Bagley organized in 1896 to jointly fund and construct the Wyoming-Darby Bench Canal to deliver it.

The project plan called for diverting water from Darby Creek just across the state line in Wyoming, putting the project under that state's purview. The group filed for a permit from the Wyoming State Engineer's Office. Smith was among the group of 13 landowners listed on the permit application. A.C. Larsen's name was listed, too, making Smith a partner in the canal development with the man he later claimed was "behind the whole thing" when he defended his murder of Neal.[171]

The same year, the Smiths welcomed their last child, Mabel. Hannah, who had just reached her mid-20s, now had five children, all under ten years old. She did not live to see them grow. Hannah fell ill and died in the spring of 1897. Her grandson attributed her death to Bright's disease, a fatal kidney disorder.[172]

Family members stepped up to help the distraught Ellington. His nephew Octave Smith made the move from Utah to the Teton Basin that spring with his brother and sister. They reached the valley on May 10, just before Hannah died.

"We called to see him next day and found his wife very sick," Octave recalled in his own memoir. "She died three days after we arrived. This was very sad because she left a family of 5 small children."

Many other members of the Smith family lived in southeastern Idaho at the time. Young Octave, known widely as Tave Smith, was asked to carry the news of Hannah's death to relatives in St. Anthony, Salem, and Rexburg.

"The next morning Uncle saddled up old Dude Rock, tied a feed of oats to the saddle and I was off," Tave remembered. "I went to St. Anthony first where I was told to go. Some relatives sent me up Snake River 6 miles to Fogg's sawmill. I came back and went on down to Salem to aunt Alsyone's. She was a sister to my Uncle Ellington Smith. I told her the sad news. Dark was approaching fast and I still had 8 miles to go. I had covered a distance of 65 miles and 8 more before me over the trackless hills of slight wagon tracks and all very strange to me."

Tave's aunt fixed him a meal, his first "since daybreak," and he rode on to Rexburg to deliver the news to more relatives. "The next day two

No Forgiveness

Octavus "Tave" Smith, circa 1897. (Photo courtesy of Church of Jesus Christ of Latter-day Saints, FamilySearch)

buggy loads of relatives started for Teton Valley."

The buggies reached Darby and found a crowd of mourners "just going to the cemetery. We fell in line, too."

Two of Hannah's sisters were in the procession. They had crossed snow-covered Jackson Pass on snowshoes and walked on to Victor where they were picked up and taken to the funeral. After the services at Hannah's grave, Tave Smith was asked to take them back. He put them in a light buggy and drove to Victor, then "... up the canyon in snow to the hub, our team got stalled so we turned the buggy around with considerable effort." Hannah's sisters put their snowshoes on to hike back over the pass.

"I told them that was the most snow I had ever seen in the summer."

He stayed in Victor that night, where his hosts told him that their son, who delivered mail to Jackson with a dog team and toboggan, would "sleep with me when he got back."

The postman son arrived at about three in the morning. "He felt like a polar bear just arriving from the Antarctic. When he got in, I got out."

Octave took the buggy back to Darby and arrived at his uncle's home just as his sister and Ellington and his children were eating breakfast.

"It was a blessing for those motherless children, for my sister Lily, stayed and cared for them that summer."[173]

Ellington did not re-marry after Hannah's death. He continued farming and relied upon his relatives and the rest of the Darby community for help caring for his children. He kept his eyes open for other opportunities and found one in 1903. Homesteader Thomas Cox wanted to sell his farm. Located a couple of miles south of his first Darby acreage, the Cox place covered 160 acres between Sorensen and Fox creeks with a road along its eastern boundary. A small spring on the rising terrain across the road provided water.

He continued to make his home at his farm north of Darby Creek but later built a new house on the Cox homestead and moved into it in 1909. His son Joe stayed at the original farm. Mabel kept house at both places. The move meant Ellington Smith now lived downhill from D.S. Neal and his family with a county road separating their farms. They shared and soon disputed use of the small stream that provided drinking water to both of them. It was a fateful entanglement that eventually left Neal dead in a ditch and Smith languishing in prison.

CHAPTER NINETEEN

Charley Wilson's account

Nick Wilson pecked out his autobiography "Among the Shoshones" on a typewriter, working in his home in Wilson, Wyoming. Skelton Publishing Company of Salt Lake City printed the first edition in 1910. The book has a clouded early history that includes alleged censorship of the original edition by the Mormon Church. As a young boy, my parents gave me a revised version of Wilson's book edited by historian Howard R. Driggs after Wilson's death. Driggs titled his 1919 abridgement *The White Indian Boy: The Story of Uncle Nick Among the Shoshones*.

In December 2024, Ken Sanders Rare Books, a Salt Lake City dealer, offered a hardcover copy of the first edition for $5,000. The shop's website described its offering as "a rare copy of the first edition, presumably suppressed by the Mormon Church. It contains an embittered account of how Wilson's fiancée was prevailed upon to become the second wife of an elderly polygamist (pp. 194-200). Allegedly only twenty copies of the unrevised first edition were issued; the remainder were destroyed prior to distribution. The text was purged of the offending section and the revised, sanitized book was issued in otherwise almost identical format in the same year (1910)."[174]

After writing, censorship, and publishing comes selling. The publisher asked Uncle Nick to travel the region to promote the book. He took copies with him on these trips and sometimes brought his young son Charley with him. Charley was the first of his three children born in Wilson, Wyoming. Their mother was the last of Nick's plural wives, Charlotte.

Many years later, Charley Wilson wrote his own book about his life in Jackson Hole. He combined his memoir with Nick's book "just as he wrote it on an old French typewriter of 1906 vintage." The reprint includes the controversial account of Nick's loss of his first love to the elderly polygamist in Utah.

Charley considered his own book a continuation of Nick's and titled the combined volume *The White Indian Boy – and its sequel – The Return of the White Indian*. Much of Charley's memoir is devoted to Nick's life in Jackson Hole until his death in 1915. Like Nick, Charley wrote his book late in his life. In its preface, he warned his readers that "I am not going to stand on exact dates for this biography, as it would require too much research and I do not have the time, as I am 83 years old and already have let too much time go by, so will suffice on approximate dates."[175]

It turns out that Charley stretched more than a few dates. He did not allow facts to get in the way of the good stories he remembered.

In his sequel, Charley recalled traveling to Idaho with Nick on one of his book-peddling trips. Charley was just nine years old. They stayed overnight with Ton Smith and his family at their farm in Darby. He knew the Smith girls, Zora and Mabel, who "came often to Jackson Hole to visit their five aunts." Zora was about 20 then and engaged to marry. Charley described Mabel as a beautiful, dark-haired girl.

He also took pains to describe the deadly trouble his brother-in-law Ellington had with his neighbor.

"Ton's land sloped to the west and a few hundred yards east of Ton's house lived another farmer, David S. Neal. There was bad blood between Ton Smith and Neal, when Nick and I visited the Smith family in 1910." The trouble was over their irrigation water, Wilson wrote.

"Their irrigation ditches came out of dual head gates from the creek which I think is called Darby Creek, and it heads under the Grand Teton Peak range on the west or Idaho side, but the peaks are in Wyoming," Charley wrote. "These two ditches ran parallel to each other for a distance, then Neal began use of the water in his land above Ton Smith, whose ditch ran south right near to Neal's house, and then turned abruptly on a right angle down to Smith's house. This ditch water was used for household use by the Smith family, for all their domestic use, as well as for irrigation."

Smith suspected that Neal was stealing his water at night, "because in the mornings the water set for the night had spread only a few yards into Smith's meadow."

Ellington told Nick and Charley that Neal took great delight in polluting Smith's drinking water. "[T]he next morning after Nick and I got there, we were all outside when Neal came out of his house carrying an overnight urinal chamber. He called, 'Hey, Smith!' We looked up, and he poured its contents into Smith's ditch! Ton was white with anger as he told my dad, 'See that! I am not going to take much more of it!'"

Nick asked Smith if he had contacted the authorities. Ton complained that the local officers did nothing about it.

"'They come up here and look at the ditch and all his waste is soon gone in the swift water. Neal always denies it! They always wait until someone is killed or something serious happens before they will act, and then it is often too late!'"

Charley remembered that after leaving Smith, Nick told him he was worried "because he could tell that Ton was about ready to take the 'law into his own hands.' I didn't know what Nick meant by that, but it was only about a week later that while we were peddling around Rexburg, Idaho, ... we heard that Ton Smith was in jail in Driggs waiting trial for murder!"

The next day Nick drove them to Driggs, according to Charley, and went directly to the jail there. Nick took Charley inside with him.

"He told the warden that he was Ton Smith's father-in-law, and we were ushered right in to see Ton. I was plenty scared when they took us through three or four iron gates, which were all locked after us, until we reached Ton's cell. ...

"Well, Ton was sitting on an iron cot and was unshaven and looked haggard to me," Charley wrote. The cell was furnished with a thin mattress with one blanket, a tin chamber pot, and a tin wash basin on a table with a tin water pitcher. There was one "flimsy chair," Charley recalled.

The boy watched while Nick and Ton embraced, then Nick asked

Ton what had happened. Charley said he sat on the iron cot beside Ellington and listened to Smith tell his story.

"'Things got worse after you left. For two mornings straight my ditch that passes Neal's house — the one we use for drinking water — was dry. ... It proved what I told you, that I thought he was stealing my water at night.'"

Smith told Nick and his young brother-in-law that a few mornings after they departed, he got up about 3 a.m. and rode his horse to the dual head gates that controlled flow into their ditches. Ellington found his head gate closed and Neal's wide open.

"I went back home. I had been getting madder and more frustrated all the time over this water problem! And when he started pouring their piss pot into our ditch — you were there!

"Well! I decided it has to stop!"

The next morning he rose about 2:30 a.m., loaded his old 45-70 rifle with "thirteen shells in the magazine and one in the barrel" and rode his horse Dick to the head gates.

"Mine was shut and all the water in Neal's ditch ... I tied old Dick to some willows close by the head gates, out of sight, and waited there for Neal. He came about daylight, and he was a-foot, but he had a shovel. It wasn't very light yet, but I could see him plainly. He started to open my head gate and I stepped out where he could see me and said, 'Alright! You water-stealing sonuvabitch!' And as he stood there with his mouth open, I shot him! Gawd Damn him! And not once! I put all fourteen bullets into his cussed carcass! And here I am!'"[176]

Well, Gawd damn, indeed.

Charley Wilson tells a good story, but that is not what happened. Smith was jailed in St. Anthony the day after the July 5, 1911 murder, not Driggs. Smith shot Neal while he was irrigating a rented field owned by another neighbor, Charlie Christensen. Neither man was near a head gate when Smith killed Neal. Smith tied his horse to a fence at a road intersection, not to some willows out of sight. He shot Neal twice, not 14 times. Smith pulled the trigger in mid-morning sunshine, not the earliest light of dawn. His own nephew Octave Smith watched him do it.

Claiming Neal provoked the murder was essential to Smith's defense strategy at trial. Charley Wilson simply repeated the claim when he wrote his story 75 years later.

Did Neal bully Smith and torment him over his water? Maybe. The trial revealed other reasons Smith may have despised and perhaps feared Neal.

CHAPTER TWENTY

May in the aftermath

The Neal brothers and their mother did not stay long to help May through the loss of her beloved husband after his funeral. She needed help and got it. Her sister Lizzie and her family lived nearby. My father said his mother sent him to live with his Grandmother Lewis in her log home, also close by. Knowing her toddler son was under the watchful eye of her mother eased May's burden. Dad stayed with his grandmother for six years, eating her meals, and sharing her evening prayers.[177]

Grief piled upon grief. Dave was dead but the momentum of his plans for the family enterprise continued to push into her life, reminding her again and again of her loss. A few days after the funeral, May received a letter from Idaho State Veterinarian J.H. Weber containing a certificate declaring that the state had recorded Neal's new livestock brand. They had planned to build a cattle herd. The state authorized the brand "DS" on the left rib of Neal cattle and the left thigh of any Neal horses. Her husband had applied for the brand certification just a month before his death.[178]

May sorted through her husband's papers. David had purchased life insurance and she found that a premium payment was due. Anxious to keep the policy current, she sent a letter and check to Continental Life Insurance Company agent Joseph Anderson. His response alleviated the worry.

"I cannot tell you how much I sympathise [sic] with you and how terribly shocked I was and still am whenever I think of [the] horrid deed of that demon who slew your husband," Anderson wrote from his office in Salem, Idaho. "Your letter containing check is at hand. I shall forward same to the home office of the company at once and I shall certainly do all in my power to help you get your money. As your husband's policy was in force until July 6th and I under[stand] his death occurred before that date, I think there is no question about your being able to collect the amount of the insurance."

The insurance agent scrawled a post script down the side of his letter that reads, "I will return note and the unpaid check for Ten Dollars." There was no need to make the payment due July 6 on a policy covering a life that ended July 5.[179]

May also had the sympathy of her congregation. Willard Durrant, the Darby ward clerk, recorded the killing in the ward's minutes book immediately below his description of the recent monthly fast meeting. "D. S. Neal was murdered in cold blood July 5, 1911 by Ellington Smith, both belonging to this ward."

Durrant's minutes of ward meetings are succinct and faithfully note the speakers at ward meetings. Unfortunately, the clerk did not record what people said. At the ward's sacrament meeting six days after the funeral, Pete Sorensen addressed the ward and was followed by five other men.

"Coun. P. Sorensen first gave a few remarks. Followed Lauritz Jacobsen, Octavius Smith, Arland Davidson, E.P. Holden, and Arnold Sorensen, each occupied a short time."

All of the speakers were relatives, friends, or acquaintances of D.S. Neal and Ellington Smith. Octavius was Tave Smith, who witnessed the murder. Holden served on the ward Amusement Committee with Neal and had been involved in the arrest of the killer. What did they tell their ward?

A few days later, Darby Bishop C.A. Larsen presided over a meeting of the Bishop's Council, the ward's top leaders. "Things concerning welfare of the ward were freely discussed."[180]

Did they talk about May and her family and how the ward could help them? What about Ellington Smith, jailed in St. Anthony? Were they concerned about Smith's adult son and teen-aged daughter, Joseph and Mabel? Did Joe need help running not one but two farms? Where did young Mabel go after her father was arrested? The bishop and his counselors must have reached out to all of them but Durrant did not record any of the discussion or the decisions and assignments made in that July 18 meeting.

The Mormon church's support and generosity for members who fall on hard times is well known. Mitch Kvarfordt, who served as a ward bishop in Ammon, Idaho in the early 21st century, believes that in 1911, the Darby ward leaders would have managed the murder crisis with an approach woven into church culture.

"The widow's needs should be addressed by the ward and the fast-

Made shortly after D.S. Neal's murder in 1911, this photo depicts his surviving children. From left, Ilah Aleen, 6; Lelia Ellen, 3; Melba May, 7; and Carmen, 4. David Lewis Neal, about 15 months old, sits at center. (Photo courtesy of the Neal family)

offering funds are to help that," Kvarfordt said. Those funds are raised each month, when members of the church are expected to fast through three meals, typically dinner on Saturday, then breakfast and lunch on "Fast Sunday." The money saved by foregoing those meals becomes a "fast offering" to the church.

The Darby ward leaders would have approached the Smith children to see what help the ward could give, Bishop Kvarfordt said. "Christlike service could a long way to help balm the feelings that would come up. Such service should not be just a one-time thing, either, but ongoing to help the family in need."[181]

Darby Bishop Charles A. Larsen would have been responsible for directing assistance for May and her family and for attending to any support necessary for Smith's children. Larsen served the ward through 1913. May's brother-in-law Peter Sorensen succeeded Larsen and served as Darby's bishop through 1921.[182] May's connection to the ward could not have been tighter. Given the self-sufficiency she demonstrated immediately after David's death and, really, for the rest of her life, it is unlikely that she accepted much charity from the church. Nevertheless, the knowledge that the ward could and would help must have allayed some of her worries.

May's mother Karen Marie had moved from Utah to the Teton Basin the previous fall to be closer to her children and their families. The murder brought her grandson into her own house. No doubt May also relied upon her mother, and her brother and sisters in the valley for the love and help she needed in those first dark months after the murder.

She also would have turned to her Mormon heavenly father. Her faith in prayer ran deep and she sought its succor each night in her bedroom throughout her life. Years later, she shared the peace she found in prayer with her grandchildren. They felt her "call the Spirit" into her room.

"When I would spend the night at her house, she would call me into her little room at the back of her house and her long white hair would be unpinned and hanging down her back to her waist, dressed in a long, white flannel nightgown," granddaughter Sue Rau recalled. "She taught me to pray there and there was the most beautiful feeling in that room each time I got to kneel with her at her bedside."[183]

There was not a lot of peace during the day. The demands of running the family's farm did not let up. Her husband had applied to the Idaho State Engineer's Office for a permit to divert water from the spring on their property for irrigation. Dave likely decided to file the application because of Ellington Smith's complaints about his use of the water. The permit would cement his legal right to put the water to use on his farm.

Less than two weeks after the murder, the State Engineer's Office recorded receipt of the application to appropriate water flowing from the "nameless spring" on his property. The application laid out plans to build a dam three feet high and 16 feet long to capture the water and enable diversion. There were problems with the application, however, and it was returned for correction on the same day it was received in Boise.

May met the bureaucracy's demands and re-submitted the application before the end of the month. State Engineer A.E. Robinson approved it on Aug. 19. The permit required starting the dam construction by Oct. 18, 1911, and completing the works for the diversion within two years. May was directed to put the water to beneficial use — that is, begin using it to irrigate crops and to water livestock — within a year after completion of the dam.[184]

CHAPTER TWENTY-ONE

The wheels of justice grind away

David was buried in the Darby cemetery and May was in her widow's weeds. In St. Anthony, the county justice system moved quickly to prosecute Smith. Eight days after the murder, Probate Judge Oliver Dalby issued subpoenas ordering Ellington Smith's nephew Octavus Smith, also known as Octave and Tave, and Harvey Loveland to appear before him in court July 25 at Smith's preliminary hearing.

When the hearing convened, Prosecutor B.H. "Bert" Miller put only Tave Smith on the stand. Loveland, once a student of Neal's at the Darby school, did not testify. Idaho Falls attorney Harry Holden represented Smith and cross-examined his client's nephew.[185]

Prosecutor Miller was new in the role. He had been elected county attorney the previous November. Miller was just 34, smart, and had grown up thoroughly immersed in the Mormon culture of Utah and Idaho. Bert's father had worked as a freighter and gandy dancer in Utah before he decided to try farming. He moved his family to Fremont County and made a land claim. Bert, who was just eight when they moved, helped his parents clear sagebrush from their homestead.

Miller attended schools in St. Anthony, then enrolled at Brigham Young College. While attending classes in Provo, he decided to pursue a career in the law after graduating. He went east to central Tennessee to attend the law school at Cumberland College in Lebanon. It took him just one year at Cumberland to complete his legal studies, and he engaged fully in Cumberland's college life. He played left halfback on the football team and served as an editor of the college annual, covering athletics for the *Phoenix*.

He knew how to talk and won an inter-collegiate oratorical contest representing the Philomathean Society. The prize gave other editors of the college annual a chance to talk up Miller's youth in the West.

"B.H. Miller, the winner in Cumberland's contest, is a native of Idaho," the brief description in the Phoenix notes. "During his earlier years, large herds of cattle and roving bands of Indians were more common to him than trolley cars or Shakespearean plays. The whiz of the lariat and the dismal yelp of the cayote were more familiar to his ears than the 'thump' of the piano or the shrill whistle of the locomotive. He early resolved to study law, and finally arrived in Lebanon where he will be graduated from the Law School with the outgoing Senior Class."

B. H. Miller's portrait as the winner of a speaking contest was published in the 1902 Phoenix Yearbook for Cumberland University in Tennessee. (Photo courtesy of the Stockton Archives, Cumberland University)

Miller graduated in 1902 at age 25.[186]

Returning home, Miller was admitted to the Idaho bar. He associated first with the Fremont Abstract Company, then joined J.D. Millsaps in a St. Anthony firm in 1907. He stayed three years "during which time he built up a fine law practice," historian Hiram French wrote, and established his reputation as a skilled attorney "possessing great tact and good judgment with a comprehensive knowledge of the law."[187]

He ran as a Democrat for the post of county attorney in 1910 and won the election. It was Miller's first successful campaign in what became an illustrious career in Idaho law and politics. The victory made him the prosecutor responsible the following summer for compiling the case to convict Ellington Smith.

THE DEFENSE ATTORNEYS

From the day of his arrest, Smith knew that he needed a good attorney. When he landed in the jail in St. Anthony, he asked people there to recommend a lawyer. He decided to tie his fate to one of eastern Idaho's prominent law firms, Holden, Holden, Holden & Holden of Idaho Falls.

The four Holden brothers earned their degrees in Nebraska, but their ambitions took them further west. They arrived in Idaho Falls around 1903 and quickly assumed prominent roles in the community's political, legal, business, and social circles. Harry was the oldest and was in his early 40s at the time of the Teton Basin murder. His brother Edwin M. Holden had been admitted to practice before the Idaho Supreme Court and decades later won election to sit as a justice on the high court, serving 18 years. Arthur Holden helped form the Idaho Falls Commercial Club, the forerunner to the Idaho Falls Chamber of Commerce. The youngest brother, J. Wesley Holden, had been elected president of the Chamber of Commerce in 1908 and was elected a state senator from Bonneville County in 1926.

The Holdens covered the bases when it came to politics. In 1910, Edwin ran as a Democratic candidate for district judge on the

Democratic ticket. Arthur ran for the same post as a Republican. J. Wesley Holden sought even higher office and entered the primary contest for the Republican nomination to become Idaho's secretary of state.

Harry Holden did not seek public office that year. Blackfoot's newspaper, *The Idaho Republican*, reported that he had good reason to stand clear of politics.

"While we are speaking of the Holden family we want to mention W.H. Holden who is also an attorney and is not yet a candidate for anything. He enjoys quite a lucrative practice and may go right along attending to business in the same pleasing manner he has done heretofore."[188]

A year later, Harry Holden spearheaded the firm's defense of Ellington Smith. He handled the defense questioning of Octave Smith in front of Judge Dalby.

THE PRELIMINARY HEARING

Octave Smith's detailed account painted a chilling picture of the killing of my grandfather and the moments leading up to it. His testimony also reveals much about the relationships of the people involved, including Ellington Smith, David S. Neal, and the witnesses of the shooting.

With a court recorder taking down the attorney's questions and the witness's answers, Miller drew out from Octave the key facts that proved to the court that Ellington Smith must be jailed until his trial. The prosecutor's series of questions showed that Octave had known both Ellington Smith and David Neal for years. Octave saw Neal working in Charles Christensen's field across the road in front of his little house at about 10 in the morning on July 5.

Octave told the court that as he weeded in his vegetable garden, Ellington rode up on a bay horse from the south. He noticed Smith was carrying a gun. Ellington and Octave exchanged good-mornings and Ellington said something about "lots of weeds" in his nephew's garden, then continued a few yards to a fence corner, dismounted, tied his horse, then climbed Christensen's fence and accosted Neal. Octave detailed their exchange as he answered Miller's questions.

Q: What did he say?

A: He asked him what he stole his water for.

Q: Is that the words he used?

A: No sir not the particular words.

Q: Just state to the Court the exact words he used?

A: He called him a Son-of-a-bitch.

Q: Did you hear Neal say anything?

A: He said he never stole any water.

Q: Was there any further words passed between Neal and Smith on that occasion?

A: I think Neal said he took his own water.

Q: Was that all in the same reply, did he say that at the same time he said I never stole any water?

A: Yes sir I think he did.

Octave did not hear any further talking but testified that both men were in plain view. He watched as Smith shot Neal with a rifle that Octave identified as a Winchester.

Q: You heard the shot did you?

Q: Yes sir.

Q: What did Smith do then?

A: He walked over closer and shot again.

Q: How far did he walk when he shot again?

A: As near as I could tell 15 or 20 yards.

Ellington Smith walked back to his horse, mounted it, and rode west on the road running in front of his house, Octave testified. He told Miller that he later walked over to where Neal lay.

Q: Was he dead when you got there?

A: Yes sir.

Q: Did you see bullet wounds on his person?

A: Yes sir.

Q: Who inflicted the bullet wounds upon the person of David S. Neal that resulted in his death?

A: Ellington Smith.

Take the witness. Miller.

Miller's questioning of Octave Smith could have taken only a few minutes before he turned over witness Smith to the defense. The transcript of Octave's testimony that day covers 31 legal pages, but Miller's direct examination covers just four and a half. The rest of the transcript records Harry Holden's questioning. Holden probed for holes in Octave Smith's memory of the event. His questions focused on many details: the wind that morning; the layout of Octave Smith's house and garden; the type and condition of fences in the area; and the proximity and actions of Octave neighbors, brothers Harvey and Oscar Loveland.

Octave testified that he had known the widower Ellington Smith and his children since moving to a house on A.C. Larsen's farm about two miles north of the murder site. There he and his uncle were neighbors. "I probably saw and talked with him every day," Octave told Holden.

The nephew and his uncle remained neighbors until Octave bought his own place in 1907. Ellington left his home north of Darby canyon in 1909 and moved to a second place he owned across the road from the Neal farm. It was about a mile south of the site of the murder.

Under Holden's questioning, Octave described how he started his morning the day of the shooting. He rose from bed at 6 a.m., before his wife, though he could not recall how much later she got up. He milked his cows. His own two small children were there along with his wife's two sisters, Essie and Ida, and they all ate breakfast together about 8 o'clock. Octave then completed his chores "and tended a stream of water I had running in the field."

He returned to the farmyard and began working in his garden with Essie, his sister-in-law who was just 13 years old. Holden wanted more details about exactly where Octave was hoeing in his garden when Ellington arrived. Tave told Holden that he was weeding his carrots.

> *Q: How long after the defendant passed your place that he tied up his horse?*
>
> *A: Just a very short time.*
>
> *Q: Where did he tie his horse?*
>
> *A: By a head gate at the corner.*
>
> *Q: By your north east corner?*
>
> *A: Yes sir.*
>
> *Q: Did you keep on hoeing?*
>
> *A: Yes sir.*
>
> *...*
>
> *Q: What direction were you facing when you spoke to him?*
>
> *A: I think I faced him.*
>
> *Q: After you spoke to him he went right on?*
>
> *A: Yes sir I don't think he stopped at all.*
>
> *Q: Did you have any reason to watch him after he spoke to you?*
>
> *A: I just happened to look up and saw him tying up his horse.*
>
> *Q: When you saw him tying his horse what did you do?*
>
> *A: Just stood there.*
>
> *Q: Did you hoe any more?*
>
> *A: I might have hit a lick or two.*

> *Q: Do you know whether you hoed any more after you saw him tying his horse or not?*
>
> *A: I may have hoed a weed or two.*
>
> *Q: Did you speak to him after that?*
>
> *A: No sir.*
>
> *Q: Did you have any reason to think there would be any trouble?*
>
> *A: No sir.*
>
> *Q: Why did you watch him then?*
>
> *A: I thought may be he was going to shoot a cyote.*
>
> *Q: You thought he was going to shoot a cyote, that was the first thought that came to you?*
>
> *A: Yes sir.*

Octave testified that he had looked at his watch at "just a little after ten" and recalled that the wind was perfectly quiet. Ellington Smith stood about 70 yards away from Octave when he exchanged words with Neal. That prompted the attorney to ask, a bit incredulously, whether Octave could possibly have heard all that was said by the two men in the field.

"I can't say that I heard it all or that I didn't hear it all," Octave replied, but he told Holden that he kept his eyes on the man with the gun.

> *Q: At the time you say you saw him going into the field you had no reason to pay attention?*
>
> *A: I had no reason to pay attention but naturally I would watch a man that was going to shoot, even if he was only going to shoot a squirell, and when I heard him talk it made me pay attention.*

As the confrontation unfolded before him, Octave said he kept moving in his garden. He watched, stunned, as Ellington fired his first bullet into Neal then quickly walked some 15 yards closer before shooting a second bullet into Neal's head. Octave said he stepped behind his house after the two shots were fired, moving closer to young Essie, who was kneeling to pull weeds.

"I told her he had shot Mr. Neal," and the girl "started to the house kind of crying." But Octave called her back. He told her to keep still but keep working.

Moments later, his wife came around the house walking toward him. Holden did not ask Octave to recount any comments between them. She took Essie back inside. Octave said he took a few minutes to put his horses in his barn before returning to the women in the house.

While he was standing in his doorway, brothers Oscar and Harvey Loveland walked over from their homes east of Octave's house. They talked. Oscar Loveland then walked back to his place and a few moments later Octave saw him "going down the road." Oscar was taking on tough duty a mile south at the Neal home. He had to deliver the news of David's death to May Neal.

As Oscar walked down the road, his brother walked out into Christensen's field, Octave testified. "He drug the dead man out of the ditch," then walked back to his house. Ten minutes later, Octave himself went into the field with Harvey.

Q: What did you do?

A: I took a canvass and covered him up. — the dead man, Neal.

Q: Did you move the body?

A: I think I straightened one of his arms out.

About a half hour later, Octave said, he joined "a number of others" who went out into the field. Who were these people? It seems likely that May would have rushed to the scene after talking with Oscar Loveland, leaving her five children at home. Perhaps the local constable was among the group in Christensen's field, as well. The transcript does not reveal when Neal's body was taken out of the field nor where it was taken.

Harry Holden tested Octave's memory of the weather conditions that morning, asking if he kept daily records of wind and temperature and if he could recall whether the wind was blowing the four days before the murder or during the days after. He wanted to know if it was reasonable to believe Miller's star witness could have heard the interchange between Neal and his killer.

Octave conceded that he did not recall the weather conditions on other days that month but stuck to his recollection that on the morning of July 5, when Neal was killed, there was no wind.

> *Q: How do you remember that then?*
>
> *A: It was a very hot still day that day.*
>
> *Q: There was considerable excitement arount there?*
>
> *A: Yes sir there was some excitement but it was [a] still and hot day, just the same.*

Holden continued to grind away, looking for a possible crack in Tave's testimony. The attorney asked about the condition of the rented field. He wanted to know the types and height of fences Octave had, and the location, number, and height of trees in his yard, apparently trying to determine whether the witness truly had a clear view of Ellington Smith and Neal. He also asked about Octave's knowledge of the victim.

> *Q: How long have you been acquainted with David S. Neal, how long had you known him prior to his death?*
>
> *A: I have known him ever since he came to the basin.*
>
> *Q: How long is that?*
>
> *A: About five years.*
>
> *Q: Has his family ever visited you?*
>
> *A: Mr. Neal has been there but I don't think his family have.*

Holden ended his examination by asking if Octave made any statement regarding the case after the arrest of Ellington Smith on July 5. Octave said an inquest had been held at farmer Ed Holden's place and his statement was taken in writing there.[189]

The questioning ended then. Two days later, Judge Dalby signed an order declaring that sufficient cause existed to believe Ellington Smith was guilty of first-degree murder and ordering him held without bail by the sheriff of Fremont County.[190]

The *Ogden Standard* reported a brief account of the hearing. Datelined from Driggs, the *Standard* report said the case "is attracting much attention in this district. Smith was apparently a quiet and unassuming man, who has lived with his daughter for a number of years past, his wife having died ten years ago. He has lived much alone and associated but little with his neighbors. He owns a fine farm and has some good animals. He has had bad luck in raising colts and at times accused his neighbors of poisoning them.

"He also claimed that he had had trouble with people regarding his water rights, but no one supposed it was of a serious nature until the morning of the shooting."

The paper described the shooting in Christensen's field, then said Smith went to a neighbor named "Mr. Plummer" and told him what he had done. Officers in Driggs were notified and Smith was arrested, the newspaper reported.

"He told Constable Eddington that he had been driven to the deed by the aggravation of Neal, and also added there were two more he was after, one of them by the name of A.C. Larson. It so happened that Mr. Larson would certainly have met Smith the same morning that Neal was killed, but for some unaccountable reason he took a different road to his home from one he usually traveled.

"The general impression in the neighborhood is that Smith had brooded so much over his trouble that the deed was committed in a fit of despondency which he was unable to withstand."[191]

Just over a month later, Prosecutor Miller filed an "Information" in the 9th Judicial District Court noting that Judge Dalby had bound Smith over to the court for trial for murder. Miller's filing stated that on July 5, Smith "Did then and there willfully, unlawfully, feloniously and with premeditation and malice aforethought, kill and murder one David S. Neal, a human being."

The filing provided a list of Miller's "known witnesses." It named Mrs. David S. Neal, Octavus Smith, Mrs. Octavus Smith, Essie Ferguson, Harvey Loveland, Oscar Loveland, William Yager, Ezra Plummer,

Constable Elijah Eddington, and Fremont County Sheriff John T. Fisher.

Three days later, on Sept. 14, Smith entered his plea of "not guilty" with the court.

CHAPTER TWENTY-TWO

The Holdens plan an insanity defense

As Smith waited in jail that fall and early winter, his attorneys prepared his defense. The eyewitness account that Octave Smith delivered in Judge Dalby's Probate Court left them little room to challenge the charge that Smith planned to kill his neighbor and did so in broad daylight without compunction.

His attorneys, Holden, Holden, Holden, and Holden decided to pursue a two-pronged strategy. Their first push would be to attack the character of the victim and suggest that he "had it coming," a common trial tactic when the basic evidence against a defendant is overwhelming.

His attorneys planned to depict Neal as a bully who regularly harassed and demeaned Smith. Ellington no doubt regaled them with stories about Neal insulting and threatening him. Neal, the Holdens would argue, was not a hard-working husband and father, nor a good church man and Christian. They would tell the jury that Neal's image as the community's trusted school teacher was a facade for a scheming land-grabber willing to pollute and steal another farmer's water to drive him off his land.

Their depiction of Neal would implant in the minds of the jury their contention that the victim had an ulterior motive: he continually harassed his neighbor to induce him to leave his farm, giving Neal's friend A.C. Larsen the chance to acquire the property at a rock-bottom price. The Holdens wanted the jurors to question how they themselves would have reacted to such abuse and conniving.

The second prong of the Holden's legal strategy focused on Smith and his state of mind the day of the murder. They planned an insanity defense. Ellington Smith, his attorneys would attempt to prove, absorbed Neal's torment and abuse until his mind snapped and he temporarily lost touch with his deepest morals. The defense would argue that when Smith shot Neal he no longer understood the difference between right and wrong and may not even have been aware of the actions he took when he rode to Christensen's place and shot his neighbor.

They well understood the foundation of their argument. The history of the insanity defense in Western civilization is long, reaching back to at least the 12th century. The argument is based on the contention that an insane person lacks the intent required to make an act criminal because they do not know it is wrong or simply cannot control their actions.[192]

Ellington Smith's defense strategy required finding local witnesses who would either help tear down Neal's reputation or portray Smith as a man of character victimized by the dead man. Smith's attorneys also needed witnesses who would buttress their argument that Smith, a man of good character, had been harassed to the point that he lost his sanity and no longer understood the immorality of murder.

The Holdens knew that Prosecutor Miller's witnesses would lay out the sequence of events and the effect of the murder on Neal's family. They knew Neal's widow May would take the stand and her testimony was certain to wring the hearts of the jury.

They put together a list of witnesses they hoped would make their case. It included Don Carlos Driggs, the president of the Teton Stake of the LDS church who had seen Smith on the day he was arrested. Smith's son Joseph and daughter Mabel Smith could testify about any run-ins with their father's neighbor. Others could testify about the neighbors' relationship or help portray Smith as a reliable farmer who paid his bills and had his community's respect. They subpoenaed two other women, Miss Eva Woolstenholm and Bernice Harris, and nine other men from Driggs and Darby, two men from Clawson, two from Rexburg, and one from Salem, all communities led by the valley's Mormon faithful.

The Holdens also needed expert witnesses to make the insanity defense, professionals in the field of psychology. Because they did not

No Forgiveness

The Idaho Falls law firm Holden, Holden, Holden, and Holden represented Ellington Smith in his 1912 murder trial. Seen in this 1906 photograph taken in their Idaho Falls office are, from left, W. H. "Harry" Holden, Edwin M. Holden, Arthur W. Holden, and J. Wesley Holden. (Photo courtesy of Rob Farnum of Holden, Kidwell, Hahn & Crapo.)

know Smith personally, the jury could view them as objective witnesses with no personal stake in the case. The Holdens found their experts when they hired two of Idaho's most prominent doctors working with people suffering severe mental illness: Dr. J.W. Givens, superintendent of the North Idaho Insane Asylum in Orofino; and Dr. Frances Poole, superintendent of the Idaho Insane Asylum in Blackfoot. The two doctors would review the case, interview Smith, and explain their findings to the jury.

Dr. Givens was one of the most well-known and respected public administrators in Idaho. He would be the star expert witness for the defense. At the time of Smith's trial, Dr. Givens had directed Idaho's efforts to identify and treat the criminally insane for more than 20 years. He had been named superintendent of the territorial mental hospital in Blackfoot in 1887, less than a year after it opened and three years before Idaho achieved statehood. He built his reputation on good care of the asylum residents and efficient administration.

The asylum, built in Blackfoot in 1886, was a source of considerable pride in the territory. A correspondent for the Wood River Times claimed the completed structure was "one of the most convenient buildings for the care of insane people that was ever erected west of the Rocky Mountains ... this building double-discounts any other structure ever erected in Idaho." And it was safe, the reporter asserted. In a fire, "the patients who occupy rooms in the third story can escape as easily as though they were on the first floor."[193]

This assertion lamentably proved wrong. In November 1889, a defective flue ignited a fire that burned through the building, killing at least three patients, and perhaps five others.

Givens telegraphed Boise, the territorial capital, with news of the conflagration:

BLACKFOOT, Nov. 24.

To The Statesman, Boise City, Idaho –

Insane Asylum burned last night. Fifty-seven patients saved; three patients known to have perished in the flames. Five others unaccounted for; may have perished or escaped.

Dr. Givens.[194]

Givens' response during the fire and to its tragic aftermath enhanced his reputation. James Hawley, a Boise attorney and future governor of Idaho, was in Blackfoot on legal business when the hospital burned. He returned to Boise with a description of a fire that "burned with frightful rapidity." Hawley told of Givens' presence of mind and courage in the emergency. Hawley also reminded Idahoans of the condition of the people that the hospital served and the challenges of caring for them.

When the hospital caught fire, Givens was roused from his bed in his apartment in the building. He immediately began directing the effort to save his patients.

"Some of the worst patients were strapped to their couches to prevent them from doing harm or damage to themselves or others. These unfortunate ones had their bands severed and were permitted to roam at large," Hawley reported. "The difficulty in rescuing the inmates of the doomed building was increased and in some instances rendered impossible from the fact that they acted like horses, and made frantic effort to get back into the building, after they had once been safely taken out."

"Dr. Givens displayed great heroism and bravery by nobly rescuing the last patient taken out — a women [sic]. The flames were burning fiercely around him, yet he ascended the ladder and carried the heavy burden back with him, when it seemed scarcely possible that the act could be accomplished."[195]

A coroner's jury that met immediately after the fire exonerated management of all blame. Opinions of the building changed. "The main building of that institution was a miserable excuse for a building of that character at best," the *Blackfoot News* proclaimed, "and from the very beginning the superintendent, the board of directors and others felt a sense of uneasiness about it."[196]

The hero Givens continued as superintendent of the Blackfoot hospital until 1895, then decided to improve his education. He stepped aside and went to New York and Baltimore for post graduate work in medicine, then returned to Blackfoot and resumed his post as director of the asylum.

When they prepared for Smith's trial, the Holdens knew that Givens had history as an expert witness. Among other cases, the doctor testified for the prosecution in a sensational Boise murder case. In early June of 1898, Charles Nelson shot the quartermaster general of the Idaho National Guard, emptying his revolver at close range into T.M. Kerr. Kerr died nine days later. Boise's *Idaho Statesman* ran long stories about the shooting, describing Nelson as an offended husband and detailing the infidelity of Nelson's wife with Kerr and allegedly others.

Nelson was defended by Boise attorneys James Hawley and William Borah, who both later became politically prominent, Hawley as governor and Borah a U.S. senator. The *Idaho Statesman*'s reporting of the 1898 trial shows that Hawley and Borah employed a defense strategy that the Holdens echoed in the trial of Smith: the victim's inexcusable acts justified his killing and the shooter was insane and not responsible for his actions.

Dr. Givens served as director of the Blackfoot hospital until 1905, building his reputation as an expert on mental health and the treatment of people society considered insane. State officials celebrated his work there. Gov. John Morrison said Idaho was "fortunate in that we have had a superintendent who is not only a skilled and experienced specialist in diseases peculiar to insanity, but who is also a good business man and a fine executive officer."

Governor Frank Gooding appointed Dr. Givens to serve as the first superintendent of the second state hospital in 1906. Givens announced he would use patients from the Blackfoot hospital to build the new asylum at Orofino in central Idaho. His inmate crew began clearing land in mid-July. The *Statesman* declared the work "probably stands without parallel in the history of the world." The inmates slept in canvas tents for months, then erected shacks to live in while continuing work over the winter. The stone and brick building, with the capacity to house 60 patients, was ready for occupation April 15, 1906, nine months later. Some pregnancies take longer.[197]

Over the next few years, Givens kept his name in the news. He pursued escaped inmates. He testified in other criminal cases involving insanity claims. He bought stock in the Lewiston National Bank and was a member of the state bankers association.[198] Harry Holden must have felt great confidence after lining up such a formidable witness to testify for the defense in the trial of Ellington Smith.

The Holdens did not rest once they had secured Givens as a witness. They also enlisted Dr. Francis H. Poole to testify. Gov. James Hawley had chosen Poole to take over the Blackfoot hospital in March 1911, just a few months before the murder of D.S. Neal. The new superintendent had worked as a doctor in Mackay, Idaho, and later in Pocatello. Poole did not have Givens' considerable knack for publicity; however, he had gained prominence in southeastern Idaho and developed valuable political connections through his involvement in a controversy over the engineering and construction of the Mackay dam. The project was underway on the Big Lost River in 1910. Newspaper reports of poor supervision of the dam's construction had wounded the re-election campaign of Republican Gov. James H. Brady. The incumbent was defeated by Hawley in the general election that fall. Poole, it turned out, was a key source for the news stories that damaged Brady.

The new governor was the same James Hawley who, along with William Borah, successfully defended Charles Nelson in the 1898 Boise murder case.

During the 1910 gubernatorial campaign, Hawley used the worries about the Mackay dam's safety to pound Brady in speeches around the state. Late in the campaign, the *Mackay Miner* published yet another story detailing the problems with the dam. Hawley used excerpts from the story in advertisements he published in papers across Idaho. The ads called the dam "an absolute menace."

In its effort to make these assertions more credible, Hawley's campaign highlighted the ties of *Miner* editor Leslie Dillingham to the Republicans and their interests. The Democrat's ads noted that Dillingham was the chairman of the Custer County Republican Central Committee and noted the *Miner* described itself as devoted to the principles of the GOP.

Neither the ad nor the Hawley campaign mentioned that Dr. Poole was a good friend of Dillingham when Poole served as the contract physician on the dam project. A few weeks after the election, news reports revealed that the incoming governor intended to appoint Poole to be the next superintendent of the Blackfoot asylum.[199]

A legislative committee convened in early 1911 to investigate the state land board's supervision of the Mackay dam project and the political controversy that followed. Poole, whose selection as the next Blackfoot superintendent by then had been announced by Hawley, was called to testify. He told the legislators that workers at the dam told him of many problems. A foreman supervising the driving of sheet steel piling, Poole said, had told him confidentially that the work was a "big joke." The project doctor added that he had traded property to move his family out of the danger zone below the dam.

Former Gov. Brady used the hearing to rebuild his reputation. He asserted that he had, in fact, informed the land board of the concerns about the Mackay dam. He also suspected a political payoff. When the committee allowed him to question Poole, Brady pushed the doctor to affirm that he knew the *Mackay Miner* editor well and that Dillingham often stayed with Poole when he had business in Pocatello. Brady forced Poole to concede that "Mr. Dillingham was active in securing your appointment at the hands of Governor Hawley to the position of medical director of the Blackfoot insane asylum."[200]

The hearing apparently did not damage Poole's appointment prospects and it certainly helped Brady. Two years later, the Idaho legislature elected Brady to represent Idaho in the U.S Senate, alongside Hawley's pal Bill Borah.

Poole ran the Blackfoot hospital for two years under the Hawley administration and was in the post when he testified for the defense in Ellington Smith's trial.

PROSECUTOR MILLER FINDS HIS OWN EXPERT

Smith's attorneys had their expert witnesses lined up. The directors of Idaho's two insane asylums were well known in the state and possessed a broad range of experience with mentally ill people, very likely more such experience than any other Idaho doctor. Their testimony could turn the case in favor of the defense. Prosecutor Miller had to find a way to respond.

The young prosecutor decided to rely on familiarity as much as expertise. He approached Dr. Ray Fisher, a general practitioner who had opened his office in Rigby in 1910. Miller knew the doctor as the county health officer. They must have crossed paths in the county offices in St. Anthony.

Dr. Fisher did not have the statewide profiles enjoyed by Givens and Poole, but he had a significant presence in Fremont County, and county residents would comprise the jury pool for the murder trial. In the fall of 1911, Fisher's duties for the county included inspecting public schools, a task that would have provided ample opportunity to meet people across the upper Snake River Valley. The *Rigby Star* occasionally reported on his activities in its pages. When he inspected school buildings, the *Star* noted it. (His presence in the *Star* would continue in the years after the Smith trial. The paper mentioned Fisher when his profession took him to medical society meetings, when he reported vital county health statistics, and when he was required to treat a gunshot wound.)[201]

Prosecutor Miller also listed Dr. W.B. West as a witness. Like Dr. Fisher, West would have been reasonably well known in the county. He was a former county physician in Bear Lake County, and practiced in St. Anthony at the time of the trial and for several years after.[202]

DEFENSE CHALLENGES AND WITNESS SUBPOENAS

While Miller put together his plans to counter the insanity arguments, Smith's defense team faced its own issues. Harry Holden was the lead attorney in the case. He had examined Octave Smith in Judge Dalby's probate court. In the months following the July preliminary hearing, an irritation in his throat developed into a significant problem that he could not ignore. He turned to the Mayo Brothers hospital in New York.

"Attorney W.H. Holden left Saturday for Rochester, N.Y., to have an operation performed upon his throat which has been troubling him for some time," the *Idaho Republican* in Blackfoot reported on Nov. 24. The paper was edited by the Holdens' political ally Byrd Trego. Trego kept the Holdens in the public eye by regularly reporting visits by Harry and his brothers to the Bingham County seat for legal or political matters. "It is considered a very dangerous operation and he avoided it until it seem imperative that something should be done to afford relief."[203]

Harry Holden survived the surgery and returned to Idaho Falls. It had been a rough year for his family in terms of health and mortality. Scarlet fever killed two of his children the previous January, a gloomy anniversary he and his wife would have observed just days before the Fremont County District Court convened the trial of Ellington Smith.[204]

Perhaps because of his throat surgery, Harry stepped back and agreed that his brother Edwin would serve as lead counsel for Smith at the trial. They had their list of witnesses, as did prosecutor Miller.

On Monday, Jan. 15, the court issued subpoenas to ten witnesses for the prosecution, Neal's widow May, Octavus Smith, Mrs. Octavus Smith,

Oscar Loveland, Ezra Yager, Ezra Plummer, Elijah Eddington, Albert Tarbet, Israel Clark, and Joe Delaney.

Later in the week, Constable George Eddington served subpoenas on witnesses for Smith's defense in Driggs, Clawson, Darby, and Chapin. The Holdens requested that Ezra Plummer and Elijah Eddington testify as defense witnesses. Others subpoenaed by the defense included Teton Stake President Don Carlos Driggs, Edlef Edlefson, Dutch Frank, W.W. Nickell, Dave Waddell, Eva Woolstenhulme, and John Pickett, the county deputy who took Smith to St. Anthony after the murder.

The Holdens also wanted testimony from several people in the Rexburg area, apparently to serve as character witnesses. The following Friday, the city's marshal served subpoenas there to Henry Flamm, Sr., Richard Smith, H.P. Jensen, Orsen Waldron, B.R. Harris, and a person identified only as Dr. Walker.

A week later, Miller asked the court to subpoena three others: H.M. Olmstead, the man who had demanded that Ellington Smith cease his abuse of May Neal when Smith was arrested; Ed Holden, owner of the farm where Deputy Pickett took charge of the suspect on the day of the murder; and Parley Driggs, whose home was near Smith's first farm and was one of the irrigators involved in the Wyoming and Darby Bench Canal project.[205]

CHAPTER TWENTY-THREE

The trial of Ellington Smith and David S. Neal

Ninth District Court Judge James G. Gwinn opened the trial of Ellington Smith on Jan. 22, 1912. It was a sensation in the upper Snake River Valley and drew large crowds to the recently completed Fremont County courthouse.

"Fully seven hundred people crowded themselves into the spacious new courtroom each day, hundreds being compelled to stand," the *Teton Peak-Chronicle* reported in its story summarizing the trial. "A great many residents of Teton Basin, where the tragedy occurred, were in attendance as witnesses and spectators, as well as numerous friends and relatives of the deceased and the accused."

It's a striking number of people in a county with under 25,000 residents. Fewer than 1,200 people lived in Driggs, Bates, Chapin, and Darby.[206]

The attorneys and many of those in the crowd knew Judge Gwinn well. He had been elected as Fremont County's probate judge in November 1910, the same election that put Prosecutor Miller in his post.

Gwinn had been involved in local politics before his election as probate judge. In 1905, he was elected St. Anthony's mayor as head of the People's Party ticket. The *Teton Peak-Chronicle* had touted his candidacy, describing him as a man of high moral character. The paper also pointed out personal qualities it expected to advance his election prospects that year, describing Gwinn as "young, handsome, and single."

The newspaper suggested those qualities "should stand in special favor with the ladies."[207] Idaho had enfranchised women fourteen years before.

Gov. Hawley appointed Gwinn judge of the newly created 9th Judicial District Court in April 1911. He represented a compromise after many members of the southeastern Idaho legal bar engaged in a "red-hot fight" for the new judgeship. The new judicial district encompassed Fremont and Bonneville counties. In late February, "... a delegation of 22 attorneys from the two counties affected descended upon Governor Hawley to protest against the appointment of Arthur Holden of Idaho Falls and to advocate the appointment of J.D. Millsaps of St. Anthony," the *Idaho Statesman* reported. (Millsaps was the former partner of B.H. Miller.)

The only objection "raised against Mr. Holden is that he has three brothers practicing law in Idaho Falls and that with him on the bench there would be too much Holden."

The idea that a Holden on the bench might somehow unfairly advantage the Idaho Falls law firm was dismissed by Gov. Hawley. He said he would have appointed E.M. Holden had Edwin been an applicant in the first place, but the radical positions taken by the feuding lawyers made it impossible to appoint any of the attorneys active in the dispute.

"You might as well try to pacify a lot of wild animals as to get the members of the bar to agree on a candidate for the position."[208] The governor handed the plum position and its $4,000 salary to Gwinn.

Gwinn, then, had served in his position for nearly ten months when he convened Smith's trial. If any ill will existed between the judge and Smith's attorneys, it went unnoticed by reporters covering the proceedings.

In the first three days of the trial, Edwin, Harry, and J. Wesley Holden sparred with Prosecutor Miller over jury selection. The Holdens used peremptory challenges to dismiss six potential jurors. Miller eliminated four other candidates. There is no court record nor any newspaper reports of the questions asked of the jury candidates by the attorneys.

The final selections were made Wednesday morning, Jan. 24. The

No Forgiveness

twelve men seated on the jury came from communities throughout the upper Snake River Valley including Haden, Lewisville, Lorenzo, Marysville, Ora, Plano, Rudy, Rigby, Rexburg, Teton, and Victor. The Rigby man, C.J. Call, was selected as foreman.

MILLER OPENS HIS PROSECUTION

With the jury seated, Miller brought his key witnesses to the stand Wednesday afternoon. He called first Ellington Smith's nephew Octave Smith, then Tave's niece Essie Ferguson. Both had witnessed the crime from Tave's garden. The crowd that jammed into the courthouse heard Octave Smith lay out the details of the shooting, giving them all a picture of Ellington riding past him and young Essie as they weeded vegetables. Tave would have described the armed rider calmly dismounting, tying his horse, crossing the road and going into the field where Neal was irrigating, then demanding to know whose water he was stealing.

Neal's response that he took no man's water but his own would have been followed by Tave's description of Ellington shooting Neal once, dropping him, then walking closer and shooting him again before returning to his horse and riding off west.

Tave recounted how Harvey Loveland pulled Neal's body out of the ditch, then his own walk into Charles Christensen's field to help cover Neal with a canvas. Somebody went to find the constable. Did Tave know who it was? Did he tell the jury that Oscar Loveland walked the road south to tell May Neal that her husband, so full of energy that morning, was dead?

The dead man's widow testified next. The court minutes list her as Mrs. David S. Neal. They do not mention her first name. Perhaps she wore the same graceful black dress that she donned for the funeral photo with her mother-in-law and her brothers-in-law the previous July. The jury certainly would have seen the dress as her mourning garb.

It had to be a grueling appearance in the witness box for May, face to face with her husband's killer. She must have recounted her breakfast with Dave that morning and his departure to irrigate the rented field.

She may have said he went out the back to avoid encountering their troublesome neighbor. She would have told the court of the arrival of Oscar Loveland at her home and his delivery of the news that her husband had been shot and killed.

It is easy to imagine her telling the jury how she absorbed the shocking news. She may have instructed Melba, her eldest daughter, to go get her grandmother to come stay with her sisters and toddler brother while their mother made her way the mile north. Or did she testify that she simply dropped everything and frantically rushed off on her bicycle to get to the murder scene, leaving Loveland and her children gaping as she pedaled away? Perhaps the shock so devastated her that she froze and had to be helped to a chair or a bed.

From the witness stand, she also must have recounted the arrest of Smith by Constable Eddington at her neighbor's house across the road. It happened just a few dozen steps away from her front porch in the bright light of a July afternoon. Did she tell the jury that it was then that she called out to Smith, "You are the man that killed my husband," then staggered under Smith's abuse?[209]

Did she hear H.M. Olmstead rebuke Smith? Could she have committed the moment to memory despite her mind swirling with the overwhelming wave of death and loss? Did she describe her fears of the future or how she sat later with her four young daughters at her feet, trying to help them understand their father was lost? Did Miller ask her to explain all of this?

The future she had dreamed with David was lost along with him. The grief must have welled up as she answered Miller's questions before the jury and that crowd of neighbors and relatives, sharing her last moments with David.

Tave Smith's wife Ellen and neighboring farmer Ezra Plummer also took the witness stand that afternoon. Ellen Smith's testimony does not appear in news reports from the trial. Plummer's testimony is reported. He told the jury that Ellington Smith rode up to his house after the shooting. Smith asked Plummer to go to his place and handle the chores and take care of his livestock until he could get word to his boys that they were needed. Plummer also testified that Smith informed him "that

Neal is laying up in a ditch in Charley Christensen's field," then said, "I guess he won't steal any more water."

Plummer told the court that Smith "looked strangely out of his eyes at that time, and did not seem to realize the crime he had committed." Smith, Plummer testified, then asked him if he could cut through Plummer's fields to get to his own farm. Plummer refused permission to cross his property. Smith instead walked his horse to an opening to the road and left.[210]

The court minutes do not say whether any of the state's witnesses were cross-examined by the defense that day. If Edwin Holden did cross-examine Plummer, he may have pushed the farmer to say more about his recall of Smith's demeanor, seeing it as an opportunity to bolster the insanity claim the defense had readied. But would Holden really have wanted to keep May, the grieving widow, on the stand any longer? More minutes with her in front of the jury would have given those twelve men more time to ponder the full emotional and economic impact of a husband's murder on a despondent young mother and her now-fatherless children.

What the court minutes do say is succinct: "Octavus Smith, Essie Ferguson, Mrs. David S. Neal, Mrs. Octavus Smith and Ezra Plummer were sworn and examined on behalf of the State. Whereupon the case was ordered continued for the day."

TRIAL DAY 4

Brothers Harvey and Oscar Loveland were called to the stand when the trial resumed on Thursday. Their testimony was needed to corroborate the statements made by Tave Smith, his wife, and her sister. The brothers heard the shots fired that killed Neal. Harvey crossed the road and walked into Christensen's field, then pulled Neal's body out of the ditch.

Testimony by Bill Yager was not reported. Perhaps he was among the group of people who gathered at the scene a half hour or so after the shooting. Constable Eddington was called to the stand twice that day, once as a prosecution witness and a second time on behalf of the defendant. His testimony proved useful for both sides as he related details of his arrest of Ellington Smith about 2 p.m. on the day of the murder.

Eddington "testified that as he approached the house Smith shook hands with him looking him straight in the eye, and saying that he knew his errand and would make no resistance," the *Peak-Chronicle* reported. The constable described Smith as "calm" when he made the arrest and echoed Plummer's description of the murderer, saying he "looked strange out of his eyes." Smith told him that he had to kill Neal because his neighbor had tormented him over water and again claimed that A.C. Larsen was at the bottom of the whole trouble.

The account of the arrest scene challenges modern expectations of a police murder investigation. Everyone involved knew each other. The constable trusted Smith's promise that he planned no further violence. He apparently did not bother to pat down the suspect. Instead, after shaking hands with the killer, the constable granted Smith's request to go back into his house to retrieve his coat and hat.

As the two men entered the house, Smith turned and asked a bystander to clean his rifle. The request rings now as absurdly weird, given 21st century expectations that police will control a crime scene and guard all potential evidence, particularly the murder weapon.

Smith and Eddington stayed inside the house together for about a quarter hour. Smith, truly calm, produced a revolver from his pocket and put it aside, telling the constable that he "guessed he would have no more use for this pop gun."

There's no suggestion in the newspaper report of his testimony that Eddington felt threatened by his suspect suddenly pulling a pistol. The two men had attended church together. Presenting the revolver was an odd moment in the constable's arrest of the suspect. It was followed by another. Smith told Eddington he wanted to retrieve a few of his papers and rummaged through a trunk for a few minutes searching for them. Then he instead took some papers that, according to Eddington, had been in plain sight the entire time.

Eddington said Smith's behavior was strange. He told the court that he believed the man was insane at the time. The comment had to be music to Harry and Edwin Holden's ears.

The constable and Smith departed the house and headed north, but they stopped at Darby farmer Ed Holden's house. (Ed Holden was not related to the attorneys.) Eddington told the court that they met Deputy Sheriff John Pickett there. Pickett took charge of Smith for transport by wagon to St. Anthony and the county jail.

Miller did not call Pickett to the stand during the initial presentation of the prosecution's case. He reserved the deputy as one of his rebuttal witnesses who would speak after the Holdens had laid out their defense. Instead, the prosecutor chose to put Sheriff John Fisher on the stand. Fisher recounted Deputy Pickett's delivery of Smith to the county jail on July 6, after they had made the trip overnight from Darby. Fisher likely would have also noted that Probate Judge Dalby issued an arrest warrant that afternoon based on the deputy's sworn statement that Ellington Smith had murdered David S. Neal "with premeditation and malice aforethought."

Sheriff Fisher told the court that when Smith arrived at the jail, he had acted as any sane person would act. The prisoner even had asked for advice on whom he should retain to defend him.

The court minutes do not indicate cross-examination of any of the state's witnesses by the Holdens that day. The minutes do state that the sheriff "was sworn and offered for cross-examination but not examined." The Holdens wanted no more of the sheriff.

Miller rested the state's case.

A SORDID ELEMENT

The Holdens launched their defense of Ellington Smith the same day. They brought both Constable Eddington and Ezra Plummer back to the stand, no doubt to burn into the jurors' minds their testimony that Smith on the day of the murder appeared to them to be out of his mind, that he looked "strange out of his eyes," insane.

Plummer told the court that he had visited Smith at his home on the evening of July 4. He said Smith acted oddly that night, "walking back and forth and looking out of the window into the dark, merely grunting when asked questions," the *Teton-Peak-Chronicle* reported. His friend's behavior convinced Plummer that "the defendant was insane at that time."

The Holdens then introduced a sordid new element to the story. They called W.W. Nickell to the stand. Nickell was a neighbor and an acquaintance of both David Neal and Ellington Smith. Nickell said that he had visited Smith on the evening of July 3, two days before the murder, to make arrangements for Smith's daughter Mabel to spend July 4 with him and his family in Victor.

On that Saturday evening, Nickell testified, he told Smith about two recent conversations with Neal. Nickell told Smith that he had been at Neal's house when Neal said there would come a time when he would "stomp" Smith's head. The second conversation occurred later, when both Neal and Nickell were working in Neal's field. Nickell told Smith that Neal revealed that he knew that Smith "was laying up" with his own daughter Mabel, and he could prove it.

The comments must have sent a ripple through the crowded courtroom. If Nickell was truthful, the claim of incest would not have surprised May. She and Dave must have discussed it. They knew Mabel, just 15 at the time, was about the same age as her mother was when she married Ellington.

Nickell and other witnesses told the court that Neal allowed his hogs to wallow in the stream that flowed from his yard to Smith's, further polluting Smith's drinking water. Neal had washed out a sore on a sick mare's shoulder and the "putrescence" from the sore ran into the same stream, he said.

The *Teton Peak-Chronicle* report says that "Nickell's testimony of the occurrence at the Neal home" was rebutted in part by both Mrs. David S. Neal and a daughter of Andrew Larsen, "who testified that Nickell had warned Neal at that time not to let Smith shoot him from ambush ..."

The newspaper's reporting and the trial minutes do not coincide. The minutes list May Neal as a witness only on Jan. 24, the day Miller opened his case. Her name is not listed among the rebuttal witnesses called by Miller later, nor is Andrew Larsen's daughter Mary. Regardless, the newspaper and, later, Judge Gwinn noted that "Nickell's veracity was impeached by several witnesses [from] Teton Basin."

Nine other witnesses were called by the Holdens on the trial's fourth day as they built their insanity case. Their testimony sustained the Holdens' argument that Smith was a quiet, industrious farmer and hammered home the claim that Neal was a bully who drove Smith to the breaking point.

Friends and neighbors of Ellington's from Salem and Rexburg were called, including Henry Flamm, Bernice Harris, H.P. Jensen, and Orson Waldram. James Henry and Jode Henry were defense witnesses who hailed from Clawson, north of Darby. Evelyn Woolstenhulme and Fred Fish came from the Driggs area. All these witnesses "established the previous good character of the accused for peace and quiet," the newspaper reported. All of the defense witnesses were cross-examined by Miller, though, again, no record exists of the questions he brought to bear.

TRIAL DAY 5

The defense brought another group of character witnesses to the stand on Friday, including Don Carlos Driggs, then one of the most prominent citizens of the little town that carried his family name. The president of the LDS Church's Teton Stake testified that he considered Smith a man of good reputation. Driggs also buttressed the defense's insanity case. Don Carlos told the court that he saw Smith when the prisoner was taken through town by Deputy Pickett on the afternoon of the murder. Smith did not seem to comprehend the enormity of the crime he had committed, Driggs testified.

Smith's sister Zoyara Avery and Smith's eldest son Joseph added family history to the insanity case. They testified that Ellington's great grandmother was insane for a long period of time, likely dying in a suicide, "and that his mother had suffered spells of insanity during which periods she could remember nothing of what occurred."

Zoyara told the court about Smith's history of childhood disease.

She testified that "while a child he suffered from typhoid fever for three or four weeks and scarlet fever for ten weeks, leaving him in a weakened physical and irritable, excitable mental condition for many years, and a chronic physical trouble."

The Holdens also produced evidence that their client likely had suffered at least two concussions. The newspaper does not specify which witness supplied this information, but the source probably was Smith's son Joseph who worked with his father on their farms. Several years before the trial, the court was told, Ellington was in an accident in which a log struck him in the face, breaking bones and knocking him backwards into a fence that he smacked with the back of his head. The blow left him unconscious.

Ellington suffered a second head injury when a horse kicked him in the head, leaving him unconscious for eight or ten hours.

These statements established the idea that both ancestry and head injuries might have affected Smith's mental condition. This line of argument carried the defense case to its two key lay witnesses, young Mabel Smith, the defendant's daughter who was a student of Neal's at the Darby school, and the defendant himself. The court minutes indicate that Mabel was followed immediately to the witness stand by her father, who would testify in his own defense.

According to the statement written by Judge Gwinn after the trial, Smith testified that he became nauseous and was stricken with a headache after hearing Nickell's claim that Neal knew Smith "was laying up with his own daughter." He left Nickell outside his house and went in to speak with Mabel. He asked her if she had heard anything about this story. The answer was no.

Smith quickly followed this denial of incest with a sordid claim of his own about Neal. He said he had asked his daughter if Neal had done anything improper to her. Mabel told him that Neal had done so on two separate occasions. "One of which," Judge Gwinn wrote, "would not be improper between a boy and girl if they were unmarried, but was improper between a married school teacher and his pupil, as the fact was in this case. The occasion, according to the testimony of the girl, was indecent but did not go beyond a proposal."

After hearing her allegations about Neal, Mabel testified that her father "ate no supper the evening when she told him of this occurrence; that early the next morning he was walking the floor, and he ate no breakfast; that she went to Victor and spent the fourth of July and did not return home or see her father again until after the homicide."

Smith testified that on the evening of July 3 his mind went blank after hearing his daughter's claims of the improper advances by Neal. He said he had "no memory of what occurred thereafter until he woke up in jail at St. Anthony" three days later, the newspaper reported. He had no memory of speaking with Octavus Smith about his weedy garden. No memory of his arrest by the constable and no memory of neighbor Olmstead's demand that he cease his abuse of Neal's stricken widow. He did not recall accusing Neal of water theft and he could not recall taking Neal's life with his rifle.

In their defense of Smith, Edwin and Harry Holden strove to destroy Neal's reputation and to convince the jury that Smith's neighbor was not the family man and community leader that people believed him to be. Instead, they claimed, the man shot to death while irrigating was a deceptive bully trying to drive an old pioneer off his farm. Far worse, they argued, the schoolteacher trusted with Darby's children was a sexual predator scheming to have his way with the peaceable Smith's teen-aged daughter. When Smith found it out, he forgot his morals in a fit of insanity and retaliated as any father might do.

Miller cross-examined Smith and his daughter before Judge Gwinn recessed the trial for the day, but no details of his questioning of them appeared in either the judge's trial report or in a newspaper. The Holdens had their expert medical witnesses lined up for the next day's proceedings.

TRIAL DAY 6

The Holdens expected to establish beyond doubt that Ellington Smith was insane when he killed Neal by bringing to the stand the two doctors who supervised the state of Idaho's hospitals for the mentally ill, Dr. Givens of the Northern Idaho Insane Asylum in Orofino, and Dr. Poole of the older state hospital in Blackfoot. The *Teton Peak-Chronicle* expansively touted Givens as the "foremost insane expert of the northwest ..."

The two doctors occupied the stand for most of the day. Dr. Poole had examined Smith while he was in the St. Anthony jail. Dr. Givens told the court that he had not examined the defendant personally but responded to hypothetical questions posed by the Holdens and by Miller in his cross examination.

"This examination of Dr. Givens disclosed the fact that he had been in close personal touch with the insane for thirty-five years," the newspaper reported. He "detailed his experience in the handling of the insane, and the outward action and appearance of every known phase of insanity." Givens' testimony "was replete with citations of cases which he described as being similar to that of Smith, and upon which he based his opinion, in connection with the facts given him by the hypothetical questions put by the defense, that Smith was mentally unbalanced at the time of the homicide."

Poole told the court that when he examined Smith, he conducted tests which revealed "unmistakable evidences of Bright's disease." Bright's disease was the then-current name for a group of diseases that cause inflammation of the kidneys. Among other symptoms, the disease can result in lethargy and general weakness. The conditions now more commonly are called nephritis.[211]

The newspaper report does not clarify how the diagnosis of kidney trouble related to the defense's insanity case. But Dr. Poole testified that Smith's "mind was slow and sluggish, and not in a normal mental condition."

Judge Gwinn also described the testimony by the medical experts in his report. "Dr. John W. Givens, of the Orofino Asylum, after hearing a hypothetical statement of the case stated that in his opinion, the defendant was insane at the time he committed the act. The testimony of Dr. Poole was to the same effect. Dr. Poole also made an examination of the defendant and pronounced him mentally unbalanced."

The defense rested its case after the testimonies of Givens and Poole.

With the day's proceedings nearing their end, Miller decided not to bring his own medical expert, Rigby physician Ray Fisher, to the stand immediately after the two defense experts. Instead, he called Deputy Sheriff John W. Pickett.

Pickett had spent more time with Smith in the 24 hours after the murder than anyone else. He took custody of Ellington from the constable at Ed Holden's place that afternoon and headed for St. Anthony. The two men, deputy and suspect, had ample opportunity to talk as they rode in Pickett's wagon some twenty-five or thirty miles. Pickett took them through Driggs, Tetonia, and Clementsville. At about midnight, Smith claimed illness and the deputy and his prisoner took shelter at Canyon Creek. They left early enough the next morning to cover the last miles to the jail by 10 a.m.

Pickett minced no words in his contradiction of the testimony of Drs. Givens and Poole. The deputy said Smith walked up to him at Ed Holden's farm and asked if he, Pickett, "had come to give him a free ride," the *Teton Peak-Chronicle* reported. The deputy testified "that on the way to St. Anthony he [Smith] appeared to be sane."

Gwinn's statement reduces Pickett's testimony to one sentence. "The officer who brought him to jail and talked with him on the way, starting with him on the fifth of July and reaching the jail on the morning of the sixth of July, said he believed the defendant was then sane."

Pickett's testimony was the last of the day. It was Saturday. Smith went back to his cell as the court took a rest Sunday. The trial resumed on Monday, the 29th.

TRIAL DAY 7

Prosecutor Miller called eleven more witnesses on the last day the court took testimony, including his own two experts, the official Fremont County Physician Dr. Ray Fisher, and Dr. W.B. West, who practiced in St. Anthony. Probate Court Judge Oliver Dalby, who conducted Smith's preliminary hearing the previous July, Sheriff John Fisher, A.M. Hudson, who worked as one of the sheriff's deputies, and District Court Clerk

A.M. Carter were among the rebuttal witnesses called by Miller.

Joseph Delaney, Neal's brother-in-law and the husband of May's sister Sarah, was the first to take the stand. Delaney's testimony was not reported by the newspaper. Presumably, he testified to help reconstruct Neal's reputation as a family man and pillar of the community. It's also likely that Delaney knew Neal's opinions of his neighbor and understood their contentious relationship.

After Delaney, Miller turned to the rebuttal witnesses he needed to challenge directly the defense claims of insanity. He turned first to the lawmen who had interacted with Smith at the county jail.

"Sheriff Fisher and Deputy Hudson and other witnesses testified that he [Smith] acted as any sane person would act, and was in their opinion sane, conversing with them as to whom to secure as counsel to defend him," the newspaper reported.

The prosecutor called other people who saw Smith the day of the shooting, including Ed Holden, Peter Lawson, and H.M. Olmstead. "While standing in front of the Holden home, Smith talked to several people," the Peak-Chronicle reported. "County Attorney Miller produced several witnesses who testified that [Smith] was sane at that time, in their judgment, and repeated their conversation with him."

The newspaper's report of testimony by one rebuttal witness, H.M. Olmstead, suggests the care that the witnesses took with their recollection of the events. Olmstead was mentioned in the story published by the *Rexburg Standard* three days after the murder.

The story said that "Mr. Olmstead, who was then on the scene, forbade" Smith from using abusive language against May after she had pointed at Smith and said, "You are the man that killed my husband."

At the trial, the court was told that Olmstead was among the people at Ed Holden's farm when Constable Eddington turned custody of Smith over to Deputy Pickett. Olmstead's testimony helped the prosecutor's case by muddling the defense assertion that Smith clearly was insane. Olmstead recalled that Smith "stared fixedly at him from the wagon, and while he seemed to know that he had shot Neal, he did not sense the enormity of his offense."

Miller called Dr. Ray Fisher as one of the medical experts he needed to counter the conclusions of the defense experts. Fisher was well known locally as a Rigby doctor and the health officer of sprawling Fremont County. Certainly, C.J. Call, the jury foreman who lived in Rigby, knew the doctor.

Fisher maintained "the sanity of the defendant under the hypothetical questions of County Attorney Miller, which differed from those of the defense ..." said the *Teton Peak-Chronicle*.

The *Rigby Star*'s short story of the trial described Fisher's testimony as he countered the assertions of Dr. Givens and Dr. Poole. "Against the testimony of these two distinguished physicians, the prosecution called Dr. Fisher, of Rigby, to the witness chair, who, after a most searching investigation, seems to have settled the question favorable to the state."[212]

Smith's attorneys attempted to rebut Dr. Fisher's testimony "by the introduction in evidence of many standard medical works on insanity," the Teton Peak-Chronicle said, "which was denied by the court."

In his post-trial written statement, Judge Gwinn did not mention his decision to reject the material the Holdens sought to introduce. The *Peak-Chronicle* asserted that the judge "was in complete touch and control at all times, and throughout the tiresome and trying days of the trial, ruled with entire and absolute impartiality on the knotty questions of the law embraced in the case."

Dr. West, the last of Miller's rebuttal witnesses, testified and was cross-examined, then Gwinn called an end to the day's proceedings.

The trial, the *Teton Peak-Chronicle* said, "were livened in every session by the brilliant objections and counter argument and repartee of counsel particularly as to admissibility of evidence of medical and insane experts on the many intricate and generally unknown phases of insanity ..."

TRIAL DAY 8

The prosecution and the defense presented their final arguments on Jan. 30. The final statements provide the last opportunity for attorneys on both sides to summarize the case they have made and to emphasize the points they consider most important to the jury's deliberation. The best attorneys find a way to capture both the hearts and the minds of the jurors.

It is a shame that the record of the final arguments by the Holdens and B.H. Miller has not survived. The *Teton Peak-Chronicle* gave each of the attorneys great credit, telling its readers that the final pleas made by Harry and Edwin Holden "are entitled to [a] place among well known eloquent appeals."

The paper extended its praise to Miller, though with less exuberance. Miller presented the state's case "in a most able and eloquent manner."

There is no detailed account of the closing arguments. The attorneys must have reminded the jury of the human and emotional impact of the murder on the families of Neal and Smith. The Holdens undoubtedly again laid out their disputed claims that Neal had driven Smith into insanity and murder through his harassment and his predatory behavior toward Mabel Smith, a vulnerable young daughter. They must have asserted again that Neal's provocations pushed their defendant into an unbalanced mental state, insanity that was confirmed by the state's premier experts on madness. Ellington Smith, the Holdens reminded the jury, could not be held accountable for killing Neal because he was insane and had lost his knowledge of right and wrong when he pulled the trigger of his rifle.

The Holdens' strategy convinced editor Byrd Trego of the *Idaho Republican*, the Blackfoot newspaper that regularly touted the legal and political work of the Idaho Falls law firm.

" ... although public feeling was at a fever pitch against the prisoner before the defense presented its case, the testimony of the family showing that Neal had persecuted them by polluting their water supply against their repeated protest, had annoyed them in many ways revealing malice, and had insulted one of the daughters just before the killing, sympathy for the defense rose to such a pitch that it is a question whether he may not be acquitted on the unwritten law," Trego's paper reported.[213] Such concise reporting of the defense arguments suggests that one of the Holdens served as the paper's source for its brief story.

In his final arguments, Prosecutor Miller would have pointed out the key facts of the case that were undisputed. Smith and Neal had a troubled relationship. Smith shot and killed Neal. The murder was plainly seen by Octavus Smith and Essie Ferguson. Other witnesses attested to the murder of Neal as he worked in Christensen's field.

Miller would have gone on to contend that Smith planned the cold-blooded murder of his neighbor, figured out where he would do it, then expected to find A.C. Larsen and kill him, too. Only luck had saved the second intended victim.

Miller also must have reminded the jury that his expert witnesses, the local doctors that the jurors knew, concluded that Smith was sane and their testimony was backed up by the county's lawmen, who saw no madness when they took the defendant to jail and locked him up.

The old farmer knew that what he was doing was wrong. In the eyes of the law, passion, or revenge based upon the "unwritten law" never serve to justify killing another human being.

Whether either prosecution or defense took time to recall the allegation that Neal knew Smith had an incestuous relationship with his daughter Mabel remains a question. Miller may simply have left it as a question in the jurors' minds. Holden had no reason to remind them of Nickell's claim.

Both defense and prosecution would have confidently assured the jury that it should find its decision easy to render. The trial minutes prepared by the court clerk say nothing of eloquent speeches. "After argument by counsel for respective parties, and the instructions of the Court, the jury retired with David McArthur sworn as bailiff.

The judge's instructions to the jury got short shrift from the clerk keeping the minutes, but not so for others in the courtroom.

"The instructions of Judge Gwinn on these points were many pages in length, and the reading of his charge to the jury consumed the entirety of the house session" that Tuesday evening, the *Peak-Chronicle* reported.

JUDGE GWINN'S INSTRUCTIONS TO THE JURY

Jury instructions comprise a key element of any judicial case. In courts today, the attorneys for both sides usually give the judge their proposed instructions in writing weeks before the trial opens. The judge decides the instruction process. A judge may direct both sides to meet to determine a set of instructions they agree upon while also making a list of instructions over which they disagree. In the final pretrial hearing, the judge will approve the agreed-upon instructions. The attorneys can make their arguments for or against any disputed instructions. The idea is to make certain that the instructions are clear before a trial begins. Nevertheless, points raised during a trial may require that a few instructions be reopened.[214]

The instructions given the jury by Gwinn may have been developed differently than in modern procedure. Nevertheless, Gwinn started with a legal definition of murder. The instructions also prescribed a method for the jury to consider the insanity defense and determine whether Smith had been proved insane when he committed his crime.

Copies of proposed instructions submitted by Miller, nineteen of them, are in the extant court records. Judge Gwinn reviewed each of them, then made a terse, hand-written note describing how he handled them. For example, Prosecutor Miller asked the judge to instruct the jury that murder is the "unlawful killing of a human being, with malice aforethought." Judge Gwinn wrote simply "Covered," on this proposed instruction and signed it.

A similar remark of "Covered" was written beneath Miller's proposed instructions regarding an insanity defense. The jury was told that the law presumes the sanity of the accused and puts the burden of proof of insanity on the defendant. The insanity must have existed at the time the offense was committed. If the jury found Smith had sufficient mental capacity to know right from wrong and the will power to decide whether to shoot Neal, it could not find him insane.

The jury was cautioned "not to confound legal insanity with hatred and revenge, or with a frenzied impulse to avenge some former wrong or grudge, or imagined wrong or grudge ..." If the jury determined that Ellington Smith acted under "some irresistible impulse to avenge some former wrong, or imagined wrong," it was instructed that it should find the defendant guilty.

Gwinn wrote "Given" on two of the instructions proposed by Miller and signed each, so it seems safe to assume they were read directly to the jury. The typewritten copy of one of them was edited slightly by either the judge or Miller. It addresses the idea of justifiable action when a person is threatened.

"The court instructs the jury that the fact of one person having threatened to take the life of another, or to inflict upon him great bodily injury, will not excuse the person threatened in becoming the aggressor, and with a deadly weapon assaulting the person making such threats," the instruction reads, "and that although the jury may believe from the evidence that David S. Neal, in his lifetime, made threats" — here thirteen words, "to take the life of, or to inflict upon him great bodily harm" are crossed out and the word "against" is inserted — "the fact of making such threats toward the prisoner will not justify a verdict of acquittal ...."

A person charged with murder is permitted to introduce evidence of threats against his own life, but such threats "should not be regarded as affording justification" to kill someone unless the person killed acts to fulfill the threats, the instruction says.

"Mere words or threats, no matter how aggravating or abusive, or profane or insulting, do not of themselves constitute a provocation for the commission of the crime of murder in any degree," the instruction concludes.

The second of these two instructions focused on Mabel Smith and Neal's alleged improper advances.

"The Court instructs the Jury, that although the jury may believe from the evidence that David S. Neal, had made improper advances to, or solicitations of Mable Smith, the defendant's daughter, this would not, in law justify or excuse the defendant in arming himself and going out and shooting and killing Neal, if you believe from the evedince beyond a reasonable doubt that he did arm himslef and go out and kill Neal." [*Spelling, punctuation, and syntax in original*].

The suspicion or knowledge of improper advances against his daughter conferred "no right to kill David S. Neal" the instruction continues, and if Smith did so, "... the killing of Neal, was and is under the law Murder in the first degree, and the Jury should so find."

If the Holdens hoped for acquittal under what editor Trego described as "the unwritten law," this instruction must have chastened them.

The judge refused to include three of Miller's proposed instructions. Two of them pertained to the possibility that the jury might find that Smith suffered from delusions or partial insanity. The judge's note on the typed instruction says, "Refused as misleading in this case."

He also refused to instruct the jury that an insanity plea should not be used to evade the law. There is no handwritten note indicating why the judge eliminated this instruction. He may have considered it simply unnecessary.

The jury was told to consider seven potential verdicts. Judge Gwinn told the jurors that they could find Smith not guilty or not guilty by reason of insanity. He explained two lesser convictions, guilty of manslaughter or guilty of murder in the second degree. The final three potential verdicts included guilty of murder in the first degree, guilty in the first degree with a penalty of life imprisonment, and guilty of murder in the first degree and imposition of the death penalty. The first potential verdict of first degree murder left sentencing to the judge. The last two meant that the jury would sentence the defendant.[215]

The judge turned the case over to the jury at about 8:30 p.m. Tuesday night, ending the arduous trial but not relieving the tense emotions of those seeking what they believed would be justice.

TRIAL DAY 9 – JAN. 31, 1912

The jury deliberated through the next five hours until 2 a.m. Wednesday. The Driggs newspaper reported that the jury "almost immediately after being locked in the jury room took their first ballot, which resulted 6 for conviction 4 for acquittal and 2 blank." A thorough discussion followed and a second ballot showed 10 for conviction, 1 for acquittal and 1 ballot blank.

"Two o'clock Wednesday morning, the third and last ballot was taken, which resulted unanimously in favor of conviction," the Driggs paper said.

With the decision made, the 12 men retired for the night with no announcement of their decision. They were back in court before Judge Gwinn at 9.am. Wednesday morning. Ellington Smith, May Neal, and the friends and neighbors of both families jammed the courtroom to hear the verdict.

Court Clerk A.M. Carter made a roll call of the jury. All were present. The judge asked if the jurors had agreed upon a verdict. Foreman C.J. Call said they had and handed the jury's written decision to the clerk. Carter read the decision.

"We, the jury, duly sworn and empanelled in the above entitled cause, find the defendant guilty of murder in the first degree, as charged in the information, and fix the penalty of life imprisonment," Carter read. The jury confirmed the statement. They rejected Smith's insanity plea without comment.

"The defendant was present with his relatives and friends and counsel at the time the verdict was made public, and although expecting an acquittal Smith gave no sign of outward emotion as Clerk Carter read the verdict which sends him to exile for life," the *Peak-Chronicle* reported.

"The effect, however, on the sisters and brothers of the convicted man was piteous in the extreme when they realized the import of the jury's findings. Tears streamed down their cheeks, and the scene which followed as they crowded around the defendant deeply affected even those who were desirous of the conviction of the accused man."

Judge Gwinn set the formal sentencing of Smith on Feb. 5. The conviction had come under a recently passed law that empowered juries to impose a sentence after a finding of guilt. Gwinn ordered the court to convene for imposition of the sentence at 2 p.m. the following Monday.

After adjourning the trial, Gwinn went to his desk that afternoon to compose his "Judge's Statement to Governor on conviction of Murder in First Degree." The statement highlights the major points of evidence and witness testimony and his assessment of it. He wrote plainly and said that Smith's defense "seemed to rest entirely upon insanity."

Near the statement's end, he wrote, "The court considers itself bound by the verdict of the jury in fixing the sentence of life imprisonment."

He signed it in bold cursive script: "James G. Gwinn, St. Anthony, Idaho, Jan. 31st 1912."

News of the verdict was reported across the state and region. In Salt Lake City, the *Deseret News* published a short, three-paragraph story in a single column, but stacked four headlines above it:

MURDERER IS FOUND GUILTY
First Case of Kind in Fremont County Resulting in Conviction
Ellington Smith Guilty
Jury Recommends Life Imprisonment for Slayer of David Neal
Great Legal Battle

The brief story described the event as "the most interesting trial" and noted the big crowds drawn to it. "B.H. Miller, though a young man, and alone on the prosecution is justly commended by many for the able manner in which he prosecuted the case."[216]

Carter's court minutes record the details of the formal sentencing hearing five days later. Smith and his attorneys listened again as Judge Gwinn confirmed that the jury had found him guilty of the July 5, 1911 murder despite his plea of not guilty.

"The defendant was then asked by the court if he had any legal cause to show judgment should not be pronounced against him, to which he replied he had not," the minutes state. Gwinn then ordered that Smith "be imprisoned and kept at hard labor in the State Penitentiary at Boise City, Idaho for the remainder of his natural life."

Smith was ordered held by the sheriff until custody could be turned over to an officer from the state prison. The next day, the judge signed another order giving Smith and his attorneys 90 days to file a motion for a new trial or to appeal the conviction. The *Peak-Chronicle* had reported the previous week that Miller and the Holdens had discussed the possibility of an appeal if a guilty verdict was reached.

There is no record that any appeal or motion for a new trial was ever made. Perhaps the Holdens reviewed the case and counseled Smith and his family against going through with an appeal. Maybe Smith simply did not have the resources to pay the costs of further legal action.

How did May react to the verdict and Smith's imprisonment? Apparently none of the reporters covering the trial talked with her. There are no direct comments from her in any of the newspaper reports of the trial and conviction. The *Teton Peak-Chronicle* story suggested that she and her relatives and friends were moved by the emotional devastation that overwhelmed Smith's family when the verdict was announced.

The weekly Driggs paper reported the verdict on Feb. 8. It used nearly word-for-word a story reported by the *Rigby Star* the day after the verdict. Somehow, the *Teton Valley News* composed a headline that got the name of the murderer wrong: "Ellerton Smith Is Convicted of Murder." The Driggs editor did append two paragraphs of his own to the *Star*'s story. Those added paragraphs acknowledge that the crime had shocked the Teton Basin community.

"Both the murdered man and the murderer are well known here, where they have lived for years with their families. Bad feeling had been know[n] to exist between the two for a long time on account of dispute about the right to water flowing through both places. Nobody had any idea the trouble had gone to the point of murder, and everyone was surprised at the result of the quarrel. The verdict, we believe, will give general satisfaction. The murderer made no attempt to escape after committing the crime.

"It is understood that the counsel for the defense will ask for a new trial."[217]

May must have experienced more than "general satisfaction." There had to be deep relief that Smith would not resume his life at his house across the road from her home. He had threatened to kill her and her children, too. If she did not say as much during the trial, she revealed the threat in letters written years later when she opposed Smith's efforts to obtain a pardon. Once he was in Boise, May knew that she and her children would be protected by the gray walls and iron bars of the Idaho penitentiary. There Smith would rue his crime far from his rifle and far from the Teton Basin.

EXCOMMUNICATION

There were other consequences for Smith. His church imposed its deepest spiritual penalty. The Mormon men of Darby ward met three weeks after his sentencing to consider their responsibilities to the shattered congregation. They had postponed action pending the results of Smith's trial. The ward minutes record nothing of their discussion but do list the action taken.

"Ellington Smith was excommunicated from the Church of Jesus Christ of Latter-Day Saints, for murdering D.S. Neal, by the Priesthood of Darby Ward, Feb. 26, 1912."[218]

D.S. Neal had been a member of the priesthood. Smith had been, too. The Darby ward made certain that Smith, a murderer, would have to look elsewhere for spiritual succor.

Maybe Ellington did ponder the future of his soul, but once he was in the pen, it did not take him long to begin scheming for his release. He would spend the remainder of his days working with friends and relatives in the upper Snake River Valley to put together pardon appeals to the Idaho governor and the State Board of Pardons.

CHAPTER TWENTY-FOUR

Smith imprisoned

No word was spoken. We stepped inside, the door closed behind us, a great key was turned in the lock and iron bars and stone walls shut me in forever ...

— Patrick C. Murphy, Inmate 2338, Idaho State Penitentiary

After his sentencing, Ellington Smith waited for four days in the county jail in St. Anthony for transportation to Boise and the Idaho State Penitentiary. His family and friends likely took advantage of that time to visit him there, much closer to their homes in Darby, Salem, and Rexburg. Perhaps Harry or Edwin Holden met with him and they decided then to give up the idea of an appeal. When his trial ended, Smith had petitioned the court to pay his witnesses' travel expenses and for their "attendance upon court," declaring that he was "without means" to pay them himself.[219] He had no way to fund an appeal short of selling a farm.

On Thursday, Feb. 8, prison officer Tom Jolley arrived in St. Anthony and made arrangements to transport Smith to Boise. He took possession of the convict from Sheriff Fisher the next day. Smith, likely restrained in leg irons, handcuffs, or both, was taken aboard an Oregon Short Line passenger train by Jolley for the long trip.[220]

Smith had the hours on the train to go over the trial in his mind and to consider his future behind bars. Why hadn't the jury believed his claims? Neal had been mean, threatening, and abusive. What else was he to do to protect his farm and defend his daughter's honor? As he stared out the window of his train car, he must have wondered if he ever would see Idaho's expansive landscape again.

Upon arrival at the capital city's railroad depot, Jolley and Smith were met by a horse-drawn cab for the final leg of the trip to the prison. Other convicted felons made the same trip. Patrick C. Murphy, who began serving a life sentence three years after Smith, recalled his arrival and incarceration in September 1915.

"I arrived, with one companion, on the early morning train, in Boise, the beautiful capital city of Idaho," Murphy wrote in a memoir of his years in the penitentiary. "We were met at the depot by a slender, dark-eyed young fellow who conveyed us to a hack drawn up at the curb and to which was hitched a pair of nervous gray horses. We climbed into the rig and the team was driven swiftly through the business section of the city and turned toward the east, out Warm Springs avenue. My thoughts were quite different from those of most tourists that land for the first time in the charming city of Boise, for I was in irons; my companion was a heavily armed guard who watched my every move."

Murphy recalled taking a deep breath when he reached the prison grounds, "wishing to inhale all of God's free air that was possible." They stopped at the prison office and a bell was rung to signal the guard inside to open the door.

"No word was spoken. We stepped inside, the door closed behind us, a great key was turned in the lock and iron bars and stone walls shut me in forever ..."[221]

Warden John Snook ran the prison. He kept it "abreast of the times" in the humane treatment and rehabilitation of its inmates but his administration operated with the understanding that the penitentiary's fundamental role is to guard the security of society.

Snook believed that Idaho's indeterminate sentence and parole law established one of the operational pillars for the administration of the prison. The law required the warden and his staff to continuously analyze the "mental, moral, and physical status" of each inmate to determine whether they could be paroled at some point after serving the minimum term imposed by a court. This operating philosophy meant the prison officers focused on more than the punishment of the criminal. The knowledge that they were continuously monitored and evaluated, Snook believed, made the prisoners aware that if they reformed, they might avoid serving the maximum time of their sentence.

Snook made a report to the governor that covered pen operations in 1911 and 1912. The report said the inmates, with one exception, were free from typhoid and other infectious diseases. Sanitation was good. A hospital had been built on the site, which ended the need to take prisoners with serious ailments to the Boise hospital. Snook noted that a small percentage of the inmates caused most of the troubles inside the pen. He addressed the problem by segregating the troublemakers , "keeping them apart from the well intentioned prisoners to improve the general standard of conduct throughout, and to relieve the authorities of the most serious difficulties encountered in discipline," historian Hiram French wrote.

Believing that regular work was good for the inmates and could save money for the state, Snook employed them inside and outside the prison. When Ellington Smith arrived, the prison, on average, held 272 inmates each day. Some of those inmates had quarried and cut stone for a new state institution serving deaf and blind Idahoans. The prison leased a farm about seven miles away where trusted inmates raised and harvested hay and grains. Within its grounds, the prison's own gardens and farmyard produced vegetables, fruit, meats, poultry, and dairy products. A tailor shop and a shoe shop made clothing for the prisoners.[222]

Snook made a practice of meeting new inmates in person. The warden met with Murphy after the new prisoner surrendered his clothes, put on his prison clothing, and ate breakfast in a holding cell.

"The warden himself took my height, weight, age, etc.," Murphy wrote.

Each new prisoner was put through an intake process that included documentation modeled on an identification system developed in the 1880s by Alphonse Bertillon, a French criminologist. The Bertillon System improved criminal identification with precise measurements of a convict's body, including height, the width and length of the head, cheek

Mugshots of Ellington Smith, prisoner No.1884, on the day he entered the Idaho State Penitentiary, Feb. 9, 1912. (Idaho State Archives, AR42-1884.)

width, and the lengths of the body trunk, outer arms, forearm, middle finger, little finger, and right ear. The measurements were listed on a card with the prisoner's name, prisoner number, and crime.

Ellington Smith's card lists him as prisoner number 1884, "Murder 1st Deg." Photographs were made showing Ellington face forward and in right and left profile.

The Idaho prison also used its own Description of Convict form. Together the photographs, the Bertillon card and the pen's form present a detailed description of Ellington Smith on the day he was imprisoned.

According to the intake documents, Smith was 52 years old and stood about 5 feet 7 inches in height. He weighed 153 pounds. His hair was brown, light, and thin, his eyes blue. His complexion was described as both fair and ruddy. For the record, his middle finger was listed as 12.5 centimeters long, apparently measured from the back of the middle knuckle.

Other aspects of his life are made plain. Farmer is his listed occupation. His father was living but his mother had been dead for 17 years. Born in Hyrum, Utah, he left his parents' home when he was 21. He had been given religious instruction and attended Sunday school as a Mormon. He still considered himself a member of that church. (His friends in the Darby ward waited two more weeks to excommunicate

Warden John Snook, middle, wears a boater as he stands on the porch of the new Idaho State Penitentiary hospital in 1912. Assistant Warden D.W. Ackley stands at right. The third man is the prison florist. (Idaho State Archives. P1968-57-68.)

him.) The form noted that he had a "Common school education" and had attended for eight years. He did not drink alcohol.

The intake document lists Mrs. Zoyara Avery, his sister, as his nearest relative, living in Rexburg. This last detail is somewhat surprising. He had five living children. He left his farms for his sons to operate. Mabel had been living with her father at the time of his crime, though with her father jailed, she had moved in with her brother Joseph on the original Smith farm north of Darby Creek. Nevertheless, Ellington listed his sister as his closest relative on the prison document, not his son and farming partner Joe nor his loyal teen-aged daughter. Maybe Zoyara already had told him that she would visit him at the prison and he wanted their relationship known to the prison authorities. Given the family's financial circumstances, his children could not afford a train ticket to see him in Boise any time soon.

In its general remarks, the penitentiary's Description of Convict document describes Smith's physical build and features as "Regular." Condition of his teeth: "Poor — Has but three teeth left." His mustache was red. He wore a size 8 boot and a size 6-and-seven-eighths hat.

He arrived at the prison with $12.45 in cash, a watch, a scarf pin, and sleeve buttons in his pocket.

The mugshots of Smith show an aging man with a deeply receding hairline and a bushy mustache that covers his upper lip. He appears to be wearing his own clothes, including a collared dress coat and a shirt with vertical stripes.

The intake documents include the Bertillon chart: a body map that used a line drawing of a naked male human being to show the location of identifying marks, such as scars or tattoos on the prisoner's body. Smith's Bertillon chart located 11 scars and a mole. The mole sat on the edge of his right ear near his face. Scars are listed on the left side of the upper lip, on his right kneecap, two on the inside of the left knee, a large scar at the base and top of the big toe of his right foot, a long cut scar at top of the big toe on the left foot, a scar on the inside base of his left thumb and, in all upper case letters, a LARGE DENT SCAR on the right side of the back of his head near the right ear.

The chart notes another scar on the side of the right buttock and one on the top of his left thumb. A vaccination scar is depicted on his upper right arm.

"FEET ARE SHORT AND THICK," the chart notes. His nose, ears and chin are listed as "Reg." In the remarks section of the chart, the inspector noted that Smith had a hairy breast, pink nipples, and short, broad feet. He also possessed a "lumpy navel."

Plainly, pen inmates retained little dignity. His last claim to privacy disappeared with a document Smith signed the day after his arrival. It gave the warden and his deputy "full power and authority ... to open all mail matter addressed to me, and to read same, and to read all letters written by me, during the term of my imprisonment in said institution."[223]

After being "Bertillioned," as fellow inmates described the process, Smith was taken for a bath, then to the tailor shop to be measured for clothing. A trip to the barber followed where he was shaved. He was assigned to a regular cell. Patrick Murphy was prisoner number 2338. "That meant 2338 prisoners had been received at the penitentiary during the sixty years it had been in existence," Murphy wrote.

Smith was given prisoner number 1884 when he arrived three years and seven months earlier.

Murphy's assertion about the numbering system is not fully accurate. Idaho Territory had imprisoned criminals since 1864 using jails in Lewiston and Idaho City. Construction of the first territorial pen building began in 1870. The first prisoners were moved into the new building in March 1872. Idaho achieved statehood in 1890 and the prison became the state penitentiary in 1891. Prison administrators began assigning sequential numbers to new and existing inmates in 1884, but did not use the system consistently until 1902 or 1903.[224]

Murphy's initial orientation to prison life ended when a prison captain took him to his assigned cell "to which I was to come when the whistle was sounded for lock-up and count every evening." He was told not to go to the prison shops without a guard, then was told how, when, and where to go at meal time.

"That night I found in my cell a library catalogue with the numbers of 4,000 books" available to inmates. "This was an agreeable surprise to me for I could at least read," Murphy wrote, "... and books promised to make less dreary those years behind the gray stone walls."

The prison library offered Smith, Murphy, and the other inmates a wide array of reading options. In a letter written in late 1914, Warden Snook informed Gov. John Haines that the pen library contained about 3,500 volumes. Among the books purchased the previous two years were the eight volumes of the *Illustrated Bible Story*, which offered religious guidance to inmates so inclined, and a 50-volume set of the Harvard Classics, which included Darwin's *Origin of Species*, reading for inmates with questions about biblical creationism and interests in science and literature.

For pure escapism, the library offered eight volumes of *Burton Holmes' Travelogues*. Other books added to the collection in 1914 included the Wild West stories of Bret Harte, *Webster's New International Dictionary*, the *Journal of Criminal Law & Criminology*, and histories of the United

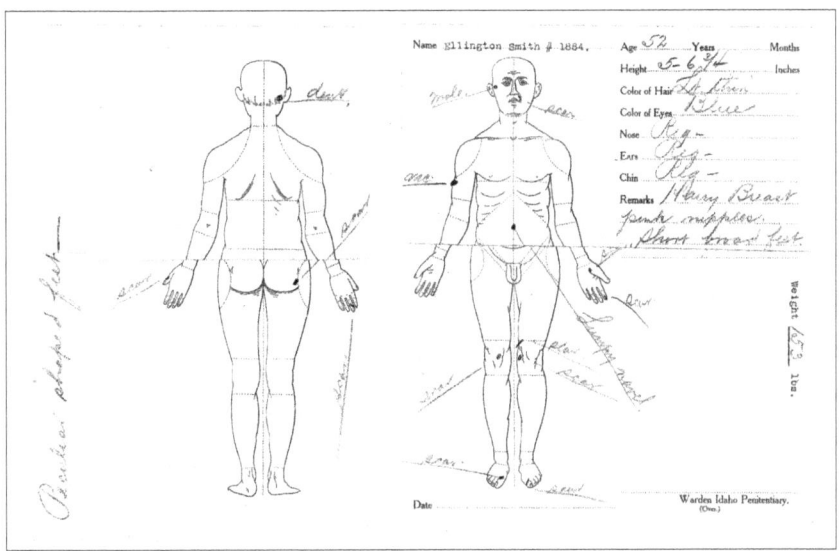

Ellington Smith's "Bertillion Chart" noted identifying marks and scars on his body. (Idaho State Archives, AR42-1884.)

States and the world. If the inmates could not find a book that interested them, there were options. Snook told the governor that "all the leading Magazines are subscribed for."[225]

When a new prisoner entered the pen, he or she immediately heard from other inmates. The polygamists of territorial Utah heard the same when they were imprisoned for cohabitation.

"Hello, fish," one inmate called to Murphy when he was first led into the prison.

Murphy tried to sort out how to handle himself and whom to trust. A long-time inmate who Murphy described as an old safe cracker, offered advice: "Do your own time. Don't let no one here draw you out in talking about your case, your past, your intentions or know your business in any way, shape or form ... I have learned from many years' experience that it is your fellow prisoner you want to look out for."

The truth of the safe cracker's observation was quickly proved to Murphy. Ten days after arriving, Murphy was pulled out of the line of prisoners leaving dinner. A guard told him to get his blankets out of his cell, then he was taken to "the hard boiled row and locked in a cell." He was in solitary confinement. Only later did he learn that a tipster seeking favor had claimed to the guards that Murphy was among a group of men planning an escape. Smith would have appreciated his reaction.

"So, here I was a stranger in a strange land; stripped of every penny and of course without friends, and starting on a life sentence by getting in bad right on the jump-off. And to think it was a fellow-prisoner who had lied to get me in solitary to further his own selfish cause filled my heart with hell and hate."

Alone in "the blackness of that cell" he fumed with a "passionate resentment against the whole scheme of life ... " During his month in solitary, Murphy found the resolve to master his anger and despair, decided to say nothing to other prisoners that he would not say to the warden, and determined to raise himself "in an honest way above the rat who had got me in solitary."

At the end of those four weeks, Warden Snook took Murphy to his office. There Snook told the rattled prisoner that his punishment in the hard boil had been a mistake. They agreed that Murphy would keep his confidences whether with prisoners or with the warden and his guards.

Warden John W. Snook sits at his packed rolltop desk in the Warden's Office while clerk H.S. Coburn stands for the circa 1912 photograph. (Idaho State Archives. P1968-57-43)

Murphy promised Snook that he would not regret allowing him the freedom of the yard again.

"Snook seemed to like the way I talked to him. He believed in fair play and would fire a guard in a minute if he knew he was trying to bulldoze or persecute a prisoner for he knew that a guard that would do that was a coward and Snook hated a coward because he himself feared neither man nor devil."[226]

This was the world Ellington Smith entered in February 1912. He had no intention of spending the remainder of his days there.

CHAPTER TWENTY-FIVE

How to get out of prison

When Idaho became a state, its newly adopted constitution directed the legislature to create a Board of Pardons that prisoners could approach for reprieve from their sentences. The legislature established the board with the state's three highest elected officials, the governor, secretary of state, and the attorney general serving on it. The governor sat as chairman.

Inmates seeking a pardon followed an application process that required them to make their intent public. They were directed to purchase a notice in a newspaper of general circulation in the county where the crime occurred. The prisoners knew the board's meetings were open to the public and received good coverage by the Boise newspapers.

In the summer of 1914, Smith took his first public step in his effort to get out of the pen. Ellington had been incarcerated since his arrest in July 1911. During those twenty-five months, he had missed his son Joe's marriage to Vergie Mae Greene and the subsequent birth of their first child. He did not want to miss more of his family's milestones.

He purchased a notice in the Aug. 25 *Rexburg Standard* announcing his petition for pardon. The notice was buried well back in the issue, on page 7. His notice fell behind a full page of news about the war in Europe, which had erupted after the late June assassination in Sarajevo of Austria's Archduke Franz Ferdinand.

The announcement of his request for pardon met Idaho's legal notice requirements in one long sentence.

"Notice is hereby given: That the undersigned, Ellington Smith has filed, or is about to file with the Secretary of the Board of Pardons of the State of Idaho, his petition for pardon of the offense for which he is now serving sentence in the Idaho State Penitentiary, namely the crime of murder committed, upon David S. Neal, in Teton Valley, on the 5th day of July, 1911, and for which he was sentenced on the 5th day of February, 1912, to be confined in the said Idaho State Penitentiary the remainder of his natural life."

The legal notice added that the petition would be heard by the board in Boise on Oct. 7. It listed C.W. Poole as Smith's attorney.[227]

A week later, on Sept.1, the notice ran again but the *Standard*'s editor, perhaps recalling the crowds that had attended Smith's trial, played it much more prominently. He placed it on page 1, beneath the paper's lead story reporting the scheduled appearance of a "Flying Machine" at the county fair, which opened that day.

The airplane story promised "three sensational flights daily" during the fair and said a skilled aviator would be on hand to explain the machine. Maybe the editor thought the two items shared a sense of freedom that his readers would appreciate.

To present his application to the Board of Pardons, Smith again retained a prominent eastern Idaho attorney, C.W. Poole, who had developed a large clientele in his six years practicing law.. He had parlayed this prominence into a political career and had been elected to represent Fremont County in the Idaho state senate in 1910. He held the seat for many years.

Poole came to the law by accident, or rather after one: he lost his right hand while operating a "traction engine" — presumably a farm tractor — on his farm near Rigby in 1903. Friends encouraged him to take up the study of law. He did, reading at home. Five years later he entered practice.

He was well known in the Mormon community, too. He had served a three-year church mission to the Samoan Islands in the early 1890s and had married the daughter of a Mormon bishop.[228]

The attorney had experience with pardon applications. He had appeared before the Board of Pardons two years earlier, in October 1912.

In that appearance, Poole represented William Ace, an inmate convicted in Fremont County of statutory rape in 1909 and sentenced to five years in the pen.

William Ace's case illustrates how politics and other social concerns complicated the pardon and parole process. Ace had applied for a pardon in early 1911 but was denied in April. He was released from prison on parole in September 1911, however, when C.G. Keller, the general manager of Keller Implement Company in Rexburg, promised to employ him for six months.

While working for Keller, Ace ran into some unspecified trouble in early 1912 that pen authorities considered a parole violation. He was arrested by the Fremont County sheriff in March 1912 and returned to the Boise prison.

Attorney Poole got involved then. On March 30, Poole wrote a letter from his Rexburg office to Warden Snook asking for a fair and thorough review of Ace's case.

"When he first returned [to Rexburg] he made an effort to live here, and during the time he was here I never heard anything about him that was improper. This being his former home, and his wife's people who are numerous and very bitter against him, took an interest in making things unpleasant for him, there is little doubt," Poole wrote.

Poole told the warden that he had made inquiries about Ace's recent behavior and found "that he has been conducting himself in a creditable manner." His client "impressed me as being very much in earnest in his desires to make good."

Justice, the state senator told Snook, demanded a fair investigation. By doing so, "you will confer a favor upon a large number of your fellow citizens of Fremont county."

Fremont County Prosecutor B.H. Miller also weighed in for Ace. "I have no personal interest in the case, but from what I have heard and know it would seem to me, if you pardon the suggestion, that before he is re-committed an investigation of some sort should be had to ascertain the correctness of the charges ... that he has violated the condition of his parole.

"A number of people have intimated to me that he is being unjustly restrained, and from what is apparent on the surface it would seem that there is indication that such is the case."[229]

Poole carried Ace's second pardon application to the Board of Pardons the following October. But it was not a propitious moment for Ace and the other pardon applicants. During the meeting, the board addressed a parole violation by one George Levy. Levy's case, like Ace's case and even Ellington Smith's, raised fundamental questions about a fair and safe system of justice. When has an incarcerated person truly paid for his or her crime? How can society safely reintegrate people who have violated its deepest moral laws after they have served due time? How far should the system go to ensure the safety of the victims of crime? How much should an efficient system cost?

George Levy was a convicted murderer and had been sentenced to death. He had avoided the gallows in 1902 only because the pardons board had found inconsistencies in the evidence used to convict him and commuted his sentence to life in prison. He later sought a full pardon and after the denial of several applications, the board in July 1911 had agreed to his release with an exile provision. The pardon required Levy to leave the United States forever. The state even paid for Levy's transportation from Boise to his former home in Brussels.

Levy proved incorrigible, however. In September 1912, Idaho officials learned that Levy had been arrested by authorities in Portland, Oregon, on a charge of white slavery. He was a pimp, though the papers did not call him one. Instead, the *Idaho Statesman* described him as " ... the lowest possible type of human being — a man who lives from the earnings of fallen women."

While Oregon and federal authorities had their own plans for Levy, Idaho pressed its interest in bringing him to justice. "It is understood that the board may demand, if necessary, that Levy be brought to Boise and placed in the state penitentiary, to serve the balance of his natural life," the *Statesman* reported.[230]

This failed pardon put an uncomfortable spotlight on the pardons board. The Levy case was on the minds of its members, Gov. James Hawley, Attorney General D.C. McDougall, and Secretary of State Wilford Gifford, and the public. But Ace's case was scheduled and Poole made his arguments on Oct. 7.

"Strong recommendations were presented by Senator Poole," the *Evening Capital News* reported. The paper also noted that Warden Snook told the board that prison authorities had information that Ace, in fact, had violated the terms of his parole.

When the board acted the next day, it refused Ace's application and granted only one pardon. It was an unconditional pardon for Frank Trimmer, also a former Fremont County resident. Trimmer's application had been backed by a petition signed by many locally prominent people, the *Idaho Statesman* reported. The signatures listed included "Judge James Gwinn of the district court in Fremont county; the prosecuting attorney [B.H. Miller], the county commissioners, and practically all county officials, as well as many influential citizens."

The application of Poole's client Ace was among five denied by the board. Undecided applications were continued. The board directed Warden Snook to contact the Portland authorities to seek the return of George Levy to the pen.

SMITH REPUDIATES HIS INSANITY PLEA

Two years later, Sen. Poole appeared again before the Board of Pardons, this time to argue for Ellington Smith's application for reprieve. The *Idaho Statesman* reported that 48 applications were laid before the board for its quarterly session, the most it had ever considered in one sitting. The cases were wide ranging with applications from criminals convicted of murder, rape, burglary, assault, grand larceny, forgery, and polygamy. The lone woman prisoner in the pen sought a pardon to avoid serving the final eighteen months of her six-months-to-two-years sentence for assault to commit murder. Idaho law gave the board the authority to determine the portion of a sentence that must be served.

On Oct. 7, Gov. John Haines, Attorney General Joseph H. Peterson, and Secretary of State Wilford Gifford heard thirteen of the cases, including Smith's. Warden John Snook attended.

Poole "made a strong plea for the release of Ellington Smith, serving a life sentence for murder. Smith was a rancher and killed a neighbor named Neal as the result of a number of grievances over water," the *Statesman* reported.

In his plea, Poole repudiated the insanity defense Smith and the Holdens made at trial. The 1912 insanity plea "was against the wishes of Smith, who wished to make no defense," the newspaper reported.

So much for the Holdens' defense strategy. If Ellington Smith "wished to make no defense" at trial, his only other options were silence at trial or a guilty plea. Poole's revelation to the Board of Pardons means Harry and Edwin Holden talked Smith out of either course. If Smith had entered a guilty plea and made no defense, he likely would have been sent to the gallows.

The Holdens must have advised Smith that his only hope for escaping execution lay in their two-pronged plan to vilify Neal and claim that Smith lost his reason to the constant abuse from his neighbor. Insanity was the heart of his defense. Recall that the statement Judge Gwinn wrote for the governor made this clear. "The defense seemed to rest entirely upon insanity."

After dismissing the claim of insanity, Poole built a different defense of Smith before the pardons board. His argument rested on "things which were said to have led up to the affair but which, on account of the character of the defense, were not brought out at the trial," the *Statesman* reported. Inferring that he had willing witnesses who were not called to testify by the Holdens, Poole said that these new statements of fact could be confirmed with affidavits.

One wonders what the attorneys at Holden, Holden, Holden and Holden thought of Poole's assertions. The senator had questioned both the legal strategy the Holdens devised and the quality of their lawyering.

The *Idaho Statesman* did not report details of the claims Poole said were not raised at trial. It's unfortunate, but the reporter had many other pardon requests to cover in the story.

Sen. Poole closed his appeal to the board by noting that Smith had a good reputation in the Teton Basin before the murder. He asserted that the sentiment of the community strongly favored Smith's release.[231] Poole had made a similar claim of community support two years earlier when he wrote his letter to Warden Snook asking for clemency for William Ace.

There are no records of opposition to Smith's 1914 pardon application. Yet the board disagreed with Poole's assessment. Neal's widow may have written to the board opposing his release. May Neal wrote letters opposing later pardon applications by Smith. The board may have acted simply on its own judgment. It had access to Smith's case file, including Judge Gwinn's statement filed after the trial.

The board granted eight of the applicants their unconditional pardons after the hearing. Ellington Smith's application was denied. The board did not list a reason for its denial.

Attorney Poole returned to eastern Idaho after his presentation to the board. Before the board announced its decisions, Poole spoke with a reporter for the *Rigby Star*. He may have anticipated the board's vote to deny Smith his pardon because he told the *Star* that his request was "to have Smith's sentence reduced as to time."[232] That is not what the notice of application for pardon published a few weeks earlier said.

The board did pardon an inmate convicted of murder, the *Star* reported a week later. He was Robert Barnes, a mechanic and foreman who worked for the railroad. Barnes "… killed a Japanese laborer in the car shops at Pocatello after the oriental made a second attack upon him. Strong petition and equally pleas in his behalf had their influence with the board."[233]

The board's denial delivered a bitter pill to Smith. The public now knew that he had lied in court about his loss of reason and his memory of the murder and subsequent arrest. He or his children and other relatives had to pay for another attorney's legal services and associated expenses, all to no avail. His hopes of freedom withered.

Family members came to see him over the years, though the frequency of visits was limited by time and travel costs. A trip to Boise required a train ticket, funds for a room and meals, and cab fare to the prison. Kate Berntson, Smith's niece who lived in Rexburg, made the trip at least once. She mentioned seeing her uncle at the prison in a letter sent four years later to May Neal. She was among many friends and family who remained concerned about Ellington.

CHAPTER TWENTY-SIX

A new governor and prison reform

Boise clothier Moses Alexander unknowingly entered the lives of Ellington Smith and May Neal when he won election as governor of Idaho in 1914. While Smith was losing his first pardon appeal that fall, Alexander put together a winning campaign centered on fiscal accountability and support for prohibition.

Alexander had moved to Boise in 1891 after leaving Chillicothe, Missouri. He planned to take his family to Alaska but decided to make a brief stop in Boise, liked the opportunity he saw there and stayed. He opened a successful clothing store that he named after himself, Alexanders, and eventually built a chain with stores in Idaho and Oregon. He was an observant Jew and joined other Boise Jews to form the Congregation Beth Israel there.

The enterprising merchant had developed a taste for politics in Chillicothe, where he had served as mayor. He took his ideas for efficient government to Boise's voters and they twice elected him mayor, in 1897 for two years and again in 1901.[234] He did not run for re-election in 1899.

When he left office in 1903, the *Idaho Daily Statesman* lauded his work, saying "Mayor Alexander gave the city the best administration it ever had."[235]

When Alexander ran for governor in 1914, his campaign made certain other Idaho newspapers relayed that praise to their readers. *The Record*, the newspaper serving the town of St. Maries in northern Idaho, was among the papers that obliged. It reprinted the *Statesman*'s 1903 editorial, then used it to heap criticism on Alexander's Republican opponent, incumbent Gov. John Haines.

"Read that well deserved tribute with care. Then turn to the history made by John M. Haines as mayor of Boise. At the close of his first term the treasury was bankrupt ... Extravagance, incompetence and corruption ran through the whole web and woof of that miserable two years," *The Record* opined. When Haines sought re-election as Boise's mayor, " ... the people of the city hurled him from power with tremendous satisfaction."

The Record told its readers that they should compare the records of the two mayors, then decide who could best serve Idaho as governor "when the state is suffering high taxes, a miserable revenue system, incompetence and machine politics everywhere."[236]

The reform-minded Democrat defeated the sitting governor. Among the other duties the new governor assumed was sitting as chairman of the Idaho Board of Pardons. Smith, his relatives, and friends eventually brought Ellington's case for reprieve before Alexander three times.

Among his ideas to improve government in Idaho, Alexander wanted to explore changes to the Idaho penal system. He retained John Snook as warden of the penitentiary, a move sustaining the status quo at the prison. But in the second year of his term, 1916, the governor enlisted Judge William M. Morgan of the Idaho Supreme Court and University of Idaho President Melvin A. Brannon in a major reform effort. They held some radical ideas to revolutionize the state's approach to punishing and rehabilitating its criminals.

"The correction of what is commonly called the criminal classes has not kept pace with civilization," Morgan told the *Idaho Statesman*. "There is an underlying reason why men and women commit crimes. It is lack of a complete understanding, or lack of full appreciation of their government and its benefits to them."

Morgan believed that the penal system should help criminals attain that understanding and appreciation of government and society.

He also believed that convicted criminals should not be released from incarceration until they proved they had achieved that high appreciation — in contemporary terms, until they had raised their consciousness — which would lead them to choose law-abiding, productive lives.

To reach his goal, Morgan wanted to change state laws guiding sentencing. The system of sentencing a convicted person for an indeterminate but limited number of years would have to end. Instead, anyone convicted of a felony would be sent to the penitentiary "until their reformation has been complete and they have learned to do right for right's sake."

A person convicted of horse theft, instead of being sentenced to serve a term of, say, one to five years, would remain behind bars until judged fit for life outside. One horse thief might be ready to leave the prison after only six months, Morgan believed. Another "might have to remain a dozen years or, perhaps, for life."[237]

Working with the warden and the university, Morgan argued that Idaho's penal system could provide both work and education opportunities that would reform most of the state's inmates.

Warden Snook had already made significant changes since taking charge of the pen in 1909. Prisoners no longer wore stripes daily. They dressed in regular working clothes unless they violated pen rules. In those cases, Snook sometimes required them to wear "a suit of black and white," according to the *Statesman*. He also had changed some of the pen atmospherics. A piano was placed in the dining room. Flowers were cultivated on the grounds. A baseball diamond was marked out.

Invited by the warden, Judge Morgan visited the pen that summer on Independence Day. He addressed the inmates, including Ellington Smith and Patrick Murphy, from a podium erected in the prison yard. Morgan spoke of the need to educate prisoners to respect, not fear, their government. He also discussed the legal reforms needed to advance his ideas.[238] Murphy later wrote about Morgan's visit.

"He wanted to get together and suggest some sane and sensible bills to be passed before the legislature for our benefit.... This he did and later one good bill he had was creating the office of Parole Officer, which the state never had before."

Murphy's memoir of life in the Boise pen also recalled the "beautiful gang of cut-throats" who pressed around Morgan after his speech in the prison yard.

"Some had the judge by the arm, some by the collar, all telling him they were innocent and shouldn't be here," Murphy wrote. "But I think he was dead wise to them for he kept one hand tightly gripped on his watch."

According to Murphy, Morgan told this crowd to take their cases to the Board of Pardons if they were innocent.

"The work I am undertaking is to reform the wrong-doer, however, if you are innocent, I can do nothing for you. It is the guilty I am after who need reforming, that need to be built up that they come back into society better men."[239]

Morgan unveiled his reform ideas to the Idaho public in October in the midst of the fall campaign season. While the judge had told the inmates of his central focus on education, he apparently had not explained that his plan's second pillar was the imposition of fully indeterminate sentences. Few of the men in prison considered a term in prison as schooling, the judge thought. Rather, they mostly saw their imprisonment as punishment for a crime committed.

Most inmates, the Judge said, would see his ideas as revolutionary and not understand that "it is for their own good."

For his part, Warden Snook thought work was essential both to reforming the criminals under his supervision and maintaining an efficient operation that was less costly, safer, and offered benefits to the state. Dozens of inmates were working on state highways that year and others worked unguarded on a state prison farm near Homedale, about 40 miles from the penitentiary. The majority of prisoners, however, remained stuck in the prison yard with nothing to do unless they contrived their own work. Snook wanted to find more for them.

"Regular work is essential to the physical and moral welfare of the prisoners," Snook maintained. "Idleness begets bodily and mental deterioration and develops vice and insanity, retards whatever improvement prisoners might otherwise be susceptible of, and inflicts a needless penalty on the taxpayers of Idaho."

The Supreme Court judge and warden were not in complete accord on the path forward for the pen and its charges. Snook told the *Statesman* that he planned to ask the legislature to appropriate funds to build a woolen mill inside the pen's walls to provide more opportunities for work. The prison's more hardened inmates, men who could not be trusted outside the pen, could work there. The mills also would employ inmates forced off road crews by winter weather.

The judge opposed the idea. Morgan "thinks they should be put out on the roads and on the state farm, but wants them sent out only after they have shown a desire to mend their ways. If they attempted no reforms he would keep them locked up inside prison walls in idleness for life," reporter Mark Shields wrote. "That, he thinks, is sufficient punishment for the most wicked criminal."

Morgan said his reform ideas required access to excellent teachers who would educate inmates about their government and society. A panel of experts would determine when a prisoner had achieved the education and reached the state of mind needed to justify release. In detail, it was a radical idea for penology at the time, but was based in the acceptance of the potential for rehabilitation. Society today depends upon medical experts to determine if and when a person involuntarily committed to a mental hospital can be released without endangering the patient or the community. Parole boards grant freedom to prisoners judged capable of living crime-free lives.

Morgan conceded that some inmates might deceive his panel of experts, win release, then turn again to crime. But Idaho already lived with the certainty that criminals who served their full prison terms sometimes did the same.

Any felon sentenced to a fixed term, "knows that at the expiration of that period he has a legal right to be discharged from the institution, whether he had been corrected or not," the judge maintained. "And the tendency is that he will harbor ill will and resentment against his government and when the time comes that we must release him, he will go forth with revenge in his heart … and the only result to be looked for is that he will, in future, cover his tracks more carefully than he has done in the past."[240]

These ideas swirled around Boise and the state as Gov. Alexander's campaign to win a second two-year term entered its final days. Warden Snook took an outsized role in the election when his relationship with Alexander soured.

The governor, elected in 1914 on a platform of efficient government and accountability, had sought an audit of the penitentiary in his first year in office. Snook didn't like it and managed to dodge the review. A controversy about management of the women's section of the pen followed. When the governor granted one imprisoned woman a reprieve on humanitarian grounds in early February 1916, Snook released her before Alexander could give her a train ticket home along with money raised to help her.

In mid-September, the warden complained loudly about the governor's veto of an appropriation to buy equipment that Snook's inmate crews could have used as they worked over the summer building a new road connecting northern and southern Idaho.

Tension between the two men continued to build. In the final days of the campaign, editorials in Boise's *Evening Capital News* sharply attacked the Republican candidates for the state's top offices. C.O. Broxon, Alexander's personal secretary and the former editor of the paper, wrote some of those pointed attacks.

Warden Snook took exception to one of the editorials which accused GOP Secretary of State George Barker of intervening to protect Snook by blocking Gov. Alexander's effort to examine the penitentiary's books.

This was too much for Snook. A few days after the editorial appeared, Snook accosted Broxon outside the governor's office in the rotunda of the state Capitol. When Broxon said he had authored the editorial, Snook knocked him to the marble floor, then continued to kick and punch the downed secretary. Broxon suffered a deep cut above an eye that required stitches to close.[241]

Accounts of the confrontation in the rotunda varied widely, but it was reported by both Republican and Democratic newspapers throughout Idaho. The fight may have turned the election in Alexander's favor. He won re-election over the GOP's D.W. Davis by fewer than 600 votes.[242]

With the election settled, Snook knew his time as warden had run out. He did not go quietly. Full of spite, Snook started the process of selling the state prison farm by advertising its livestock for sale. He maintained that the governor had told his campaign audiences that he planned to give up the farm. The governor fumed then walked out of a subsequent meeting of the state Board of Prison Commissioners when he saw Snook in attendance. Snook agreed to leave, the governor returned to the meeting and the board terminated the effort to auction the farm's livestock and equipment.[243]

Snook resigned at the end of December. Alexander appointed Frank DeKay, a former sheriff of Bingham County, to replace him.[244]

Moses Alexander campaigned for governor in 1914 on Prohibition and fiscal responsibility. He signed Idaho's Prohibition Bill on March 1, 1915, in a ceremony attended by officers of the Women's Christian Temperance Union, including Mrs. Warren Chipp, (X over her head), several Boise ministers, and the superintendent of the Anti-Saloon League. C.O. Broxon, Alexander's secretary, stands at left, next to the desk. Warden John Snook punched Broxon to the marble floor of the Capitol rotunda in October 1916, near the end of the gubernatorial election campaign. (Idaho State Archives. P1960-114-9)

CHAPTER TWENTY-SEVEN

Ellington bides time while May fends for her family

Ellington Smith watched the days slowly pass from his cell in prison. He followed penitentiary rules. He got a job in the prison kitchen. He served his time but it cost him. He missed more family milestones while he aged behind bars, including the birth of another grandson and the marriage of his daughter Mabel.

In the Teton Basin, son Joe ran the farms and must have written letters to his father discussing crops and the weather. Someone may have mentioned seeing a notice in the Jackson paper that reported his father-in-law Nick Wilson had joined a few other friends on a fishing trip to the lakes at the base of the Tetons in the summer of 1914.[245]

His daughter Mabel left the family farms, though exactly when she did is uncertain. She must have sent a letter to him in prison to tell him she had married barber Wesley Mulherin in Sumatra, Montana. The wedding was in December 1915 and she was 18, an adult. Sumatra lies far from Boise. Ellington probably never met his son-in-law. Certainly he was told when Nick Wilson got sick late in the year and died. A letter might have included the death notice published in the Jackson's Hole Courier on Dec. 30, 1915. The old frontiersman "had been feeble with age for some time, and the recent sick spell was more than his strength could endure," it said.

Ellington's own father died about eight months later. Adam Smith had been living in Rexburg with Ellington's sister for a couple of years. If

Ellington happened to see the right issue of the *Statesman*, he could have read a brief notice that reported his father's death at 91.[246]

May continued on in Darby, trying to keep her farm and to scratch up cash for necessities. She had her cows and would depend on them for many years. She sold their milk and cream and the butter she made in her wood churn.

In late June 1913 she made a trip to Utah to participate in one of the rituals most important to members of the Mormon Church. She went to the LDS temple in Salt Lake City where she received her endowment and was sealed to her husband D.S. Neal. Mormons know that when they reach the afterlife, if they have been sealed in the temple and if they are judged virtuous and true to the gospel revealed by Joseph Smith, they will live with their families for "time and eternity." Family genealogical records note that all five children, Melba, Ilah, Carmen, Lelia, and David, also were sealed to their parents on that June trip.

May relied on her family and saw them often. Pete and Lizzie were neighbors. May's mother Karen Marie [Mary K] helped her with the children and kept David at her home. Her sister Sarah and husband Joe Delaney and her brother Elie and his wife Roxie were rearing their own children, the cousins that May's children played with often.

The church remained at the center of the family's social life. May taught her children to love their family and their church. Their Heavenly Father was their best friend.

May served as president of the Darby ward's Primary Association for several years. All her daughters attended Primary meetings during those first years after the murder and Smith's trial. Her toddler David might have been carried along. By 1915, he was old enough to attend his own first Primary classes.

Primary classes provide religious instruction to Mormon children until they are about 12 years old. The church still relies upon its Primary Association to awaken the consciences of its youngest members. My own Primary teacher in the Idaho Falls 18th ward instructed our class to imagine the conscience as a triangular spinner inside the chest that whirred and stirred the heart when a lie crossed our lips, or we treated someone meanly. We were taught the Golden Rule and were warned that a higher power watched our every move, knew our every thought. Songs reinforced the teaching.

Jesus wants me for a sunbeam
To shine for him each day
In every way try to please Him
At home, at school, at play.

A sunbeam, a sunbeam
Jesus wants me for a sunbeam
A sunbeam, a sunbeam
I'll be a sunbeam for Him.[247]

Summer in the Teton Basin brought welcome outdoor activities, picnics, family reunions, and in July and August, "berrying." Many of the Teton Valley's roads feature stretches lined with chokecherry bushes. The berries were picked to make jelly for toast and purple chokecherry syrup to pour over sourdough pancakes.

"We all learned to work," her daughter Carmen recalled years later. "My jobs were washing dishes, cooking breakfast, mopping floors and one job I really liked in the summer, taking the cows to graze on the hills above our farm."

May had taught Carmen to appreciate nature and the ordinary pleasures of spring that brought flowers and new lives to the animals that lived around them.

"I'd follow the little mountain stream into our small canyon and find the pussy willows as they came out. There were tiny little pussies on reddish-green willow stems to very large. One as big as one inch long on the golden willows my dad had planted on the little ditch that we got all of our water from for drinking, house use, and for watering our garden berry patch and fruit trees, as well as water for the animals."

Her long walks following the cows took her through meadows with columbine, blue bells, and paintbrush.

"I knew where the birds' nests were as well as the wild chicken nests.

May Neal, front, stands in a community raspberry patch with daughters Carmen, left, and Ilah, who wears a hat. The mouth of Darby Canyon can be seen at right. Circa 1914. (Photo courtesy of the Neal family)

One time I found a fox den, but learned later Mother knew it was there long before I did."

They tended a raspberry patch just north of their house. "We picked and sold many quarts of them and always had bottled raspberries and jam in the winter," she remembered.

Families also knew, and often kept secret, the locations of good huckleberry patches on the slopes of the Tetons or in the Big Hole Mountains on the valley's west side. People looked forward to the outings. They filled pails with berries and sometimes went home with a story of an encounter with a critter or an account of a chance meeting with a neighbor. Occasionally, the children returned with a moral lesson they had not expected.

My cousin Diana Larsen Black, Melba's daughter, received one of these from her grandma one day in the 1940s. Diana remembered that they were picking away on opposite sides of a line of chokecherry bushes when Grandma Neal called to her with advice she recalled often the rest of her life.

"Diana?"

"Yes, grandma?"

"Don't ever be a hypocrite," May instructed.

Diana said her grandmother's lesson was easily learned, though sometimes difficult to keep.

May kept her children close and invited their friends to come to the farm to stay and play. She made them salmon sandwiches, oatmeal cookies, lemonade, and, sometimes, a freezer of ice cream. "We would go off into the hills, have a picnic and get so tired we just fell into bed at night," Carmen wrote.[248]

School classes resumed each fall although teachers had to wait for some to complete their harvest work. They dug potatoes and helped stack hay. Once the crops were in, the last mild days of Indian summer gave hunters time to search out deer, elk, and moose. Fool hens, the blue grouse Carmen called "wild chickens," could be found, too. The mountains surrounding the valley and the riparian habitat along its many streams still held healthy wildlife populations.

When winter took hold, it could close down the valley for days at a time. Blizzards shut roads and stopped train traffic in and out of the basin. Snow piled up in drifts that could make simply getting about the farmyard difficult, let alone getting to school or into Driggs for food and other supplies. The drifts might not melt away until mid-April, or later.

During the coldest of those days, holes had to be cut in ice to haul water for farm animals and domestic use. Woodcutters used sledges to haul logs out of the valley's forests, selling them for home cooking and heating.

In homes heated with wood stoves, fires did not last the night, making mornings chilly for everyone. Once the morning fire caught, there was no forced air and ducting to distribute the heat, even many years later. Diana Black said that as a young girl in the 1940s, she slept upstairs in her parents' Darby home. The only source of heat was whatever warmth wafted up the stairway. Her mother would warm her school clothes on a downstairs stove and bring them up to her.

May steered her children through each season while running the farm. In the summer of 1915, she filed for a patent on the Darby homestead. President Woodrow Wilson was halfway through his first term, two years before he took the country into World War I. The Neals certainly had "proved up" on the original land claim, turning it into a productive farm. Nevertheless, May was not awarded the patent for another ten years. Calvin Coolidge signed her patent four days after Christmas in 1925, granting her title to 204.6 acres: the 160 acres in their original claim and another 45 acres adjacent.[249]

CHAPTER TWENTY-EIGHT

1917
Smith and friends push for a pardon

With Snook ousted, Frank DeKay took over as warden of the Idaho State Penitentiary and its 232 inmates on Jan. 1, 1917. Ellington Smith did not want to remain among them. He launched a new pardon effort but decided that this time he would not pay an attorney to represent him before the Board of Pardons. He turned instead to a petition effort and letter-writing campaign to secure his freedom. It was directed by his niece Kate Berntson.

The pardons board now included Gov. Alexander and two new members, Attorney General T.A. Walters and Secretary of State W.T. Dougherty, both elected in November. The board met on the first Wednesday of the first month of each quarter. Smith and his friends and family targeted the April meeting for his next push for freedom. The board's rules still required applicants to publish legal notices in newspapers in the county where they had committed their crime. They also were required to notify local authorities in the justice system, then file their application with the board at least three days before the board convened.[250]

Ellington handled the paperwork from the penitentiary, pecking it out on a typewriter. By this time, Fremont County had been divided to create Madison County. The Idaho legislature subsequently split the Teton Basin from Madison County, establishing Teton County with Driggs as the county seat in 1915. Smith had to publish his notice in the

Driggs paper.

Kate Berntson coordinated the pardon campaign's effort in the upper Snake River Valley from her home in Rexburg. She worked with many others to circulate copies of a petition and secure letters supporting the pardon request.

On Jan. 18, the *Teton Valley News* published Smith's notice of his intent to request a "full and absolute pardon" at the next meeting of the Board of Pardons.

May Neal or one of her friends saw the legal notice. May quickly wrote a letter protesting Smith's application. [Spelling and punctuation in original]

> Darby Idaho
> Jan. 27, 1917
>
> Dear Governor —
>
> *Again I find it necessary to beg of you to act justly in the case of Ellington Smith when he puts in his plea for pardon. Last May he ask to be pardoned and I wrote you consurning the matter and told you all the facts of the case on July 5th 1911 Ellington Smith brutally shot and killed my husband because he said my husband stole his water and left me a widow with five small children the oldest of which is only 12 years old now the youngest my only boy is six years old. Smiths girls are both married and his boys are men and may be all married by now. So he has no one to care for and he has made the statement that he will kill me and all my family if he gets liberty. So if he ever gets freedom my life will be in danger and so will my dear little childrens. You surely acted justly last time I wrote you and I hope and pray you will this time.*
>
> *Thanking you for your past great favor. I remain Very*
>
> *Respectfully*
>
> *Mrs. D.S. Neal & children* [251]

My grandmother's reminder to the governor that she had written to him in May 1916 to protest an earlier Smith pardon request is puzzling. Her reference cannot be corroborated. Smith's penitentiary file at the Idaho State Archives holds no official record documenting a 1916 pardon application. The files of Gov. Alexander at the archives do not contain a letter written by May Neal in 1916.

Nevertheless, May was truly worried after seeing Smith's notice in the *Teton Valley News*. Her fears surfaced again in a letter she wrote a few weeks later to the General Land Office in Blackfoot. The request for her homestead patent was pending there.

"Would it be possible for this patent to be made out in favor of my children so there would be no settling up on the land in case I should die," she wrote. "My children's names are Melba May age 13 Ilah Aline age 11 Carmen age 10 Lelia Ellen age 8 and David Lewis Neal age 6."

Her letter was returned with an official date stamp and a concise note from whomever in the Blackfoot land office handled her correspondence. The bureaucrat knew nothing of her worries and simply penned a concise note on her original letter: "Consult a local lawyer if you want to transfer your land to your children."[252]

Among her other activities, May was writing for the *Teton Valley News*, producing one of the short, chatty columns that the paper's local correspondents compiled from the valley's corners. Each column appears under the name of a community with no byline. May's notes relayed the doings in Darby. She gathered the bits for her column at the many church meetings in Darby, by staying alert to a neighbor's absence when she bicycled into Driggs, and noting when different vehicles or horses stood in someone's yard.

Her "Darby" column published Feb. 22 includes news about several families including her own and Smith's. She even mentioned Andrew Larsen, the family friend Smith had sought to kill after gunning down her husband.

"We are having another spell of that horribly blizzardy weather," the column notes, then May announced that a death had prompted her mother to make a trip back to Utah.

"Mrs. Mary K. Lewis was called to Marion, Utah, last week on account of the death of her niece Mrs. Crissie Mitchell. Before she reached her destination, she received word her great grandson was dead."

The reader might pause here to ponder the fragility of life in those last decades before the world discovered antibiotics and made more progress in the development of effective vaccines. Mary K left Darby to grieve one family member and suddenly found herself mourning two.

The local correspondents' reporting from each of the valley's communities reminds that people living in rural Idaho in 1917 viewed time and space differently than residents today. In the days before dependable, comfortable automobiles and better roads, people made extended stays when visiting relatives or friends. A house filled for days with visitors may have been trying for the hosts, but hospitality

Gov. Moses Alexander. (Idaho State Archives. P1972-72-239)

was admired.

"J.H. Heuser returned home from Sandy, Utah, on the 19th."

"Bryan Barney of Bates visited his cousin, Mrs. Alice Heuser, from Saturday of last week until Tuesday of this." That's a four-day stay with a cousin living just a few miles away.

"Mr. And Mrs. Bert Murdock visited with Mrs. Neal and family Sunday afternoon." May must have bumped into young Joe Smith, because she mentioned Ellington's son and his wife in a column, too.

"Mr. and Mrs. J.E. Smith and children are visiting relatives in Teton City." It became an extended stay. On March 8, May's Darby column reported that the Smiths had returned and were accompanied by Barbara Green, who "will visit with her sister for some time."

Her Feb. 22 column ends with this odd item: "J.S. Brock, C.B. Valentine and Billy Jacobson are bailing hay for A.C. Larsen at Chapin."[253]

Baling hay in February? Larsen must have had a loose stack of hay that he needed to bale to make it easier to feed to his livestock or to sell to some other farmer.

May did not acknowledge Smith's pardon plans in any of her Darby columns, despite the local interest in it. The Smith clan continued its drive to free Ellington. On March 3, they began circulating a petition in Driggs, calling for Smith's pardon.

PETITION TO THE HONORABLE
STATE BOARD OF PARDONS
Boise, Idaho.

> We the undersigned citizens of the United States and residents of the State of Idaho, residing at the various place set opposite our names, do respectfully petition your honorable board, that you do grant an absolute pardon to Ellington Smith, who on or about the 6th day of February 1912, was convicted of the charge of first degree murder, in the District Court of the Ninth Judicial District of the State of Idaho, in and for the County of Fremont, at St. Anthony,

Idaho, and having been sentenced by said court to serve a term of life imprisonment in the Idaho State Penitentiary, situated at Boise, Ada County, State of Idaho.

The text of the petition was typed above three columns of lines. The first column on the left was for signatures, the middle column for the signee to list his or her occupation, and the third for signees to list their residence. The first person to sign it was attorney B.W. Driggs. Driggs doubled down when he signed a second copy of the same petition. Both were submitted to the board.

The canvasser carrying the first copy of the petition took it to Tetonia and Felt, both north of Driggs, and gathered more than forty signatures. Mostly farmers and ranchers signed it, although P.R. Breckenridge listed himself as a cowhand. Wayne Henrie of Tetonia was a mechanic.

The second copy was circulated in Driggs and holds signatures of a number of local officials and businessmen. Attorney Douglas Hix was the first to sign it, followed by M. Byrne, the probate judge, Teton County Sheriff P.P. Robinson, attorney B.W. Driggs again, then local merchant Victor Hegsted.

As is often the case with petitions, not all the signatures are legible. Some people listed their occupations and the community they lived in. Others did not.

Driggs postmaster J.A. Edlefsen signed as did S.F. Johnson of the local Studebaker dealership. The superintendent of the Teton County school district signed.

The second petition was taken south to Victor for at least eighteen more signatures. Most of those who listed occupations said they were farmers or ranchers. The petition may have been left on a counter at the town's general store, B.F. Blodgett & Company, for customers to review and sign. One of the owners, C.M. Hatch, was a vocal supporter of a Smith pardon. He also had served on the jury that convicted Ellington.

In all, 136 men and women signed the documents, a good showing in the rural valley. Despite the interest in Smith's incarceration, *Teton*

Valley News publisher and editor F.C. Madsen did not devote an inch of copy about the circulation of the pardon petition among his readers. There's not a mention of it in the March copies of the *News* held by the Marriott Library at the University of Utah.

The petition drive alarmed May. A.C. Larsen's wife stopped to see her on Sunday, the day after Smith's advocates started circulating it in Driggs. They must have discussed the potential influence of the petition on the pardons board. She decided to write Gov. Alexander again about her fears. She did so two days later. [*Spelling and punctuation in original.*]

> *Driggs, Idaho*
> *March 6, 1917*
>
> *Governor Alexander Head of Board of Pardon*
> *Boise Idaho*
>
> *Dear Governor,*
>
> *I am sorry to be compelled to bother you so much. But again I am brought to worry over the fact that Ellington Smith might be pardoned. As I understand some of his friends and relatives were circulating a petition in his behalf in town on Saturday last. I have told you all the facts and conditions before and as he has said he will wipe me and my family off the earth for testifying against him, I can't help but having a horror of him being freed.*
>
> *I again ask of you to act justly & wisely and as you would want others to do if your wife and five babies were crually robbed of their dear husband & father because some man thought our dear papa was taking water that did not belong to him when he wasn't.*
>
> *Thanking you for past favors I remain,*
>
> *Yours Very Respy,*
> *Mrs. D.S. Neal & children*[254]

Seeking more political support, Smith's relatives reached out to

Madison County state Sen. John Pincock for help. Pincock used his Senate stationery when he wrote his letter from Sugar City and told the governor that he had known Smith for decades.

> *"I knew him many years during the time he lived at Salem, Idaho, that was before and after he was married, also prior to his going to Teton Valley to live,"* Pincock wrote. *"During all the time his life and habits were that of an honorable honest hardworking man. I never heard of him having trouble with anyone.*
>
> *"I hope you will be able to give these facts due consideration and that you will see your way clear to give him some relief."*[255]

It is a cautious letter, not a resounding request for an absolute pardon. There is no mention nor any defense of Smith's crime. Perhaps Pincock hoped the governor and the board would, at the least, reduce Smith's sentence. As an elected official, Pincock could tell his constituents that he had honored their request for his official help.

Whether Smith or his advocates ever saw the senator's letter seems doubtful. But they kept up their lobbying of the board with more letters from prominent people in the valley. Despite Smith's excommunication, they enlisted local church leaders to join their cause. Don Carlos Driggs had served as a defense witness in 1912. Writing as president of the Teton Stake of Zion — and using the stationery of the stake presidency — Driggs composed his own letter supporting Smith's bid for freedom. Like Pincock, the stake president said he had known Ellington for years, twenty-seven to be exact, and told Gov. Alexander that the murderer had a "splendid reputation up to the time he committed this murder ...."

The fact of the killing did not seem to reduce the church leader's appreciation of Smith. Perhaps Driggs was moved by his belief in Christian mercy. The letter continues with Driggs adding, "... a great many of his old acquaintances and friends feel that he should be pardoned and I understand that a strong petition is being filed on his behalf."

Driggs's letter also opened a new line of argument for Smith, a caveat about his future living arrangements. The stake president said that he made his recommendation "… with the reservation that he does not come back to this part of the country to reside in the future. I understand that Mr. Smith would be willing to agree to this."[256] Maybe the stake president knew of May's fears for her safety and the safety of her children.

Kate Berntson pursued another aspect of her plan to free her uncle: enlisting the support of the members of the jury that convicted him. She sent letters to them and included a form letter for them to sign and send back to her. It included spaces for the former jurors to date the letter and list its point of origin at the top. Below the text of the form letter, a line marked out space for the juror's signature. The form letter reads:

To the Honorable Board of Pardons of the State of Idaho.

Gentlemen:

As one of the jurors in the case of State vs. Ellington Smith, I respectfully request your Honorable Board to grant his application for a pardon.

It is my belief that the law has been vindicated by his imprisonment for nearly six years including the time he was confined in the Fremont county jail awaiting trial, and that his pardon will be approved by the people of this section, generally.[257]

Berntson probably approached all 12 members of the jury. Items from Smith's records as an inmate at the prison show that three of the jurors signed forms to be submitted to the Board of Pardons before its April meeting. A.F. Rawlins of Teton City signed his form letter on March 26; J.E. Hunt of Ora signed his on March 31. Wintry weather nearly thwarted Berntson's effort to enlist C.M. Hatch in Victor. She wrote to Hatch on March 28, but "snow blocades" delayed his receipt of it, he told her, until three days later.

"I have read the contents, and I hasten to sign the request to the State Board of Pardon that Ellington Smith now be given his freedom," he wrote to Berntson. Hatch expressed hope that the pardon would be "speedily granted and that Mr. Smith is in good health …." In a postscript, he worried that his signed form would not reach her in time. The letter did. The board did not meet until April 4. Berntson put her heart into the effort to free her uncle. It seems certain that she went to Boise for the board hearing and carried the form letters herself to present to the board.

CHAPTER TWENTY-NINE

Ellington pleads his case for reprieve

Ellington Smith himself composed what he thought would be the key to his pardon, his own statement of explanation, regret, penance, despair, and hope. He typed it a few days before the April meeting of the Pardons Board.

"I, Ellington Smith, hereby petition your Honorable Board for a pardon," he wrote. He laid out his version of the dispute with his neighbor, then described the murder for which he was serving a life term in the pen. The statement contains many errors, some significant, others of little importance. Among the former, his description of the confrontation and shooting was a lie. Among the latter, he misspelled his victim's name. Other errors can be attributed to the changeability of human memory. How many times had he turned over each moment of the day he shot Neal and the days leading up to the murder? His recollection of the murder changed over his years in prison to mollify a troubled conscience.

" ... the facts and circumstances surrounding the killing by me of D.S. Neill are as follows:

"In 1903 I bought a farm in the Teton Basin, about four miles from Driggs, Idaho. On said farm was a small creek called a spring branch. A half interest in the water in said creek became mine, legally, by reason of my purchase of said farm, and the remaining half of said water was the property of a man named Sorenson. There was at all times sufficient water flowing in said creek for our domestic use and for the irrigation of gardens and during high water in the spring there was sufficient water to irrigate other crops."

Sorenson was Pete Sorensen, D.S. Neal's brother-in-law. But Sorensen did not move to Idaho until 1906, when he, Lizzie, David and May drove their wagons to the Teton Basin from Utah.

"In 1907 or 1908, Mr. Neill filed on the adjoining farm and erected buildings across the road from my place, and shortly thereafter began to annoy me systematically in many petty ways, induced so to do, in my opinion, by another man who desired to purchase my property for less that it was worth."

This other man was Andrew Larsen, also known as A.C. Larsen. Larsen had been involved in the Darby Bench Canal project along with Smith and others to deliver water to their farms north and west of Darby Canyon. Smith thought at the time of the murder and still believed at the time of his pardon request that Neal and Larsen conspired against him.

"In the fall of 1909 I put up a stack of mixed oats and alfalfa and while I was staying at another farm Neill allowed his hogs to run loose about my stack until they had ruined it, although I called his attention to the damage they were causing me and requested him to shut them up."

Smith, a farmer with many years of experience in Salem and the Teton Basin, had to know that Idaho is a fence-out state. In the West's fence-out states, landowners must put up fences to keep ranging livestock off their property or away from areas they need to protect. Smith could have fenced his stack to keep the hogs out of it. A more accommodating neighbor might have kept the hogs penned or even have helped Smith do the work to fence his stacks.

The pardon statement asserts that once when Smith was showing Neal the damage his hogs had done, "he had a revolver on him and was very angry and I believe that I was in danger of my life."

There is no way to verify nor to disprove this statement. Smith did not suggest that Neal directly threatened him with the gun by pointing it at him, only that he had a revolver "on him."

Smith told the board that Neal allowed his livestock to run loose and "drink from my ditch, the water in which became so contaminated that it was unfit for household purposes and I had no other source of supply. Neill had a mare with an open, running fistula sore on her and she would drink out of my ditch while the matter from said sore would drop into the water." Other people witnessed it, he said.

Consider another perspective here, as Ellington compiles his long list of grievances. At the preliminary hearing two weeks after the murder, his nephew Tave Smith testified that Ellington had not moved to the place across from Neal until 1909. Before that move, he lived at his farm north of Darby canyon, on the acreage served by the Wyoming and Darby Bench Canal. When Smith moved to his farm a mile south of Darby canyon, the Neal family was well established across the road from his new home, having moved there in 1906. Smith knew that his neighbors kept livestock, and he knew they were upstream from his residence that depended on the spring branch running through Neal's place for its drinking water. More cordial neighbors might have worked out a solution.

As his statement proceeded from his complaints about contaminated water, Smith revived the claim that Neal stole water from him, threatened to harm him, and manhandled his daughter.

"On numerous occasions Neill, without my consent, used my water for the purpose of irrigating his crops, and I went to him three different times and requested and demanded that he not interfere with my water as I required all of it for my own crops," Smith wrote. "He paid no attention to my requests and demands and utterly ignored my rights and continued to steal my water and apply it to his own use."

Ellington did not say if he reported this alleged theft to local authorities. Neal had denied taking Smith's water and said he used only his own. The discord plays throughout their relationship.

In Smith's view, he was an innocent forced to suffer and persevere under continual harassment from his neighbor. "At different times he abused me without cause or provocation and made threats against me to other persons. He informed one William Nichols that he would 'stamp my damned head off.'"

Here Smith referred to W.W. Nickell, who testified for the defense during Smith's trial. Ellington's pardon statement to this point recounts defense claims made during the trial. From this point on, however, his recollection of the events nearly six years earlier shifts and does not comport with the evidence gathered immediately after the crime and as recounted at trial.

"In the spring of 1911 my daughter, Mabel, was driving home the cows when Neill met her and sought to induce her to go with him into the brush on the pretext of looking for a cow and when she refused he took hold of her and used her roughly. Mabel did not inform me of this occurrence until shortly before the killing. In July 1911, I was irrigating alfalfa and had barely enough water to cover my ground and on the morning of the fifth I discovered that Neill had diverted more than one half of my water supply to his chicken house. He was not using it for irrigation purposes and had taken it merely to deprive me of it, as I thought.

"Later on that day I started for my other farm and took my rifle with me. I met Neill on the roadside near another farm he had rented. I charged him with stealing my water, with having treated me like a dog for years, and with having endeavored to ruin my girl and we quarreled violently. He would not agree to conduct himself properly in the future and cursed and abused me as though I were a pickpocket and in a moment of long-suppressed and ungovernable rage I shot him."

This polished recollection of events embellished and altered the facts of the murder. Smith created it over his years behind bars, turning the awful day of the murder over and over in his mind as the time slowly passed. He changed details and made it his story of justification.

When he had testified in his own defense during his 1912 trial, Ellington told the court that he could remember nothing after the evening of July 3, when Mabel told him of Neal's improper advances. He remained unconscious until he found himself in jail in St. Anthony three days later. The brief conversation with his nephew about a weedy garden, accosting and shooting Neal, riding off and telling Ezra Plummer that Neal was dead in the ditch, his arrest at home by Constable Eddington, and the long trip to St. Anthony with Deputy Pickett were all lost to him, he had asserted from the witness stand five years before. He was under oath.

Under the carefully crafted strategy devised by Harry and Edwin Holden, Smith's inability to remember anything that happened over those three days was essential to his insanity plea, the foundation of his defense. This was the defense he repudiated in 1914. By 1917, his memory had returned. He cultivated it, growing it into a tale of an angry confrontation with his abusive, predatory neighbor that set loose his ungovernable rage.

But the confrontation he described in his appeal for a pardon never happened. Tave Smith watched his uncle ride up and tie his bay horse to his fence. Tave heard him accost Neal. It was Ellington Smith who did the cursing, demanding that the "son of a bitch" tell him whose water he was stealing. Neal replied with the last few words he ever uttered, none of them curses. Then Ellington shot him. Twice.

There was no violent quarrel, no request that Neal behave properly, no black words from Neal. Tave Smith and his young sister-in-law Essie would have heard all of it. In 1917, Ellington Smith created a new story of the murder in his attempt to present his deed as a justifiable homicide, hoping that a violent quarrel with a thieving, vulgar, sex predator might win him his freedom.

Ellington also told the board that in his case justice had been served. He tapped out a painful ode to contrition, deep contrition that racked his soul, contrition that he hoped might appeal to the hearts of the men on the pardons board.

"Since I killed Neill I have suffered the torture of the damned," Ellington wrote. "The knowledge that I am responsible for the death of one of my fellows is greater punishment to me than any that incarceration in the penitentiary can possibly be. I would exchange places with Neill tomorrow and my rash act will torment me as long as I live."

He hoped this pain and this contrition would resonate with his readers. Take a look inside yourself, his appeal suggests. How would you or anyone feel after experiencing an overwhelming rage that whipped you into shooting down another human being?

He had been a peaceable man, Smith added.

"Prior to my difficulty with Neill I had never had any trouble of any kind or character with any man."

He implored the board to consider his behavior during his incarceration. He had been a model inmate who had "strictly observed the rules and regulations laid down for the conduct of prisoners," he wrote. He had piled up credits for good behavior.

He had aged in prison and it was hard on him.

"I am now 57 years of age and crippled by rheumatism to such an extent that my left arm is shrinking away and all but useless. My life record shows that I am not a criminal at heart."

He asserted that he had been imprisoned long enough and argued he was not truly to blame for the murder.

"For several years I submitted quietly to the tyrannical conduct and vile abuse of Neill and I feel that, in the eyes of God and man, I have suffered sufficiently to atone for the fearful crime I committed when in a moment of uncontrollable frenzy, I killed him."[258]

His pardon statement left much unsaid. He did not address the devastating impact the murder of D.S. Neal had on May Neal and her five children. He submerged Neal's family, never even mentioned them. But the families had lived as neighbors for two years. Melba Neal, Neal's eldest child was just seven years old, half Mabel Smith's age when Mabel's father killed hers. Melba may have been too young to have shared much childhood friendship with the neighbor girl across the road. But Mabel and her father had to see Melba and her sisters often, whether just passing one another on the road, picking chokecherries from the bushes that flourished near their homes, riding horses, or tending livestock. Neal's wife and daughters shared both Darby school and the Darby ward's meeting house with Smith and his children.

Yet Smith admitted no remorse for depriving May of her husband and her children of their father. He did not suggest to the Board of Pardons that the "torture of the damned" encompassed any pain for the sorrow and loss that washed over Neal's family. He did not worry or lament that he had turned their promising future into one of doubtful prospects.

Ellington wanted the pardons board to focus on him and his declining health, his good behavior during his years behind bars, and

No Forgiveness

his belief that even God knew he had paid the price of atonement. He promised to be good.

"I pray your Honorable Board to grant me a full and absolute pardon and should you see fit to do so I beg to assure you that my life henceforth will be such that you will have no cause to regret your action," he wrote.

The board did not agree.

In addition to May's plaintive letters reminding Gov. Alexander of Smith's threat to destroy May and her children, the board had Smith's trial record in hand. Inmate 1884's file included Judge Gwinn's statement to the governor written immediately after the trial jury convicted Smith.

May Neal, her face showing the wear of years working on her farm largely on her own, stands with her children in snow in front of the family home circa 1918. Front row, Lelia, David Lewis, Carmen; back row, Melba, Ilah, and May Neal. (Photo courtesy of the Neal family)

Gwinn laid out the case presented by Prosecutor Miller and the defense argument of insanity. Gwinn's report acknowledged W.W. Nickell's testimony recounting Smith's reaction to the claim Neal had threatened to beat Smith and that Neal said he could prove Smith was guilty of incest with his daughter. These were the comments that Smith's attorneys claimed had tipped their client into insanity. Nickell may have been the most important lay witness for the defense after Mabel and Smith himself. But the judge told the governor that during the trial, Nickell was shown to be an unreliable witness. Judge Gwinn pointedly noted that the Holdens had not risen to Nickell's defense when their witness's integrity was questioned.

The pardons board knew that Ellington had dropped his insanity defense in his 1914 pardon appeal, claimed his attorneys had coerced him to say he had lost his mind, then failed to call important witnesses. He instead justified his "uncontrollable frenzy" by painting Neal as a foul-mouthed villain. In 1917, the board could see how Ellington's recollection of the murder differed radically from the account given under oath to the Probate Court by Tave Smith just days after the crime and again at trial six months later.

TIMING

Smith's pardon application was one of ninety-two submitted for the Board of Pardons meeting in April. There may never be a perfect time for a prisoner to seek pardon or parole, but this particular meeting certainly was not the best for Ellington. A controversial decision in December again had focused statewide attention on the board. The controversy was rooted in a 1914 embezzlement scandal involving the former state treasurer and his deputy. The two men, both Republicans, had been convicted of stealing tens of thousands of dollars from the Idaho treasury. The deputy had petitioned the Board of Pardons for reprieve the previous fall. The board considered the matter some six weeks after the November general election. It was the last meeting of the board in Gov. Alexander's first term, and the panel then included

Secretary of State George Barker and Attorney General Joseph Peterson. Both Barker and Peterson were Republicans and both were lame ducks: Barker had failed to win re-election; Peterson did not run.

The two men took the opportunity and voted to reduce the sentence of Fred Coleman, the former deputy state treasurer. It was not Coleman's first application for a pardon. His most recent attempt had been rejected in July. The pardons board initially denied Coleman's new application on the first day of the December meeting when Barker joined Alexander in voting against it. But when the meeting continued the following day, Barker called for a reconsideration of the vote on Coleman's application. The two Republicans then voted 2-1 over Alexander's objection to fix Coleman's sentence at two and one-half years with credit for good time served. The decision meant the former deputy treasurer would be freed in mid-February 1917.

Two years before, Coleman had been sentenced for a term of thirty months to ten years after pleading guilty to embezzling $22,000 from the state treasury (worth nearly $700,000 today). His boss Treasurer O.V. Allen also had confessed to embezzlement and had been sentenced to a term of five to ten years in the pen.[259] The treasury scandal severely damaged the administration of Gov. John Haines and helped propel Alexander to his victory in the 1914 gubernatorial election.

With the turn of the new year, the lame-duck Republicans were out of office. In the first days of January 1917, Gov. Alexander convened a Board of Pardons now made up entirely of Democrats. They voted to rescind the board's December decision in the Coleman case.

The governor justified the rescission by noting that the previous board had violated its own rules that should have prohibited another application from Coleman for six months following its July denial of his pardon request. The board also justified its reversal by noting that Coleman never had revealed what had been done with the public funds stolen by him and his former boss.

Coleman and his friends in the Republican party challenged the rescission of the reprieve in a subsequent lawsuit. They prevailed when a district court judge declared the December Board of Pardons decision binding. Coleman walked free on Feb. 22.[260]

The reprieve did not sit well with many Idahoans. Ralph Knepper, the publisher of the *Kendrick Gazette* in north Idaho, was watching. He reminded his readers that Coleman had filed six applications for pardon beginning in October 1915, just ten months after being sentenced.

"As soon as the criminal is warm in the pen he begins pathetic appeals to a venal pardoning board to be set at liberty, and his success is usually assured if his friends are in the majority on the board."

Knepper saw the state's indefinite sentencing law as an underlying problem. "Our judges should be men of fearless honesty and after a fair trial should fix the sentence definitely," he wrote. "The pardoning board should have no jurisdiction except when errors would be uncovered or new evidence had been found which would have affected the pronouncement of the sentence."

In another skeptical editorial on March 9, titled "That Pardon Board," Knepper accused the board of concluding that "Judges and Juries have not done their duty. Its members made up of petty politicians believe that there are many men inside the prison walls who have been improperly sentenced." He declared that "the notorious Coleman got off with an inadequate service in the pen for the offense committed" and promised that the public would watch the pardon board "with interest" in the coming months.[261]

It was under this cloud of controversy that the board convened on Wednesday, April 4 to consider Ellington Smith's pardon petition and those of so many others. The board pardoned or imposed shorter definite sentences to five prisoners the first day of its meeting. Four more men were pardoned the next day; three had been convicted of forgery, one for violating liquor laws.[262] The board met again Friday to complete the long docket. In the week, it gave pardons or granted clemency to twenty-two inmates serving time for such crimes as kidnapping, grand larceny, statutory rape, sodomy, arson, forgery, and burglary. The last woman in the pen, Dolly Underwood, was pardoned effective June 29. She had been convicted of car theft in Bonner County.

Ellington Smith was not among those reprieved. Secretary of State Dougherty confirmed the decision turning down Smith's application in a note sent to Warden DeKay on April 9.

"Please be advised that at a meeting of the State Pardon Board held on April 6th, 1917, the application of Ellington Smith was denied."[263]

The board apparently did not believe the public would tolerate turning murderers out of their cells. Even so, Editor Knepper in Kendrick challenged the board's clemency.

"The *Gazette* fully understands its meager influence but nevertheless it cannot help using the influence it has in opposition to that over righteous pardon board which is nullifying the solemn actions of our courts of justice," he wrote. "Were there any extenuating circumstances, any new evidence or anything to show that Justice had miscarried, the case would be different; but when a board composed of mere ordinary men will set itself up to decide when a criminal has had enough and thus condemn the acts of our courts, it is time to call a halt."

And there's the rub with the legal system. Everyone in it is a mere ordinary human. This debate ran through the 20th century and continues today. Progressive thinkers remind the public that reform is as much an obligation of the penal system as punishment. Prisoners ultimately will be released and need skills and a society that will accept them.

Hardliners on crime argue that criminals, especially violent felons, must be punished first. Reform is a secondary consideration. They championed the imposition of "three-strike" laws to ensure punishment of chronic criminality, or mandatory minimum sentencing that establishes certainty of punishment.

In April 1917, the pardons board determined that Smith had not had enough of the penitentiary. Its decision must have been a stinging blow for Smith and his supporters. They had devoted considerable time and energy to secure his freedom. Smith's sister Zoyara and his niece Kate went to see him at the prison after the board meeting. They must have told him they would not be deterred. Another appeal was coming very soon, in just three months. But it came after international events had changed state priorities.

THE WAR ARRIVES IN IDAHO

The Idaho Board of Pardons voted to deny Ellington's pardon application on April 6. On the same day in Washington, D.C., the United States declared war on Germany.

Gov. Moses Alexander immediately turned his attention to Idaho's role in the war effort. He established a state "war council" that met in mid-April to mobilize state resources in support of Uncle Sam. The governor instructed the adjutant general of the Idaho National Guard to call all its men into service to be ready for emergency work.

The forward-thinking Alexander recognized an opportunity to use the nation's war effort to build the state. Among many other moves, the war council sought federal financing for an irrigation project on the Payette River at Black Canyon between Emmett, Idaho, and Horseshoe Bend. State officials expected the project to irrigate 19,000 acres.

"All departments are made secondary to agriculture, and all executive heads of the state agree that the greatest work is to make the fields of Idaho produce the largest possible crops," a Blackfoot newspaper reported.

The war council also planned to make low-interest loans available to farmers. The council members discussed storing coal, wood, and other supplies in various places around the state. The state mine inspector was dispatched to Salt Lake City to ask officials of the Oregon Short Line to build a spur line off the tracks serving Driggs to reach coal deposits in Teton County.[264]

The war effort imposed new duties on Alexander and the state. Congress passed the Selective Service Act in mid-May. It set up recruitment quotas for each state and mandated the establishment of draft boards in every county. Idaho ultimately sent more than 19,000 recruits and draftees to serve the U.S. armed forces in the war.[265]

CHAPTER THIRTY

May remarries and Ellington's niece tries again

I know very little about my grandmother's romantic life beyond the few letters that David wrote to her from the Normal School in the years before they married. May kept no diary. After her husband's murder, she plunged into the challenge of providing for her five children. She kept the family's finances together and worked toward patenting their homestead.

Her mother lived nearby and assisted with the children, especially son David, and with the livestock and their gardening. Mary K contributed to the family enterprise in other ways, too. As she had in the Weber Valley in Utah, Mary K served women in the Teton Basin as a midwife. Though she would accept no cash for her services, neighbors who needed her help birthing a child must have dropped off a sack of potatoes occasionally or provided some other compensation in thanks.

May stayed strong in her church. She served her ward as one of the leaders of its religious-education programs for its children. She attended Sunday services and other meetings regularly. She certainly would have met bachelors at ward meetings and in Driggs and the surrounding rural communities.

She kept a letter from one of these bachelors. It was written in 1916 by William Davies after he had departed the Teton Basin to work in a Nevada gold mine. The mine was at Seven Troughs, near present-day Lovelock, Nevada. It's a funny, brief letter in pencil on lined paper. Davies told May about his adjustment to life there.

> "So far I am working regular. Wages are good. Air is esccellent considering we are working under ground. My friend is here with me. Mr. Lewis from Cardiff South Wales. Our Boss is a Londoner. There are 3 saloons here 35 miles from a depot. Southern Pacific R.R. I am quite at home here. Under the condition I am in."

He discussed the fierce winter weather and said he had heard that a pair of their Teton Basin friends "are going to be married. Is that right." He wished her good health and signed the letter. A late thought came to mind because he turned the page upside down and wrote a final note in tiny script above the salutation. It is a coy expression of interest in the 36-year-old widow. He asked if her nephew Leland Sorensen, Lizzie's son, had found his own partner.

> "Tell him I am working in the Gold mine. No more herding sheep tell him. Let him know I dropped you a card. Make him smile. I often tease him last summer about getting Auntie May never would give me his consent some times he would be cross." [266]

And that's it. There's nothing more from Mr. Davies, at least no letters that May kept. Did she write back and shut him off? Did she read and burn other letters he mailed from Seven Troughs, erasing further evidence of a love interest?

Davies' attempt to woo her from afar, if it was one, failed. Another man emerged from the Darby ward. He was Lauritz Jacobson, whom she saw regularly at the Darby meeting house. Jacobson was another immigrant from Utah. He had been active in the Darby ward for years before the Neals moved to Idaho. He had been made a High Priest in 1913 and served as a ward teacher and as an officer in the Young Men's Mutual Improvement Association. May was president of the ward's Young Ladies Mutual Improvement Association in 1916 and 1917 as her daughters entered their teenage years. Though "MIA" classes are separated by gender, the church has a long tradition of staging MIA social events that bring a ward's children together in plays, pageants, and dances. As the leaders of the ward's MIAs, she and Jacobson would have crossed paths often.[267]

No Forgiveness

The 18th ward MIA of my youth in Idaho Falls introduced me to the box step, the waltz, and the cha-cha a half century after May and Jacobson taught the Darby ward's teen-agers how to dance. In fact, my grandmother may have favored the art and taught dancing to her young charges. I once asked my father why he disliked the long hair sported by the teen boys of my youth but never batted an eye when he heard about the Twist, the Jerk, the Locomotion, and other new dances of the 1960s. He smiled and talked about his mother. She had told him that the parents of her youth were scandalized when, in the Gay '90s, they saw couples bend at the waist and dance "with their heads together, arms wrapped tight around their necks, and their butts sticking out." My father, who at the time favored a crew cut, didn't worry about the latest dance craze.

A romance developed between May and Lauritz Jacobson. They married on May 16th, 1917, the day before May's 38th birthday. News of the wedding traveled quickly to the Smith family. If May had moved on from widowhood, perhaps her attitude about a pardon for Ellington might also have changed. Kate Berntson did not wait long to find out.

Berntson's family and friends put in motion a second drive seeking a pardon for her uncle in June. They renewed the plan followed for the April appeal: circulate petitions; enlist prominent local citizens to sign them and to write letters in support of the application; and continue to seek backing from the members of the jury that convicted Smith.

There was one significant change in the plan, which Berntson hoped would, at last, turn the minds of the members of the pardons board. She decided to enlist the victim's widow in the effort.

She waited a month after May's wedding to Lauritz Jacobson, then wrote a letter to her. She addressed it to Mrs. David S. Neal, not Mrs. Jacobson, perhaps feigning ignorance of the recent marriage. The letter was direct. She wanted May to consider Mormon ideas of the afterlife as part of her calculation in seeing justice served. Berntson also wanted May to temper her ideas of earthly punishment. The letter acknowledged May's feelings of loss but asked her to consider the eternal punishment awaiting Berntson's aging, sick Uncle Ellington. The final argument in her plea for May's support of a reprieve was the idea first raised by Teton

Stake President Don Carlos Driggs in his March letter to the governor. Berntson told May that Smith would not return to the Teton Basin and his farms.

> *Dear Mrs. Neal,*
>
> *We are taking steps to obtain the pardon of my Uncle Ellington Smith and write you to inquire if you would object to his being pardoned. We can imagine how terribly you feel about this matter, but my uncle is approaching old age and is in very poor health, and after he has lived out the balance of his days with a smitten conscience for the crime he has committed, he still has to atone for this deed hereafter; therefore, we feel like obtaining a pardon for him if possible.*
>
> *My mother Mrs. John L. Farnes, of Rexburg, and I visited my uncle this spring at Boise and therefore know the true condition of his failing health and feel assured that he will not live to exceed two years longer behind the prison walls.*
>
> *If he is pardoned he will not return to the Teton Basin but will locate elsewhere.*

Maybe Kate Berntson planned to take in her uncle at her Rexburg home. Perhaps her mother, Ellington's sister Zoyara, had space for him at the Farnes residence. In any case, Ellington would not return to live near May and her children.

Berntson also acknowledged May's neighborly attitude toward Ellington's sons, who continued to work the family farms, including the acreage just across the road from May's house.

> *We have learned from his sons that you have been very kind to them for which accept our thanks.*

I often have wondered how May Neal dealt with the presence of Smith's family so close to her in Darby. It seems her heart was big and her thinking clear. She did not hold Ellington's children responsible for

No Forgiveness

their father's crime. Instead, she was kind to them. It fits the memories of her carried by my older cousins. They remember a devout Mormon grandmother who lived her Christian values.

As Berntson had done with the jurors the past winter, she included a stamped, addressed envelope for May's response with her pleading letter.[268]

If May used that self-addressed envelope to respond, there's no record of it. If she replied, she would have politely turned down the request to give her husband's killer his freedom. She did put Berntson's letter to use, however. Smith's and Berntson's allies had not yet begun circulating the new petitions. The letter from Kate alerted May to their latest plans. She waited a few days, then composed another letter to Gov. Alexander and included Berntson's letter with it.

> *Driggs, Idaho,*
> *June 24, 1917*
>
> *Dear Governor*
>
> *I am sorry to bother you so much, but inclosed you will find a letter that shows plainly that Ellington Smith's people are trying or going to try to get him pardoned again and I am in such fear and horror of him when I hear that there is any danger of him being set free. I can't do any other way than appeal to you for help. For me and my dear little children would be in danger all the time if he were free as well as others for there are others (three that I know of) in the valley whose lives he has threatened.*
>
> *Do you think there will be need of another petition to keep him there some of my neighbors told me to ask you as they are sure they can get plenty of signors in a short time.*
>
> *Thanking you for all past favors and begging you to help me again, I am*
>
> *Yours Very Respectfully*
> *Mrs. D.S. Neal and children*[269]

The fearful memory of Smith's threats against her had not faded. Gov. Alexander had to have seen and felt that fear and horror in each of the letters she sent to him. This is the only letter in which she mentions the possibility of circulating a counter petition. It would have made plain the doubts that the family and friends of D.S. Neal held regarding a pardon for Ellington and shown that the Smith clan's claims of general support for his reprieve were inaccurate.

May did not mention her recent marriage to Lauritz Jacobson to the governor. Instead, she signed her letter as the widow of D.S. Neal. She may have worried that Alexander might assume her new husband provided security for her and the Neal children or that her second marriage meant that she had left the past behind. More likely, however, is the possibility that she feared that signing her letter as "Mrs. Jacobson" would confuse the governor. He was familiar with Mrs. D.S. Neal.

In late June, Smith suffered another emotional blow when his daughter Mabel died of tuberculosis in the hospital in Miles City, Montana.[270] On April 1, Mabel and her husband Wesley Mulherin had welcomed the birth of a son, Jack, at their home near Sumatra, Montana. But baby and mother became sick. Doctors had been treating her and her infant son for more than a month before Mabel succumbed.

In Rexburg, Kate Berntson stepped up her efforts for her uncle. She convinced a fourth member of the 1912 jury, T.W. Whittle of Marysville, to sign the same form letter that three other jurors had signed in March. It likewise claimed that a pardon for Smith "will be approved by the people of this section generally."

Petitions for Smith's freedom were circulated in Rexburg and Driggs that expressed the same sentiment. "He possessed and still possesses the respect and confidence of the people generally and we believe that his pardon will meet with the approval of a large majority of our citizens."

New wording in the petition downplayed the severity of Smith's crime. The petitions that were circulated in March stated plainly that Smith "was convicted of first degree murder." The petitions of June and July did not mention murder at all.

> We have known Mr. Smith for many years and know that during his long residence in said Fremont county and prior to the unfortunate encounter because of which he is now incarcerated in the Penitentiary, he was a peaceable, law-abiding and exemplary citizen, and had never had any difficulty of any kind or character, to our knowledge.[271]

The cold-blooded killing had become an "unfortunate encounter." Perhaps the Smith family believed more signatures would be forthcoming if people were not reminded that Ellington was a murderer. The word "peaceable" again described Smith. Other supporters used the word to describe him in separate letters to the Board of Pardons. The adjective had become what lobbyists these days call a "talking point." Berntson wanted the board members to think of her uncle as a quiet, amenable man.

In Driggs, postmaster J.A. Edlefsen and merchants Victor, Glen, and Orville Hegsted signed the "unfortunate encounter" petition along with W.F. Robertson, the county's auditor and recorder. Berntson enlisted Robertson, who also served as the Clerk of the District Court in Driggs, to organize prominent local residents to write personal endorsements of Smith's pardon application. He was an efficient organizer. The letters that he solicited were submitted on his official clerk stationery.

The first of these letters was written June 25 by Teton County Commissioner E.B. Edlefsen. Edlefsen, like Robertson, had been appointed to his post by Gov. Alexander when Teton County was separated from Madison County in 1915. He was one of the first Mormon pioneers in the basin and a former bishop of the Driggs ward. His letter is succinct. It does not note his position as a commissioner, but Alexander must have recognized his name.

"I understand the application of Ellington Smith for Pardon comes up for hearing on July first. I trust that his case will meet with favor and that he be pardoned," Edlefsen wrote. "I have been intimately acquainted with the applicant [Mr. Smith] for more than thirty years and have had many business transactions with him. I have always known him to be of a peaceable, honest and trustful nature."

A few days later, merchant Victor Hegsted penned a similar letter. Like the petition that he also signed, Hegsted told the board that the people of the community backed clemency. "... and that points largely to the thought that while he could not be justified in the crime that there are mitigating circumstances enough to warrant the community here in believing he deserves some relief at this time."

Hegsted knew about the need for relief, having run afoul of the law and early 20th century Mormon social norms himself. He represented another aspect of Mormonism's plural marriage history. He had lived in Salem, just north of Rexburg, and served as bishop there for five years. But Hegsted made a "post-Manifesto" polygamous marriage with a Ricks Academy instructor, Hannah Grover, in May 1904. It was a controversial step among the Salem Mormons. Hegsted lived apart from Grover for about ten years. Hegsted and Ada, the first wife that he publicly acknowledged, resided in the upper Snake River Valley while Hannah Grover and first one, then two, then three of their children kept a home in Salt Lake City. Ada died in 1912. Two years later, Victor married Hannah in a civil ceremony and she joined him in Driggs — and mainstream society — in late May.[272]

The couple was well known and respected locally. Victor Hegsted had served as Fremont County clerk while living in Salem.[273] A few years after he supported the Smith pardon effort, he was elected to represent Teton County in the Idaho Senate.[274] Hannah was active in the Driggs ward, serving in the Relief Society and worked "very zealously" in the ward's Primary.

Victor Hegsted closed his letter to the pardon board with a few words of worry about Ellington's health. "While in Boise a short time ago, I met Mr. Smith, and I feel sure that unless released by the Honorable Board of Pardons, that the grim reaper will soon grant what is asked of the Honorable board in giving their favorable consideration at *this time*." [Hegsted emphasis].

The penitentiary file for Inmate 1884 contains three more letters sent on Robertson's Clerk of the District Court stationery. All the writers were prominent residents of the Teton Basin. One came from Douglas Hix, an attorney practicing in Driggs. He earlier had served as Fremont County attorney and as secretary of the Idaho State Senate during the legislature's 1905 session.[275] Driggs postmaster J.A. Edlefsen and Robertson himself authored the two other letters. Each maintained the petition theme that Smith was a good man driven to a calamitous deed by his victim and that his declining health in prison should spur an immediate reprieve by the board.

Hix told the board that he had attended Smith's trial and knew "little things" brought out during that trial that "... if the Board could know and understand them, it would warrant them in moderating the verdict of the jury, now that Smith has given the full measure of his life to the state.

"It certainly cannot afford the people of the State of Idaho, any pleasure to keep to the last hour of his mortal existence a man who was a worthy citizen up to and until the paroxism of anger that resulted in the death of Neal, who gave Smith an accumulated and continuous burden of affliction," Hix wrote. He essentially repeated in a few words the defense case built by the Holdens in the 1912 trial.

"Smith stood this until something snapped in his mental make up, and he took in his hands the last wild law by which man's inhumanity to man has caused so many of us to mourn." Hix pleaded for the board to grant Smith "some small degree of happiness before his life is gone."

Like so many others, postmaster Edlefsen said he knew nothing but good of Smith "up to the time of his trouble with Neal." Court Clerk Robertson informed the board that Smith for ten years had been one of the very best customers at his general merchandise store and "whose word we always considered 'As Good as the Gold.'

"While the crime for which he is now languishing prison could not be justified, there are circumstances surrounding such actions at times that aggravate people to overstep the bounds of sane reason." This last comment marks the line of insanity without contradicting Smith's denial of his insanity plea.

Teton County Superintendent of Public Schools Cecil Price urged the board to pardon Smith in a short note written on his official letterhead. Like others, he used the word "peaceable" in his description of the murderer.

"Up to the time of his unfortunate trouble with Mr. Neal I had always held Mr. Smith in the highest esteem. Mr. Smith was an honest citizen, a successful farmer, and a peaceable neighbor."

The supporters of pardon and clemency minimized and justified the crime to rehabilitate Smith's reputation. They made certain that the pardons board recognized their status as pillars of the community by using official stationery for their letters. These church, civic, and business leaders wanted the pardons board to see the man they remembered and believed in: honest Ton Smith, the man who worked his farm and paid his bills, the man who lived a peaceable life but was driven to murder by a tyrant neighbor.

They made no mention of the paranoid man who thought someone among his neighbors poisoned his colts and told law officers that he wanted to kill others after shooting Neal. They did not see the desperate murderer who struck fear into May Neal's heart. None of them mentioned May Neal and her children and the losses they suffered.

The "unfortunate encounter" petitions that circulated in the Driggs area were signed by forty-eight people in all, including Ellington's son Joseph. Also among them was A.M. Carter, who noted on his signature line that he was "Auditor and Recorder of Fremont County at [the] time of Ellington Smith's hearing at St. Anthony, Idaho."

In Rexburg, the hard-working Kate Bernston obtained signatures from many members of its business community. Those signing included the Madison County sheriff, the manager of the Mountain States Telephone and Telegraph office, the local druggist, a restaurateur, a bookseller, a garage operator, and farmers and ranchers. A couple of printers signed, too, including Kate's husband, P.W. Berntson.

In all, however, fewer than 100 people signed the second petition.[276]

THE ATTEMPT TO WIN MAY'S APPROVAL

The effort to convince May Neal to consent to Ellington's release did not rely solely on Berntson's letter. A two-man delegation went to see her at her new husband's home. My father David Lewis Neal told the tale of this encounter a few times during my childhood. I asked him to tell it again in the summer of 1984 during a family camping trip in Island Park. I recorded the conversation. Dad recalled that Smith's family was motivated by Ellington's declining health to seek his release.

> *Dad: Because, well, he was sickly. Anyhow, it was kind of a comical deal because these two guys come there to ask her. My mother had married another guy by name of Jacobson and I was, it was after I was seven years old. And we was living on his place at the time. These guys come and they wanted to get him out of prison because he was sick.*
>
> *Dan: Were these relatives of his?*
>
> *Dad: I don't know. I think it was his lawyer or somebody like that. I don't know because even seven years old, you don't remember people like that. But I do remember one thing. They come in there and they was talking to Mother and she found out what they was there for.*
>
> *You know what she done? She went into the kitchen. She got a tea kettle full of scalding water — in them days they always had a tea kettle full of water — and that's the first time I ever heard my Mother swear. And she come in there and, and she says, "You dirty sonsabitches, you get off'n this place or I'll scald you to death."*
>
> *And she had that tea kettle ready to pour the water on them. And, boy, you don't think you've ever seen two guys get the hell off of some place, boy they took off!*
>
> *And that's the last time I ever heard of them.*[277]

The Board of Pardons did not meet on the first Wednesday of July that year since it fell on Independence Day. The meeting was rescheduled for the last day of the month. Smith was ready. He had surmounted the legal hurdles in the way of his pardon. He had purchased legal notices and alerted the county officials whose job purview included public safety.

Some of the brightest, most important people in his home community backed him.

The highest hurdle was not a legal matter. It was the judgment of the board, those "mere human beings." Gov. Alexander had articulated what his own favorable judgment required in a memo to the state prison board several years earlier. He had written out his ideas when he was seeking legislative authorization to create and fund a prison chaplain and a state parole officer.

"I deem society needs protection and the sentence of incarceration is not put upon the unfortunate merely to punish him, but to protect society and assist the prisoner to reformation," Alexander wrote.

The *Idaho Statesman* reported the results of the pardon board's July 31 meeting the following day. The newspaper's story included a remark the governor made at the outset of the session, one that must have made the hearts of those attending as allies of pardon applicants soar.

"We ought not to be bothered by technical evidence. It takes up hours of our time. The technicalities are immaterial to me. I care nothing about them," Alexander told those assembled for the meeting. Kate Berntson and her mother Zoyara must have been among them. "We are not a board of law. We are a board of mercy. We don't want to be bothered by law."

But with Smith's threats to kill May Neal, her children, and others ringing from her letters, the governor must have worried that the contrite Smith still had murder lurking in his heart. The board was discreet with its mercy. "Twenty-four prisoners were pardoned, four had their sentences reduced, 12 cases were continued and 16 applications were denied by the state pardon board," the *Statesman* said.[278]

For Smith and his family, the July answer from the pardons board was the same answer given in April. Secretary of State Dougherty wrote Warden DeKay on Aug. 1. "Please be advised that at a meeting of the State Board of Pardons on July 31st, the application of ELLINGTON SMITH was denied."[279]

On the same day in far away Montana, Wes Mulherin and Mabel's sister Zora Mayer reached Butte with Mabel's ailing infant son to "consult an infant specialist," the Sumatra newspaper reported, then declared, "who we are glad to say greatly benefited the child."[280]

Zora kept the baby and took him home with her to Jordan, Montana. It was a long way from Butte. Jordan lies in east-central Montana, south of the Fort Peck Indian Reservation. Zora tended the baby there but the treatment recommended by the Butte specialist did not bring him back to health. Ellington's grandson Jack Mulherin succumbed to tuberculosis ten days later. Jack did not live five months.[281]

Over just four months that spring and summer, Ellington Smith had lost his daughter and grandson and what had seemed his best chances at gaining his freedom.

CHAPTER THIRTY-ONE

Ellington engulfed

The gray walls of the Boise penitentiary had swallowed Ellington Smith. He was in its belly, his arm shriveling and his body aching with rheumatism. His family and friends had mounted two major campaigns to win him a pardon but failed. They could not overcome the fears behind May Neal's objections nor the pardon board's concerns about setting free a murderer.

Smith's daughter and her infant son were buried in Montana in the Miles City cemetery. Saddened, discouraged, and grieving, Ellington must have felt hope evaporate.

Warden DeKay, like his predecessor Snook, kept many of the inmates busy with work inside and outside the prison. Some learned to farm. DeKay took advantage of those who possessed other skills. A Blackfoot man who visited the penitentiary in September found former Idaho state treasurer O.V. Allen, the mastermind fraudster who embezzled tens of thousands of dollars from the Idaho treasury, working as a bookkeeper in the pen office "taking a keen interest in the business end of the institution." The former treasurer earlier had worked at one of the state prison farms in Owyhee County, the man reported.[282]

DeKay also worked the inmates in the pen's own gardens and fields, and building Idaho's roads. A crew of twelve convicts, "honor men," labored on roads in eastern Idaho's Swan Valley that fall, the warden reported in an annual assessment sent to the governor and the Board of Prison Commissioners.

Inmates on the road-building crews were paid 50¢ a day. They wore ordinary clothing, as did the men working on the prison farms. Inmates were not paid for their labor on the prison farms, but they generated some cash for themselves by occasionally finding work on neighboring farms.[283]

More than half the inmates sent to the pen were working outside its walls at one time or another that year, all overseen by unarmed guards. "In the management of the prisoners, I have employed the honor system," DeKay told the prison board. "The general conduct of the inmates being good and but few instances occurring which required punishment."

The use of prisoners to build roads had its critics. The state's highway department claimed that private contractors cost less when prisoners had to be transported across the state, then housed and fed closer to the project site.[284]

Some of the inmates who remained inside the prison made jewelry or worked leather or other materials to produce items that could be sold in the prison library. One of those men, J.M. Coplin, saw his request "to get a dozen good cow or ox horns" published in a Boise newspaper. The inmate promised to pay 12-and-a-half cents each for the horns.[285]

Five convicts escaped state custody in 1917, but none escaped the prison itself, DeKay reported. Two fled the state hospital at Blackfoot. One escaped from the Lava Hot Springs Sanitarium. (Ellington might have enjoyed working at Lava, where he could have taken advantage of the hot pools to treat his aching joints.) Two other prisoners escaped from the prison farms, DeKay wrote.

"However, considering the number of men employed outside of the walls, the percentage of escapes has been remarkably low."

The penitentiary kept a herd of dairy cows that supplied its milk and butter. The prison's gardens and orchards produced fruits and vegetables. "We have canned approximately eleven hundred gallons of tomatoes besides a large quantity of fruit," he wrote. "In addition, we have dried various amounts of apricots, peaches and corn. The root-cellars are well filled with potatoes and vegetables sufficient to supply the needs of the Prison until the next crop becomes available."

The state legislature agreed with Gov. Alexander's request to create

Trusted inmates, including Ellington Smith, staffed the kitchen and dining room in the Idaho State Penitentiary. Most of the food served was produced at the prison. This 1912 meal offered stew, potatoes, corn on the cob, and bread. (Idaho State Archives. P1968-57-25)

a position for a chaplain and parole officer. Rev. James Leitch was appointed to the new post. DeKay lauded his work, saying that Leitch "has worked completely in harmony with me in the various departments of the Prison and in the making of our paroled prisoners successful in the resumption of their proper relation with society, — only two men paroled during this period failing to make good."[286]

The pen opened the year 1917 with 232 male and female prisoners on hand. At the end of November, it incarcerated twenty fewer. The count represented significant turnover. The pen accepted eighty-nine newly convicted felons during those eleven months. Eight parole violators and two escapees were returned to their cells. Some 115 prisoners left the pen. Forty-four were pardoned, eight reprieved, and twenty-three paroled. Three inmates were discharged by court order and thirty-three completed their sentences. One prisoner died.

Outside the prison, the World War and America's growing involvement in it dominated the nation's life. Idaho's newspapers filled their pages with stories about draft boards, army camps, farm work for the effort, and the work of the Red Cross. The state's war effort reached behind the penitentiary walls in October. The Red Cross asked the prisoners to knit socks and sweaters for the doughboys. The proposed knitting was part of a national effort to make warm clothing for the American soldiers fighting in France. The knitting campaign resulted in some unexpected consequences for the prison, but that was a year away.

Shortly after the new year in eastern Idaho, Dr. Fisher was dealing with an outbreak of scarlet fever in Lewisville, south of Rigby. He acted quickly and convinced the local school board to close the school to help limit spread of the disease. The doctor also quarantined three infected people on Butler Island in the Snake River.[287] The disease had plagued southeastern Idaho in the late 19th and early 20th centuries and remained a mortal threat until the development of antibiotic therapy in the 1940s.

But a different disease, a new one, brought a cataclysm to the U.S. and the rest of the world in 1918. The flu was first identified that spring when more than a hundred soldiers living in close quarters at Camp Funston in Kansas became ill.[288] The disease became a pandemic. It killed an estimated 675,000 Americans and at least 50 million people worldwide, a far higher mortality than combat deaths in the war.

The flu's spread across the U.S. was sporadic. In September 1918, it had reached the Teton Basin. The Darby ward discontinued meetings and all church gatherings because of the flu. It was one more worry for May. She and Larry Jacobson had a new baby to protect. Their son Joseph had been born that spring.

The state Board of Health sent telegrams to all county health officers announcing the prohibition of "public assemblages and operations of place of amusement" after Oct. 10. The board allowed public and private schools to remain open but the order otherwise applied to all indoor public gatherings including political rallies, Liberty Loan rallies, theaters, and dance halls.[289]

The state's newspapers that fall were filled with stories about the flu in Idaho and across the country. People were given advice similar to that offered by the Centers for Disease Control a hundred years later during the Covid epidemic of 2020: watch for fevers, body pains, and depression; cover coughs and sneezes; stay home if sick; avoid crowding in public and even at home.[290] Masks were favored in some communities but not in others. Preventives and alleged cures were offered in newspaper advertisements.

At the penitentiary, Ellington Smith had won the trust of the warden and his guards. In his pardon statement he described himself as a strict observer of the pen's rules and regulations. DeKay made him one of the prison's night cooks. In July, while working one of his graveyard shifts, Smith fell down an elevator shaft. The *Idaho Statesman* reported the fall as an accident. There was no mention of problems with the elevator. How Smith found himself teetering at the brink of the shaft at 2 a.m. was not reported.

Ellington broke his left arm in two places in the fall. It was the same arm he had told the pardons board was "shrinking away and all but useless."[291]

With his broken arm, it's unlikely that Smith began clacking knitting needles for the war effort, but other inmates were productive..

"There have been knit to date 350 pairs of sox, 20 sweaters, 5 pairs of wristlets, 2 mufflers," Kate DeKay, the warden's wife and the prison matron, told the *Statesman* in mid-September, "besides making over 32 pairs of sox and 4 sweaters that were sent into the local Red Cross chapter by other Boise knitters incorrectly made."

The matron considered the clothing production "a most excellent record when you take into consideration the knitters are constantly coming and going, entailing a vast amount of time and patience in teaching new beginners." She said that yarn shortages had limited the amount of work that the knitters could accomplish. There were other possibilities for inmates intent on doing their bit for the war. Mrs. DeKay said that her husband allowed one man to "cultivate a tiny patch of ground inside the walls, on which he raised a few hills of potatoes, and sold them for 70 cents and turned the entire amount to the Red Cross fund."[292]

It's unlikely that Ellington Smith was the man who grew spuds for the war effort. He did, however, find time to make another application for a pardon. There's no evidence that his niece mounted a third petition drive in support of it. State archives hold no further letters from his supporters nor any new letters from May Neal to the governor in either Smith's penitentiary file or among Gov. Alexander's papers. Perhaps Smith simply advanced the same material compiled in 1917 to the board. He may have pointed to his July fall as further evidence of his declining health.

The pardons board was active in 1918. In January, it had ruled that a Mexican citizen convicted of murder should be executed by hanging. At the same meeting, the board freed twenty-two prisoners, eighteen men and four women, almost all of them convicted either of burglary or grand larceny.[293]

In March, Gov. Alexander told state residents that he expected an exodus of pen inmates convicted of minor offenses. They were needed for the war effort.

"I shall lay before the board the question of granting many of these prisoners a chance to earn a living to support their families and help the food production of the country with their labors and thereby help win the war."

Criminals convicted of serious crimes would not be turned out of the pen, he added. "A man who commits murder, assaults a woman or a child, plunders a treasury or a bank, although he may be well supplied in worldly goods, will not get much consideration from me ... I expect to make a careful investigation of the convicts in the penitentiary to find those able-bodied men who can be trusted to work on the outside."[294]

The governor's comment about plundering a treasury was pointed directly at former state treasurer O.V. Allen. *The Meridian Times* reported on March 18 that the board had declined to parole Allen, who had seen opportunity in the war effort. "He asked to be allowed to work in the ship yards, helping with his 'bit' to aid the government in the war."[295] He truly wanted out of prison. Maybe Allen did his bit by turning to knitting socks after he got the bad news from the board.

Smith watched as the board of mercy granted pardons or commutations to another dozen inmates in April, all forgers, embezzlers, and burglars. He must have seen that applications from three inmates convicted of murder were denied.²⁹⁶ Still, he made one more try. His request was among at least forty applications for pardon or parole considered by the pardons board at its fall meeting.

"Freedom will come as a Christmas gift this year to 10 prisoners in the state penitentiary," The *Idaho Statesman* reported after the meeting. Ten others were told they would be released over the coming two months. Three were promised release at the completion of their minimum sentences. "Final discharges were granted three who have been on parole."

Sixteen other applications were denied, though the newspaper named only three of those inmates. One was former treasurer Allen. The two others, John Otis Ellis and T.E. Hawkins, were Wobblies, members of the International Workers of the World who had been convicted in northern Idaho for "criminal syndicalism."²⁹⁷

Smith's application for pardon is not mentioned in the Boise paper's story. Nevertheless, Warden DeKay received a familiar letter from the Idaho Department of State regarding prisoner 1884 immediately after the meeting.

Oct. 3, 1918.

Frank E. DeKay, Warden,
Idaho State Penitentiary,
Boise, Idaho

Dear Sir:

This is to advise that at a meeting of the State Board of Pardons held October 2, 1918, the application for pardon of
ELLINGTON SMITH
was taken up, considered, and denied.

Yours very truly,
W. T. Dougherty
Secretary of State ²⁹⁸

No Forgiveness

Alexander had stayed true to May Neal and to the personal policy he had announced to the Idaho public the previous spring. He did not support pardoning a murderer. Smith and his niece had run the course with the Board of Pardons.

CHAPTER THIRTY-TWO

Smith's last months

The routine of prison days, the reliable rules and regulations, defined Smith's last months of life. His arm broken in the July fall in the elevator shaft must have healed. He went back to his night shift in the prison kitchen.

He could peruse the Idaho news brought to the pen library. The flu continued to rage in communities across the state. The situation was dire in some, including Nez Perce, a community of 600 residents in north Idaho. In mid-October, the town reported 300 cases of flu and appealed to the city of Lewiston for aid. The city responded, sending thirty nurses, five doctors, a druggist, and a burial crew. "The situation is serious beyond description," a special dispatch in the *Idaho Statesman* said.

The state Board of Health said it had received reports of six deaths and 186 new cases statewide on Oct. 25. In Boise, the local board of health quarantined all flu cases. Both Boise hospitals were filled "almost to their capacity now owing to the influenza epidemic, for which careful nursing is a necessity if pneumonia is to be avoided," the *Statesman* reported. Any worsening of the epidemic might make it necessary "to commandeer some large vacant house" to convert into a temporary hospital.[299]

More war news came to the prison in late October. Warden DeKay and his wife learned that their son, Frank, Jr., had suffered shrapnel wounds and that he had been gassed. He had been serving in France since the previous Christmas after enlisting in the medical corps. The

War Department telegram to the DeKays described their son's wounds as "not serious."[300]

In mid-November, Smith's routine days were disrupted when two inmates found a better use for the Red Cross knitting yarn.

"Using yarn furnished to inmates of the Idaho penitentiary by the Red Cross for knitting sweaters for soldier boys, two prisoners, one a life term, braided a rope 25 feet long with which to scale a 20-foot wall and make their escape Sunday morning at 6 o'clock," the *Statesman* reported.

Fred Gruber, the murderer sentenced to a life term, and Fred George, a convicted robber, ran from the prison to the wood yards of Boise Payette Lumber. Officials believed that the escapees hopped a westbound train near the lumber company's yards late that morning. The escapees had braided an inch-thick rope and attached an iron hook that they used to grab an iron guard rail on the outside of the south wall of the pen. They covered the metal hook with a sock to deaden the sound of it hitting the guard rail, then used the yarn rope to climb out of the prison yard.

The men cut the prison lights to allow them to scale the wall unseen. Both men, the newspaper said, worked as waiters in the prison dining rooms and had been released from their cells at 6 o'clock that morning along with cooks to go start their work.

"Some 16 men were released along with the two who made their escape but seemingly they had no knowledge of the latter's plan, for they made no effort to take advantage of the opportunity presented," the *Statesman* reported.

The newspaper printed the prison's complete description of the men, clearly taken from their "Bertillion" cards. The warden added a final clue that might lead pursuers to their quarry.

"Warden DeKay says that both men are expert cornet players and that they may seek employment in an orchestra."[301]

By December, the influenza epidemic was abating in some parts of the intermountain region. In Blackfoot, J. H. Jacobson returned from an extensive business trip the first week of December and told the *Idaho Republican* editor Byrd Trego what he had seen of the epidemic.

Jacobson said that throughout Idaho and adjacent states he had found the situation improving. In Spokane, the disease had "run its course." In Butte, Montana, however, the epidemic had "broken out in some strength and everything, including saloons, barber shops and cigar stores are tightly closed." To avoid crowding, grocers in the copper-mining town delivered directly to customers' homes.

"The compulsory wearing of masks is not in force at any place Mr. Jacobson visited, and he was surprised on reaching Blackfoot to find all citizens wearing masks."[302]

The danger had not passed, however, and in December, the flu slipped into the penitentiary. Warden DeKay had quarantined the prison in October, a decision that ended all visits by relatives and friends. Despite the isolation, an inmate sickened in the second week of the month. Dozens of inmates became ill over the following days.

"According to Mr. DeKay, Doctor Collister and other prison officials have been unremitting in their care for the comfort of the sick there, and every precaution has been taken to prevent the contagion from spreading among the well inmates." The afflicted prisoners, fifty-three of them, were isolated in the prison hospital.

Ellington fell ill despite the precautions and died of pneumonia on December 19. He was 60 years old and had completed his life sentence. A much younger inmate, Frank Jones, just 24, also died that morning.

"Smith was serving a life sentence for murdering a man in Fremont county, January, 1912, in a quarrel over an irrigation ditch," the *Statesman* reported the next day, confusing Smith's 1912 trial date with the 1911 killing. Ellington had been incarcerated in Boise for six years and ten months.

"He was considered a model prisoner while in confinement and a favorite with everyone connected with the prison because of his affable disposition. A sister of his and a daughter live in Driggs, Idaho, where the body will be sent for burial."[303]

CHAPTER THIRTY-THREE

Last stories and a burial mystery

When the train carrying Ellington Smith's body chugged into Driggs and wheezed to a stop at the Oregon Short Line depot, Ellington's son Joe stood on the platform in his heavy winter coat, waiting to welcome his Aunt Zoyara and cousin Kate Berntson.

Kate's husband P.W. stepped off the car with the two women. They had boarded the train in Rexburg to accompany Ellington's body back to the Teton Basin. The Smith clan planned a short service at Joe's house, then would take his body to the cemetery for burial.

But Joe Smith wasn't the only one waiting at the depot for the train. Pete Sorensen, Joe Delaney, and Elie Lewis huddled on the platform, too. With the train stopped, they strode to the baggage car. The baggage clerk rolled the door open, sliding it wide aside. He dropped a bag of mail on the platform and eyed the farmers lined up in front of him.

"You gentlemen need something? Waiting on a package?"

Elie answered. "We're here to make damn sure you don't unload any caskets here today."

"What do you mean?"

"Ain't this train hauling the body of Ellington Smith? Coming from the Boise pen?"

"It is and my orders say it comes off here."

"Your orders are wrong. That casket does not come off," Elie said. "That sonuvabitch is not going in the ground anywhere near my sister's husband."

Joe Smith and Kate heard this exchange but stayed back. They quickly conferred with Zoyara and Kate's husband.

"I'll go get Victor Hegsted and a couple of others," Joe said. He walked back through the depot and headed toward Driggs' Main Street. His relatives turned back to follow the confrontation at the baggage car. Kate, ever her uncle's advocate, could not stay quiet and stepped towards the men. She was angry.

"Haven't you people had enough? When's it enough for you?" She stepped towards Elie. "I told May he wouldn't last two more years in that dismal hell and now here he is, dead in his coffin, just like I said."

She looked to the sky, then turned her gaze back at Elie and the others. "When is it enough?" she demanded. "Please. Just stand back."

The baggage clerk did not want a confrontation with anybody. Saying nothing, he turned back into the car, then reappeared with two more mail bags and piled them in front of Elie and Delaney and the now-crying Kate Berntson. At the end of the short train, the conductor descended from the caboose's steps. Smiling and holding his pocket watch in his hand, he walked to the baggage car. The clerk caught his eye and nodded at the men in front of him.

"Mr. Woodcock, what's going on here?" he asked the clerk.

"These gentlemen say we can't unload the casket from the pen."

"Do they?" The conductor turned to Elie and Pete. "What's the issue?"

"You're not unloading that murdering bastard here. Take him somewhere else, down to Victor or, better, back to Boise."

"Now boys, we can't do that. The ticket says take the casket here. The Short Line has hauled it here and we're taking it off."

"No, you're not." Pete Sorensen, a man of few words, had had his say.

The conductor understood that he was out-numbered. He was a man of sense.

"Arthur, get the rest of the Driggs packages off. I'll find the constable."

As the conductor walked into the depot, Elie and Pete and Joe Delaney shuffled uncomfortably. They were not violent men. The idea that what they were doing might involve the law had not really occurred to them. They were there because May could not bear the idea that

Ellington Smith would await his judgment day in the same holy ground that held her David.

"We'll tell old Eddington that the body's got to go somewhere else. He'll understand. He arrested Ton right after he shot Dave," Delaney said.

They never saw Constable Eddington. While they waited on the platform under Kate Berntson's now clear-eyed glare, Joe Smith returned with Victor Hegsted and a half dozen others. They had guns.

"My Dad's coming off," Joe said, staring hard at Elie and Pete. "He's coming off or some other people are going to get buried."

Elie and Pete look around. They had no guns, just their determination.

"That sonuvabitch has no right to the Darby cemetery, Joe," Elie said. "He killed my brother dead. He might as well have shot May that day. It killed her when we buried Dave. You know. You seen her that day, her and her kids, and you've seen her since."

"He's coming off, Lewis. He's coming off and we're taking him to Darby to lie with his wife."

Now, none of this is true. I made it up. But Smith family oral history lies behind the scene. Ellington Smith's great granddaughter Susan Smith Foster told me that her family told a story about the Neals' attempt to prevent Smith's burial in Darby. She didn't grow up with the tale because her generation knew little of Ton Smith. She did not know her great grandfather had died in prison. In 1972, she asked her father Spencer, the son of Ellington's son Joseph, about the murder that put him there. She wanted to know why she had not learned of it as a child. "He said they were not allowed to talk about it," Foster told me.

Two generations after the murder, her family elders had no desire to see old ashes stirred. Foster learned the details of Ellington's conviction for murder and of his death in the prison after she began her own genealogical research in the early 1970s. Foster wrote letters to the Idaho State Board of Correction in January 1973. The penitentiary had begun the process of moving from the old prison into a modern facility several miles south of Boise's downtown. Inmates had rioted in 1971 (and would again in March 1973),[304] spurred in part by overcrowding, complaints about guards, and other poor conditions at the old pen.[305]

Foster's first query to the pen earned a one-page response with only the basic outline of her great grandfather's imprisonment. She wrote a second letter asking for more detail. The appeal prompted R.D. Newberg, the board's records administrator, to pull Smith's penitentiary records in the Idaho Department of Law Enforcement Building Archive Section. He copied the complete file and printed two photographs from the original negatives made of Smith when he arrived at the prison.

Newberg told Foster that he occasionally received "letters such as yours" referring to a relative who had been imprisoned in Boise. He said he generally devoted little time to them, then added, "However, in your case, you seem extremely sincere in factual information, rather than being just curious as most of the letters are."

His letter expressed hope the material would advance her family research. "Incidentally, there is no charge for the enclosures, compliments of the Idaho State Penitentiary."[306]

Mr. Newberg was a state bureaucrat who took his service to the public seriously. Foster described him as a "sweet little man." She was living in St. Anthony at the time and continued her research into Ellington's life at the Fremont County courthouse. There she "got the transcript of the trial," she said.

Foster shared these papers with my cousin Diana Black, who shared them with many of May Neal's descendants. A full transcript of the January 1912 trial is not among the papers. The documents did include the transcript of Octavus Smith's testimony during Ellington's preliminary hearing before the probate court, however, along with numerous other documents from both the probate and the district courts. Tave Smith's testimony aside, the most important among these is Judge Gwinn's summary of the trial that he prepared for the governor. Foster believes the documents show that some evidence relating to D.S. Neal's alleged sexual misbehavior toward Mabel Smith was not allowed in the trial. [I could not confirm that assessment.]

Foster talked about her discoveries with her family and friends. Word of the documents reached Wendell Gillette, a Victor businessman interested in local history. He talked to her about writing a story. She held back.

Later, during a visit to the Darby cemetery, Susan bumped into Paul Delaney. Delaney was May Neal's nephew and briefly a student of D.S. Neal's at the Darby school. Foster and Delaney began talking about the murder, the trial and subsequent events. Before long, the conversation became a "heated discussion," she recalled.

"He remembered the whole thing," Foster said. She was shaken by the emotions the murder still evoked. "I didn't talk about it much after that."

Susan Smith became Susan Foster in 1969, when she married Randall Foster. She learned later that years before her wedding, Randall's grandfather had purchased Ellington Smith's farm opposite the former Neal homestead. He acquired the farm by paying back taxes owed the county. Ellington's son Joseph Smith had died and his wife Vergie left the property and apparently ignored the tax responsibilities. When Randall inherited it, the Fosters became full-time farmers.

Foster recounted a concise version of the Smith family's story of a confrontation at the Driggs train depot in 1918. "Some people" met the train carrying Ellington's body, Foster said, and tried to stop the crew from unloading his casket. A standoff held until members of the Smith family rode horses to the depot and demanded that "the body come off for burial or other people would be buried."

A second Smith family story that D.S. Neal's body later was dug up and re-buried further from Smith's grave was told to Foster by her mother's father.[307]

Both stories illustrate the hold that the murder of David S. Neal and the trial and incarceration of Ellington Smith had on both families. Arising from some kernel of truth, these near-myths should not be brushed aside. I decided to try to verify them, but I could not find any timely reports in upper Snake River Valley newspapers of a funeral for Ellington Smith nor accounts of a confrontation at the Oregon Short

Line depot in Driggs.

I reached out to Janet Penfold, the contact for the Driggs-Darby Cemetery District listed on the Teton County, Idaho official website in 2024. I asked Penfold if she had a sexton's diary or any record that might suggest D.S. Neal's body was moved from its first burial plot or of any record that an attempt was made to prevent Smith's burial in Darby.

Penfold found no record of evidence for either story, but her research produced one more mystery.

"I'm sending all the information I have. I'm afraid we have a missing body," she told me in an email message. "Smith has a marker but his body is not buried there."

In our email exchange, she included digital photographs of the note cards in the cemetery records for "Block 4, Lot 2 E. Smith."

"E. Smith is Ellington Smith. His grave is grave 1 of Blk 4 Lot 2," the handwritten card notes. "He has a marker by his wife in BLK 22 Lot 6, but his body is not there."

The second card says the grave in Block 22 holds "'Infant' Smith No marker" and "Louise Smith." The card includes birth and death dates for both Hannah Louise and Ellington Smith.

Penfold questioned whether Smith's body ever left the penitentiary.

"Just speculation but in those day[s] prisoners got buried at the prison. I'm guessing he is in Boise at the prison cemetery."[308]

The historic Idaho penitentiary does have a cemetery, a potter's field of sorts, where some of the inmates who died while incarcerated were buried. Not all the graves have markers.

A check with state record keepers seemed in order. Jim Riley, the government records archivist for the Idaho Historical Society, responded after asking a former administrator of the old pen what might have happened to Smith's body.

"It looks like he found the same information as you did," Riley wrote. He referred to the Dec. 20, 1918, *Idaho Statesman* story that reported Smith's death and which stated that Smith's body would be returned to Driggs where he had family.

"He [Ellington] isn't buried up at the Old Pen though, at least that eliminates one probability," Riley said. "But there is still the issue of a missing body."[309]

Epilogue

My grandmother Carrie May Neal died in 1956. During the forty-five years after the murder, she thought often about her husband David and the killing that changed the course of her life and the lives of their children. In her faith she was no hypocrite, yet she worried about her life after death, and talked to her children and grandchildren about the reunion with David that she expected in heaven. Would he, could he, a young man when he died, still love her, a wrinkled, gray-haired wife?

She managed to hold her family together with the help of relatives and friends in the Darby community and her great faith in her church. Still, she must have spent hours in prayer in the days following her husband's murder, trying to understand why her God allowed this calamity into her life and the lives of her very young children. The same emotions must have surged again each time she had to contend with Smith's efforts to be freed from prison.

My father inherited his parents' wedding portrait, May's rocking chair, and a few other personal items. Among the last was a book, *Teachings of the Prophet Joseph Smith*. The book is a compilation of the original LDS prophet's theology. Its publication was directed by LDS Church Historian Joseph Fielding Smith, a grandson of Hyrum Smith, brother of the church founder. May wrote her name in the copy she left to my father.

The historian Smith believed the book would promote faith by presenting the prophet's divinely inspired "utterances" in a more accessible way, organized by spiritual topics. When I first picked up May's copy of the *Teachings* years ago, it fell open to page 339. She must have turned to the page often.

MURDERERS HAVE NO FORGIVENESS

A murderer, for instance, one that sheds innocent blood, cannot have forgiveness. David sought repentance at the hand of God carefully with tears, for the murder of Uriah: but he could only get it through hell; he got a promise that his soul should not be left in hell.

The section informs the faithful that murderers "could not be baptized for the remission of sins for they had shed innocent blood." A murderer's only hope lies in conversion to the true gospel, which might lead Jesus to blot out the sin "when the time of refreshing shall come from the presence of the Lord."[310]

Perhaps in the years after she had battled to keep the old farmer Ellington Smith behind bars and the decades that followed, my grandmother found some spiritual resolution in this passage.

For me, it is impossible to pin down the true cause of the murder so many years after Ellington Smith committed the crime. I have thought long about W.W. Nickells' claim that my grandfather, the Darby school teacher, discovered that Smith had engaged in an incestuous relationship with his daughter. At the time of the shooting, Mabel was roughly the same age as her mother Hannah Louise had been when she married Ellington. Had Smith, whose own family raised questions about his sanity, somehow envisioned Mabel as her young mother?

Or was it Mabel's assertion that my grandfather had attempted to seduce her that drove Smith to murder? The claims that the neighboring farmers had a contentious relationship, that Neal verbally abused Smith, and that the old farmer's mind was weak were made convincingly at trial by Smith's attorneys. Smith's own son and sister believed that two farm accidents damaged Ellington's brain. After his conviction, however, Smith was adamant that he was not insane and denied the defense so carefully constructed at trial.

Whether Ellington Smith will suffer spiritual penalties in his afterlife, I leave to the faithful to discern. Here on Earth, a stream of sorrows cascaded over both families. The Smiths lost a father, brother, and uncle to the prison's gray walls and finally to the flu. Mabel slipped away to Montana. Her older brother Joe held the farm together with Vergie but their children never met their grandfather.

May struggled alone for seven years after the murder, then married Larry Jacobson and had two children, Joseph and Isabel, with him. Some of my cousins believed that Jacobson drained May of her assets before they divorced. After the split with Jacobson, she and her seven children lived in near-poverty. Their poor prospects pushed my father David Lewis Neal to drop out of high school to go to work as a sheep herder, earning cash to help his mother.

If his father, the Normal School graduate, had lived, I believe he would have insisted that his son attend college, too. Without a college education or even a high school diploma, my father herded sheep, hauled wood, and worked for valley farmers that, during the Great Depression, he sometimes had to chase down to demand his pay. He married Gladys Hanson, the daughter of his father's old friend and fellow teacher Alma Hanson. Dave and Gladys had three children and were dirt poor. In the depth of the Depression, L.G. Neal told me that his parents moved the family from a home they called the cold house to one they called the leaky house.

The Rural Electrification Act of 1936 relieved their poverty with the regular paychecks Dad earned stringing wire in South Dakota, Wyoming, and Idaho. A year or so after the U.S. entered World War II, Dad found a living as a railroad brakeman and, eventually, a conductor. His marriage to Gladys ended in divorce, separating him from his three children. He met my mother who was working at a cafe in Ashton where the Union Pacific train crews liked to buy lunch.

With a high school and college education, my father might have become a professional, a teacher like his father or a chemist like his own eldest son. He never would have worked throwing switches and tracking passengers and freight. He would not have met my mother serving trainmen in that Ashton cafe. That leaves me a product of Fate. I suppose everyone is. Do I owe my existence to Ellington Smith and the murder he committed? Should I thank him?

For those who believe, Mormon theology says no. I learned this during high school when I left the public campus for the church seminary that stood nearby. We crossed an irrigation ditch that separated the church and state schools. In the seminary, I was taught that in the existence that precedes life on earth, each human being already waits as an independent spirit. When the time comes for each spirit to begin his or her earthly existence, human DNA does not matter. Where the Mormon god would have placed me and my siblings if my grandfather had lived, mere human beings cannot know.

Daniel Neal

Endnotes

1. *The Rexburg Standard* (Rexburg, Idaho), "David S. Neal Killed at Bates," 8 Jul 1911, p. 1.
2. *Kamas Courant Supplement* (Kamas, Utah) "David Neil Shot," 12 Jul 1911.
3. *The Evening Standard* (Ogden, Utah) "Smith Now Held on Murder Charge," 3 Aug 1911, p. 2.
4. FamilySearch. "United States Census, 1910." Entry for Andres Larsen and Annie M Larsen, 1910. Accessed Thu Oct 05, 2023. https://www.familysearch.org/ark:/61903/1:1:MLH2-GWZ .
5. Bagley, Emanuel; et al; "Application for a Permit to Divert and Appropriate the Water of the State of Wyoming, 1896." See: Application for permit, 1896: Wyoming State Engineer's Office file, Permit #1332. Thyra Thomson Building, Casper, WY. Digital copies available at seo.wyo.gov.
6. Larsen, A.C., Hill, D.B., Winger, Arthur. "Affidavits signed April 10, 1906, asserting timely completion of the Wyoming and Darby Bench Canal and beneficial use of water diverted in Wyoming." See: Application for permit, 1896: Wyoming State Engineer's Office file, Permit #1332. Thyra Thomson Building, Casper, WY. Digital copies available at seo.wyo.gov.
7. "In the Matter of the Application of Ellington Smith for Pardon, April, 2, 1917. Smith, Ellington," File number 1884, Box number 2470, Records, Idaho State Penitentiary, 1869-1973, AR00042. Idaho State Archives.
8. Gwinn, James. "Judge's Statement to the Governor on Conviction of Murder in First Degree, Jan. 31, 1912. Smith, Ellington," File number 1884, Box 2470, Records, Idaho State Penitentiary, 1869-1973, AR00042. Idaho State Archives.
9. *The Teton Peak-Chronicle*, (St. Anthony, Idaho) "Ellington Smith Gets Life Sentence," 1 Feb 1912, p. 1.
10. "Deputy Pickett's statement and the arrest warrant; Smith, Ellington," File number 1884, Box 2470, Records, Idaho State Penitentiary, 1869-1973, AR00042. Idaho State Archives.
11. Church of Jesus Christ of Latter-Day Saints. *Hymns Church of Jesus Christ of Latter-Day Saints, Revised and Enlarged*. The Deseret News Press (1961).
12. Deseret Sunday School Union, 1909. *Deseret Sunday School Songs*, 1937 Edition.
13. Church of Jesus Christ of Latter-Day Saints. *Hymns Church of Jesus Christ of Latter-Day Saints, Revised and Enlarged*. The Deseret News Press (1961).
14. Smith, Joseph. *The Doctrine and Covenants*, Section 57, p. 89-90; Sec 58 V 52, Church of Jesus Christ of Latter-day Saints, (1952) p. 93.
15. Mulder, William and Mortensen, A. Russell, editors. *Among the Mormons – Historic Accounts by Contemporary Observers*. A Bison Book, University of Nebraska Press. (1973), p. 73.
16. Brodie, Fawn. *No man knows my history: The Life of Joseph Smith The Mormon Prophet*. Alfred A. Knopf. (1972), p. viii.
17. Mulder and Mortensen. *Among the Mormons*, p 102-103.

18 Brodie, Fawn. *No man knows my history: The Life of Joseph Smith The Mormon Prophet*, p. 458.

19 Turner, John G. *Brigham Young - Pioneer Prophet*, The Belknap Press of Harvard University Press (2012). p. 112.

20 Arrington, Leonard J. *Brigham Young - American Moses*, Vintage Books, A Division of Random House, Inc., New York. (2012), p. 206.

21 Black, Diana L., Neal and Lewis genealogy records. Family papers.

22 Turner, John G. *Brigham Young – Pioneer Prophet*, p. 185.

23 The Church of Jesus Christ of Latter-day Saints sent missionaries to Denmark in 1849. https://www.churchofjesuschrist.org/study/history/global-histories/denmark/dk-chronology?lang=eng

24 Turner, John G. *Brigham Young – Pioneer Prophet*, p. 70.

25 Young, Gary D. "Morgan Lewis of Kamas Valley, Utah." Copy in author's possession.

26 Ashore, Melvin L., and Haslam, Linda L. *Mormons on the High Seas*. Third Revised edition. Historical Department, The Church of Jesus Christ of Latter-day Saints, Harold B. Lee Library, Brigham Young University, Provo, Utah (1990).

27 Stratton, Laura Lynn Lewis. *From Old to New - The Life and Times of Daniel Lewis and His Two Wives*, Utah Printing Co., Salt Lake City, Utah (1995).

28 Wikipedia. "Emma Smith," https://en.wikipedia.org/wiki/Emma_Smith

29 Long, E.B. *The Saints and the Union*, University of Illinois Press, (1981), p. 6.

30 Ibid., p. 18-19.

31 Young, Gary D. "Morgan Lewis of Kamas Valley, Utah."

32 Arrington. *Brigham Young - American Moses*, p. 283.

33 Long, E.B. *The Saints and the Union*, p.44.

34 Young, Gary D. "Morgan Lewis of Kamas Valley, Utah."

35 Black, Diana. Lewis family genealogical records. Family papers.

36 Marie Peterson, ed. *Echoes of Yesterday, Daughters of Utah Pioneers of Summit County, 1946*, p. 51.

37 Turner, John G. *Brigham Young – Pioneer Prophet*, p. 217.

38 Hampshire, David; Bradley, Martha Sonntag; and Roberts, Allen. *History of Summit County*, Utah State Historical Society and the Summit County Commission, Salt Lake City, Utah (1998) p. 76.

39 Familysearch.org. https://www.familysearch.org/tree/person/details/KWVW-2QB

40 Black, Diana. "John Neel family genealogy sheet." Family papers.

41 *Doctrine and Covenants*, Section 132, p. 239-245.

42 Ulrich, Laurel Thatcher. *A House Full of Females: Plural Marriage and Women's Rights in Early Mormonism, 1835-1870*. Alfred A. Knopf (2017), p.240.

43 The Church of Jesus Christ of Latter-day Saints website: https://www.churchofjesuschrist.org/learn/lion-house-temple-square?lang=eng; Savage, C.R., photograph: Lion House, built by Brigham Young, Salt Lake City. L. Tom Perry

Special Collections, Harold B. Lee Library, Brigham Young University.

44   Mulder and Mortensen. *Among the Mormons*, p. 399-403.
45   Wikipedia. https://en.wikipedia.org/wiki/Eli_Houston_Murray. Also, Utah Department of Cultural & Community Engagement, "History to Go"; https://historytogo.utah.gov/territorial-governors/
46   Nye, Bill. *Remarks*, Thompson and Thomas, Chicago (1901), p. 199.
47   Ibid. p. 418-420.
48   Ulrich, Laurel Thatcher. *A House Full of Females*, p. xiii.
49   Turner, John G. *Brigham Young – Pioneer Prophet*, p. 196.
50   Turner, John G. *Brigham Young – Pioneer Prophet*, p. 265-300.
51   *Reynolds v. United States*. www.oyez.org/cases/1850-1900/98us145. Accessed 23 Nov. 2021.
52   Coates, Lawrence G., Boag, Peter G., Hatzenbuehler, Ronald L., and Swanson, Merwin R. "The Mormon Settlement of Southeastern Idaho, 1845-1900," *Journal of Mormon History*, Vol. 20, No. 2 (Fall 1994), p. 45-62; University of Illinois Press; Mormon History Association. https://www.jstor.org/stable/23286599
53   Bigler, David L. *Forgotten Kingdom: The Mormon Theocracy in the American West, 1847-1896*, (Kingdom in the West; v. 2) Arthur H. Clark Company, Spokane, WA, (1998), p. 354.
54   Doctrine and Covenants, p. 257.
55   Mackley, Jennifer. "Wilford Woodruff's Witness: The Development of Temple Doctrine," http://www.wilfordwoodruff.info/p/wilfords-wives.html
56   Neal, May Lewis's "History" of Karen Marie Lewis. Family papers.
57   Saints by Sea. "A Compilation of General Voyage Notes," https://saintsbysea.lib.byu.edu/mii/account/932; and Jensen, Andrew. *History of the Scandinavian Mission*, Deseret News Press, Salt Lake City, (1927).
58   Hansen, H.N. (1971) "An Account of a Mormon Family's Conversion to the Religion of the Latter Day Saints and of Their Trip From Denmark to Utah," The Annals of Iowa 41(1), 709-728. https://doi.org/10.17077/0003-4827.11120; Also Saints by Sea. "Reminiscences of H. N. Hansen," https://saintsbysea.lib.byu.edu/mii/account/943
59   Saints by Sea. "Autobiography of Andrew Christian Nielson," (Ms 2735 282), pp. 4-6. (CHL) https://saintsbysea.lib.byu.edu/mii/account/945?keywords=Christian+Nielson&mii=on&netherlands=on&europe=on&scandinavia=on&sweden=on
60   Saints by Sea: "Autobiography of John Smith" (MS 8305 3 #1) pp. 10-12. (A) https://saintsbysea.lib.byu.edu/mii/account/946?keywords=John+Smith+Autobiography&mii=on&netherlands=on&europe=on&scandinavia=on&sweden=on
61   Hansen, H.N. (1971) "An Account of a Mormon Family's Conversion to the Religion of the Latter Day Saints and of Their Trip From Denmark to Utah," *The Annals of Iowa* 41(1), 709-728. https://doi.org/10.17077/0003-4827.11120
62   Author's conversation with Laura Lynn Lewis Stratton, Jan. 16, 2022.
63   Young, Gary D. "Morgan Lewis of Kamas Valley, Utah."

64 Stratton, Laura Lynn Lewis, *From Old to New - The Life and Times of Daniel Lewis and His Two Wives*, p. 43.

65 *The Coalville Times* (Coalville, Utah), "Letters from Correspondents," 8 Nov 1901; p. 1.

66 Sorensen, Mary Elizabeth Lewis, an untitled personal life sketch. Family papers.

67 FamilySearch. "International Genealogical Index (IGI)," database. Entry for John Austin Neel; submitted by ldcrow26832 [identity withheld for privacy]; no source information is available. Accessed 5 December 2021. https://familysearch.org/ark:/61903/2:1:9V15-T5S.

68 FamilySearch. "International Genealogical Index (IGI)," database. Entry for Therese Amelie Guarm; submitted by jddavis90031 [identity withheld for privacy]; no source information is available. Accessed 5 December 2021. https://familysearch.org/ark:/61903/2:1:MGHG-L5V.

69 Author's correspondence with historian Laurel Thatcher Ulrich, Nov. 16, 2021.

70 FamilySearch. "Ancestral File," database. Entry for Daniel Bigelow (467D-S2); record merged from multiple submissions. Accessed 5 December 2021.https://familysearch.org/ark:/61903/2:1:MWQV-B2L.

71 FamilySearch. "Ancestral File," database. Entry for Clara Fredricka Ostensen (20V0-CM); record merged from multiple submissions. Accessed 5 December 2021. https://familysearch.org/ark:/61903/2:1:M7KX-6PM; FamilySearch. "Ancestral File," database. Entry for Permelia Meachem. (2B3T-GW); record merged from multiple submissions. Accessed 5 December 2021. https://familysearch.org/ark:/61903/2:1:M7LG-73Q.

72 Marie Peterson, ed., *Echoes of Yesterday*, Daughters of Utah Pioneers of Summit County, (1946), p. 214.

73 Ibid., p. 325.

74 Black, Diana, Lewis family genealogy sheets. Family papers.

75 The LDS Church directs internet readers to scriptural references at "Doctrine and Covenants," 7:2 and John 21:20-23. See https://www.churchofjesuschrist.org/study/new-era/2017/11/to-the-point/are-john-the-beloved-and-the-three-nephites-actually-still-on-the-earth-if-so-what-are-they-doing?lang=eng

76 *The Book of Mormon*, 3 Nephi, Chapter 28, Church of Jesus Christ of Latter-day Saints, Salt Lake City, Utah, (1961), p. 452-454.

77 Stratton, Laura Lynn Lewis, *From Old to New - The Life and Times of Daniel Lewis and His Two Wives*, p. 52.

78 Bigler, David L., *Forgotten Kingdom: The Mormon Theocracy in the American West, 1847-1896*, p. 308. Also the website of the Church of Jesus Christ of Latter-day Saints, "Church History Topics," https://www.churchofjesuschrist.org/study/history/topics/john-taylor?lang=eng

79 Ekins, Roger Robin, *Defending Zion: George Q. Cannon and the California Mormon Newspaper Wars of 1856-1857*, (Kingdom in the West; The Mormons and the American Frontier, v. 5) The Arthur H. Clark Co., (2002), p. 11-16. Also online at https://www.churchofjesuschrist.org/study/history/topics/george-q-cannon?lang=eng. (Accessed May 23, 2025.)

For an explanation of the LDS Church hierarchy, see https://www.churchofjesuschrist.org/learn/global-leadership-of-the-church?lang=eng. (Accessed May 23, 2025.) The church organizes its congregations into wards, equivalent to an administrative parish. A bishop leads each ward. Each ward has quorums of "high priests," "seventies," and "elders." A group of wards forms a stake. Each stake is directed by a stake president, who is advised by two counselors.

80 Stratton, *From Old to New - The Life and Times of Daniel Lewis and His Two Wives*, p. 162.

81 Ibid., p. 54.

82 Lewis mission diary, p. 54 - 55. Copy in author's possession.

83 Saints by Sea, https://saintsbysea.lib.byu.edu/mii/account/1366; "Diary of William F. Rigby's" and Stratton, *From Old to New - The Life and Times of Daniel Lewis and His Two Wives*, p. 71-72.

84 Sorensen, Mary Elizabeth Lewis, Personal life sketch titled "Mary Elizabeth Lewis Sorensen," (circa 1953). Family papers.

85 Stratton, Laura Lynn Lewis, *From Old to New - The Life and Times of Daniel Lewis and His Two Wives*, the land sales were made on July 18, 1887; p. 157.

86 *The Salt Lake Herald* (Salt Lake City, Utah), "It Caused a Breeze," 18 Sep 1888, p. 8.

87 Bigler, David L., *Forgotten Kingdom: The Mormon Theocracy in the American West, 1847-1896*, (Kingdom in the West; v. 2), p. 326-330.

88 *Deseret News* (Salt Lake City, Utah), "Surrender of Apostle George Q. Cannon," 19 Sep 1888, p. 8.

89 https://genealogytrails.com/utah/state/history/history_territorial.html

90 *The Salt Lake Herald* (Salt Lake City, Utah), "It Caused a Breeze," 18 Sep 1888, p. 8.

91 *The Salt Lake Herald* (Salt Lake City, Utah), "The Cannon Case," 18 Sep 1888, p. 4.

92 *The Salt Lake Herald* (Salt Lake City, Utah) 19 Sep 1888, "The Third District - Five Mormons Sent to the Pen. Yesterday," p. 8

93 Siefrit, William C., *Utah Historical Quarterly*, 1985 - Vol. LIII - No. 3 – "Prison experience," p. 224; quoting M. Hamblin Cannon, ed., "The Prison Diary of a Mormon Apostle," *Pacific Historical Review* 16, 1947.

94 Cannon, Hamlin, "The Prison Diary of a Mormon Apostle," *Pacific Historical Review* 16, 1947, p. 395-397

95 Bashore, Melvin, "Life behind Bars: Mormon Cohabs of the 1880s;" *Utah Historical Quarterly*, 1979 - VOL 47 - no 1; p 24; see footnote 1. Digitized by J. Willard Marriott Library, University of Utah, 2009. UHQ 1979 - Volume 47 - no 1 - Life Behind Bars | Department of Cultural and Community Engagement | J. Willard Marriott Digital Library (utah.edu)

96 Ibid., p. 33, quoting Rudger Clawson, *Penitentiary Experiences*, p. 38-39.

97 Seifrit, William C. "The Prison Experience of Abraham H. Cannon," *Utah Historical Quarterly*, Vol. LIII, Willard Marriott Library, University of Utah, 1985. https://collections.lib.utah.edu/ark:/87278/s6jm2905/423015

98 Bigler, David L. *Forgotten Kingdom: The Mormon Theocracy in the American West, 1847-1896*, (Kingdom in the West; v. 2), p. 348-349.

99 Ibid., p. 341, citing Smith, Joseph, Jr., *History of the Church*, 5:324, 336.

100 Ibid., p. 346-347.

101 Ibid. p. 353.

102 Woodruff, Wilford, and Snow, Lorenzo, "Official Declaration," *Doctrine and Covenants*, p. 256-257.

103 Bigler, David L., *Forgotten Kingdom: The Mormon Theocracy in the American West, 1847-1896*, (Kingdom in the West; v. 2), p. 365.

104 Stratton, Laura Lynn Lewis, *From Old to New - The Life and Times of Daniel Lewis and His Two Wives*, p. 83.

105 Young, Gary D., "Morgan Lewis of Kamas Valley Utah."

106 Utah State Archives and Records Service, Third Judicial District Court, Summit County, Civil Case Files, Series 26613, Lewis Case 271.

107 Michelle Hill for Utah Humanities. 2012. "Early Education in Utah," Utah Stories from the Beehive Archive. Accessed Feb. 8, 2022. https://www.utahhumanities.org/stories/items/show/239.

108 Hampshire, David; Bradley, Martha Sonntag; and Roberts, Allen. *A History of Summit County*, p. 232. Also Michelle Hill for Utah Humanities. 2012. "Early Education in Utah," https://www.utahhumanities.org/stories/items/show/239.

109 Stratton, Laura Lynn Lewis, *From Old to New - The Life and Times of Daniel Lewis and His Two Wives*, p. 83-84.

110 Hampshire, David; Bradley, Martha Sonntag; and Roberts, Allen. *A History of Summit County*, p. 232

111 Park, John R. "Second Report Of the Superintendent of Public Instruction Of the State of Utah For the Biennial Period Ending June 30, 1898, Salt Lake City, 1899." p. 188. General Library of the University of Michigan, Presented by Dept. of Public Instruction. https://www.google.com/books/edition/Report_of_the_Superintendent_of_Public_I/mbqgAAAAMAAJ?hl=en&gbpv=1&dq=Summity+Stake+Academy+Utah&pg=RA2-PA52&printsec=frontcover

112 Ibid. P. 191.

113 Author's conversation with Diana Black. March 27, 2019.

114 *The Coalville Times* (Coalville, Utah), "The County News – Peoa," 18 Mar 1898, p. 5.

115 *The Morning Examiner* (Ogden Utah), "Ogden Brevities," 14 March 1905, p. 5.

116 University of Utah. "Annual of the University of Utah including the State School of Mines and the State Normal School, Salt Lake City, 1901-1902," p. 25 and p. 66-78.

117 FamilySearch. "United States Census, 1900," database with images. Entry for Ellen C. Neel and Franklin S. Neel, 1900. Accessed Sep 17, 2023. https://www.feamilysearch.org/ark:/619903/1:1:MMRL-PPY.

118 The house, built in 1892, still stands.

119 Utah History Encyclopedia. Haymond, Jay M., "The Telephone in Utah." https://www.uen.org/utah_history_encyclopedia/t/TELEPHONE.shtml

120 University of Utah, "Annual of the University of Utah including the State School of Mines and the State Normal School, Salt Lake City. 1901-1902." p. 22.

121 *The Salt Lake Tribune* (Salt Lake City, Utah) "J.W. Neill convicted of rape," 18 Jun 1899, p. 11.

122 *The Coalville Times* (Coalville, Utah) "Neel Gets Five," 21 July 1899, p. 1.

123 *The Salt Lake Tribune* (Salt Lake City, Utah). "Heavy Charge Lodged Against Joshua W. Neil at Peoa," 24 Dec 1899, p. 7.

124 *The Park Record* (Park City, Utah). "Neel Again in Trouble," 30 Dec. 1899, p. 4.

125 Nye, George L. Reports of Cases determined in The Supreme Court of the State of Utah including portions of the October Term, 1899, and February Term, 1900, Vol. 21, Callaghan & Co. (1901), p. 151-158.

126 *Deseret News* (Salt Lake City, Utah)."District Court Business"; 21 Apr 1900, p. 7.

127 *The Salt Lake Tribune* (Salt Lake City, Utah). "Neel must go to jail" 16 Jun 1901, p. 3.

128 *The Daily Utah Chronicle* (Salt Lake City, Utah). "The Societies," 5 Nov 1901, p. 14.

129 *The Salt Lake Tribune* (Salt Lake City, Utah). "There are Ninety-Nine," 1 June 1902, p. 4.; *The Deseret Evening News* (Salt Lake City, Utah). "State University Graduation Day," 4 June 1902, p 1. ; *The Salt Lake Herald* (Salt Lake City, Utah). "Large Graduating Class," 1 June 1902, p. 2.

130 Utah State Archives and Records Service, Third Judicial District Court, Summit County, Civil Case Files, Series 26613, Lewis Case 271.

131 *The Coalville Times* (Coalville, Utah). "District Court," 18 Jan 1901, p. 1.

132 CPI Inflation Calculator; https://www.officialdata.org/us/inflation/1903?amount=40.

133 *The Coalville Times* (Coalville, Utah). "County News – Marion," 26 Sep 1902, p. 8.

134 *Box Elder News-Journal* (Brigham City, Utah). "Honeyville Happenings," 22 Oct 1903, p.4.

135 Neal, May Lewis, letter to Eleazer Lewis, July 18, 1904. Family papers.

136 Neal, May Lewis, letter written to Eleazer Lewis, Nov. 30, 1904. Family papers.

137 Driggs, B.W. *History of Teton Valley*, edited by Lewis J. Clements and Harold Forbush, 1970. p. 158 - 160.

138 Holt, Kristin. "What is a Calico Ball?" May 31, 2018. http://www.kristinholt.com/archives/1572.

139 *Salt Lake Tribune*, (Salt Lake City, Utah). "Calico Ball Held," 27 Jan 1906, p. 10.

140 *The Park Record*, (Park City, Utah). "Park Float," 28 Oct 1905, p. 3.

141 Neal, May Lewis, and Neal, D.S., letter written to Eleazer and Roxie Lewis, May 12, 1905. Family papers.

142 Klass, Perri, *A Good Time to Be Born - How Science and Public Health Gave Children a Future*. W.W. Norton & Company, New York, NY, 2020, p. 5.

143 Institute of Medicine (US) Committee on Palliative and End-of-Life Care for Children and Their Families; Field, MJ., Behrman, RE., editors. "Chapter 2, Patterns of Childhood Death in America." *When Children Die: Improving Palliative and End-*

144. Neal, May Lewis, and Neal, D.S., letter written to Eleazer and Roxie Lewis, May 12, 1905. Family papers.
145. Stratton, Laura Lynn Lewis, *From Old to New - The Life and Times of Daniel Lewis and His Two Wives*, p. 92.
146. Ibid., p. 90.
147. *The Coalville Times* (Coalville, Utah). "County News – Marion," 10 Nov 1905, p. 4; 8 Dec 1905, p. 4; and 15 Dec 1905, p. 4.
148. Stratton, Laura Lynn Lewis, *From Old to New - The Life and Times of Daniel Lewis and His Two Wives*, p. 92.
149. Sorensen, Elizabeth. "Mary Elizabeth Lewis Sorensen," (circa 1953). Family papers.
150. Hansen, Margaret. "A New Home," a high school theme written in 1944 or 1945. Copy supplied by Michele West.
151. National Park Service. "About the Homestead Act." https://www.nps.gov/home/learn/historyculture/abouthomesteadactlaw.htm; and "Homesteading in Idaho." https://www.nps.gov/home/learn/historyculture/homesteading-in-idaho.htm. Accessed March 17, 2025.
152. Corey, J.N. Fremont County Recorder, "No. 17647 Possessory claim," filed July 11, 1907. Copy among family papers.
153. Idaho Statutes. Title 58, Public Lands, Chapter 9, sections 901-901.
154. Darby Ward membership records. Church of Jesus Christ of Latter-day Saints, Church History Catalog
155. Author's telephone conversation with the Teton County, Idaho, County Clerk's Office. Feb. 15, 2023.
156. State of Idaho Teacher's Second Grade Certificate, issued Dec. 5, 1909. Family papers.
157. Neal, D.S., letter to Charles Hugh Neal, June 8, 1910. Family papers.
158. Neal, D.S., letter to Ellen Christiana Stevens, Feb. 6, 1910. Family papers.
159. Neal, D.S., letter to Charles Hugh Neal, June 18, 1910. Family papers.
160. Forbush, Harold S. *Education in the Upper Snake River Valley*, Ricks College Press, Rexburg, Idaho, (1992), p. 361.
161. D.S. Neal signed the student examination and attendance reports as teacher, then signed the backs of the cards as school principal. Family papers.
162. Neal, L.G. *The Murder of David Steven Neal - A True Story*, McCall, Idaho: Self-published, (2003), p. 9.
163. *Deseret News* (Salt Lake City, Utah). "Narrow Escape," 1 Feb 1883, p. 13.
164. Wilson, Elijah Nicholas. *Among the Shoshones*. Bookcraft Publishers, Salt Lake City, Utah (1969).
165. Ancestry.com. www.ancestrylibrary.com/family-tree/person/tree/56593088/person/46449785651/facts?ssrc=&ml_rpos=2

166 Ferrin, Nellie Wilson. "Biography of Nick Wilson," transcription of Ferrin's biographical sketch taken from the *Jackson Hole Guide* newspaper, Jackson Hole Historical Society and Museum. A second transcription is available at the archives of BYU-Idaho in Rexburg.

167 Wilson, Charles Alma. *The Return of the White Indian*. University of Utah Press (2005), p. 157.

168 Ferrin, Nellie Wilson. "Biography of Nick Wilson." Jackson Hole Historical Society and Museum, Jackson, Wyoming.

169 Ibid. Also Wilson, Charles Alma. *The Return of the White Indian*. University of Utah Press (2005), p. xviiii-xx. Wilson's book lists the deaths of three sons in 1891 and notes that the death dates of two daughters and two sons are not known.

170 Darby Ward manuscript history and historical reports, 1891-1971. Church History Catalog.

171 Bagley, E. Scan of "Application for a Permit to Divert and Appropriate the Water in the State of Wyoming." Wyoming State Engineer's Office. Aug. 26, 1896.

172 Smith, Eugene Ellington. *Life Story of Eugene Ellington (Enoich-Nick) Smith*, (circa 1985), p. 1. Copy in author's possession.

173 FamilySearch. Smith, Octavus; "Untitled memoir." (1938). https://www.familysearch.org/tree/person/memories/KWCH-VJ6

174 Ken Sanders Rare Books. Accessed Dec. 10, 2024. https://www.kensandersbooks.com/pages/books/49018/elijah-nicholas-wilson-uncle-nick/among-the-shoshones.

175 Wilson, Charles A. *The White Indian Boy* and its sequel *The Return of the White Indian*, University of Utah Press, 1985. p. xv.

176 Ibid., p. 207-209.

177 Author's taped interview with David Lewis Neal, summer 1984 in Island Park, Idaho.

178 Brand certificate from J.H. Weber, state veterinarian, mailed to May Lewis July 11, 1911. Family papers.

179 Anderson, Joseph. letter to Mrs. D.S. Neal, July 14, 1911. Family papers.

180 Darby Ward manuscript history and historical reports, 1891-1971. Darby ward general minutes. LR2145 11. LDS Church History Center, Salt Lake City, Utah.

181 Author interview of Mitch Kvarfordt, Oct. 23, 2018. Kvarfordt is a former bishop of the Ammon 4th ward, Ammon, Idaho.

182 Jensen, Andrew. *Encyclopedic History of The Church of Jesus Christ of Latter-day Saints*, Deseret News Publishing Company, Salt Lake City, Utah (1941) p. 173. https://catalog.churchofjesuschrist.org/assets/a6485840-8cb3-4f4c-bf9c-a3219a76017c/0/185

183 Rau, Sue. Letter to the author, Feb. 8, 1993. Family papers. Rau is a daughter of Carmen Neal Lloyd.

184 Permit No. 7584 issued Aug. 19, 1911; State of Idaho, Engineering Department, Boise, Idaho. Family papers.

185 Fremont County Probate Court minutes signed by Judge Oliver C. Dalby. Undated but July 25, 1911, inferred. Smith, Ellington, File number 1884, Box number 2470,

Records, Idaho State Penitentiary, 1869-1973, AR00042. Idaho State Archives.

186 Phoenix Yearbook (1902) p. 105. Stockton Archives, Cumberland University, Lebanon, Tennessee. And a personal communication with Joshua Baxter, archivist, Cumberland University, April 8, 2021.

187 French, Hiram T. *History of Idaho*, p. 1196.

188 *The Idaho Republican* (Blackfoot, Idaho). "Maybe Holden, Maybe Not," 22 Apr 1910, p. 4.

189 Vaughan, G.C., stenographer. Transcript of testimony taken in Fremont County Probate Court in *State of Idaho vs. Ellington Smith*. July 25, 1911; transcript submitted July 27, 1911. Case CR1911-1337. Smith, Ellington, File number 1884, Box number 2470, Records, Idaho State Penitentiary, 1869-1973, AR00042. Idaho State Archives.

190 Commitment order signed by Probate Judge Oliver C. Dalby, Fremont County Probate Court, July 27, 1911. Smith, Ellington, File number 1884, Box number 2470, Records, Idaho State Penitentiary, 1869-1973, AR00042. Idaho State Archives.

191 *The Evening Standard* (Ogden, Utah). "Smith Now Held on Murder Charge," 3 Aug 1911, p. 2

192 FindLaw. Accessed March 20 2023. https://www.findlaw.com/criminal/criminal-procedure/the-insanity-defense-history-and-background.html.

193 *Wood River Times* (Hailey, Idaho). "Idaho's Insane Asylum," 1 Feb 1886, p. 3.

194 *The Idaho Statesman* (Boise, Idaho). "A Sad Affair – Burning of the Lunatic Asylum," 26 Nov 1889, p. 2.

195 *The Caldwell Tribune*, (Caldwell, Idaho). "The Burning of the Idaho Insane Asylum," 30 Nov 1889, p. 2.

196 *Blackfoot News*, (Blackfoot, Idaho). "The Insane Asylum," 30 Nov 1889, p. 8.

197 *The Idaho Statesman*, (Boise, Idaho). "Patients Build Their Own Home," 27 March 1906, p. 2.

198 *The Idaho Statesman*, (Boise, Idaho). "Wants Dam," 16 Jan 1911, p. 3.; *The Caldwell Tribune* (Caldwell, Idaho). "Nampa Gets Institute," 12 May 1911, p. 3.

199 *Montpelier Examiner* (Montpelier, Idaho). "Dr. Poole Will Be Supt. of Asylum," 30 Dec 1910, p. 1.

200 *The Idaho Statesman* (Boise, Idaho). "Land Board Was Fully Advised As To Dam," 12 Feb 1911, p. 5.

201 *The Rigby Star* (Rigby, Idaho). "Inspected Public Schools," Dec. 14, 1911, p. 1; "Honor Washington's Natal Day," Feb. 26, 1912.

202 *Montpelier Examiner* (Montpelier, Idaho). "Commissioners Proceedings," 24 Jan. 1902, p 1; *The Idaho Republican* (Blackfoot, Idaho). "Taken with Appendicitis," 26 Oct. 1917, p. 1.

203 *The Idaho Republican* (Blackfoot, Idaho). "Harry Holden in Hospital," 24 Nov. 1911, p. 4.

204 *The Bingham County News*, (Blackfoot, Idaho). "Blackfoot Day by Day," 12 Jan. 1911, p. 6; *The Idaho Republican*. untitled column of notes, 20 Jan. 1911, p. 5.

205 Witness subpoenas issued week of Jan. 15, 1912, Ninth Judicial District Court records. Smith, Ellington, File number 1884, Box number 2470, Records, Idaho State Penitentiary, 1869-1973, AR00042. Idaho State Archives.

206 U.S. Census Bureau. "Thirteenth Census of the United States Taken in the Year 1910 – Statistics for Idaho. Reprint of the supplement for Idaho, 1913." Accessed on Jan.28, 2025. https://www2.census.gov/library/publications/decennial/1910/abstract/supplement-id.pdf.

207 The *Teton Peak-Chronicle* (St. Anthony, Idaho). "Odd Fellows Installed Officers," 22 Jan 1903, p. 1; "Local News," 17 Sep. 1903, p. 6; Untitled local notes, 2 June, 1904, p. 8; "Local Happenings," 29 Sep. 1904, p. 6; "Notice to Band Members," 30 March, 1905, p. 1; "St. Anthony City Election," 6 April, 1905, p. 1; "Local Happenings," 20 April, 1905, p. 8.

208 The *Idaho Statesman* (Boise, Idaho). "Protest Storm Breaks," 22 Feb 1911, p. 5, and "Bitter Fight for Judgeship is Ended," 1 Apr 1911, p. 8.

209 The *Rexburg Standard* (Rexburg, Idaho). "David S. Neal Killed at Bates" 8 Jul 1911, p. 1.

210 The *Teton Peak-Chronicle* (St. Anthony, Idaho). "Ellington Smith Gets Life Sentence," 1 Feb 1912, p. 1; and "Judge Gwinn's Statement to Governor on conviction of Murder in First Degree ," Jan. 31, 1912.

211 HealthMatch. https://healthmatch.io/kidney-disease/what-is-brights-disease#overview.

212 The *Rigby Star* (Rigby, Idaho). "Justice Vindicated - Strong Arm of the Law Finally Runs down a Murderer," 1 Feb 1912, p. 1.

213 The *Idaho Republican* (Blackfoot, Idaho). "Murder Trial at St. Anthony," 2 Feb 1912, p. 1.

214 Author's conversation with attorney Mark L. Aronowitz of The Spence Law Firm, Jackson, Wyoming; May 25, 2023.

215 Miller, B. H. "Proposed instructions with notes from Judge Gwinn." Smith, Ellington, File number 1884, Box 2470, Records, Idaho State Penitentiary, 1869-1973, AR00042. Idaho State Archives.

216 *Deseret News* (Salt Lake City, Utah). "Murderer Is Found Guilty," 3 Feb 1912, p. 12.

217 *Teton Valley News* (Driggs, Idaho). "Ellerton Smith Is Convicted of Murder," 8 Feb. 1912, p. 1.

218 Darby Ward, Teton Stake. "Darby Ward general minutes, 1884-197." https://catalog.churchofjesuschrist.org/record/cd079b06-1ca0-4c66-b58c-4cbe5fe24047/0?view=summary&lang=eng, accessed Nov. 8, 2023.

219 Affidavit of Defendant filed in Ninth Judicial District Court, Jan 31, 1912. Smith, Ellington, File number 1884, Box 2470, Records, Idaho State Penitentiary, 1869-1973, AR00042. Idaho State Archives.

220 The *Bingham County News* (Blackfoot Idaho). "Pen For Life," 12 Feb 1912, p. 1.

221 Murphy, Patrick C. *Behind Gray Walls*. Caxton Printers, Ltd. Caldwell, Idaho (1920), p. 12.

222 French, Hiram T. *History of Idaho*, Vol 2. p. 685-686

223 Smith, Ellington, File number 1884, Box 2470, Records, Idaho State Penitentiary, 1869-1973, AR00042. Idaho State Archives.

224 Johnstone, Rachel S. *Inmates of the Idaho Penitentiary 1864-1947 - A Comprehensive Catalog*, compiled and arranged by Johnstone; Idaho State Historical Society, Boise, Idaho (2008).

225 Undated letter from Warden John Snook to John M. Haines, governor of Idaho. Box 30. Records, Idaho State Penitentiary, 1869-1973. AR2-10. Idaho State Archives.

226 Murphy, Patrick C. *Behind Gray Walls*. p. 25.

227 *The Rexburg Standard* (Rexburg, Idaho). "Notice – Before the Board of Pardons," 25 Aug. 1914, no page number

228 French, Hiram Taylor. *History of Idaho*; p. 1212.

229 Ace, William aka Titsworth, File number 1581, Box number 2470. Records, Idaho State Penitentiary, 1869-1973. AR00042. Idaho State Archives.

230 *The Idaho Statesman* (Boise, Idaho). "Boise Convict Arrested In Portland," 21 Sep 1912, p. 3; "Many Applications To Be Considered By Board," 2 Oct 1912, p. 5; and "Levy Will Come Back to His Old Home," 3 Oct 1912, p. 5. See also Levy, George aka Blome, File number 854, Box 2470. Records, Idaho State Penitentiary, 1869-1973. AR00042. Idaho State Archives.

231 *The Idaho Statesman* (Boise, Idaho). "Travel Together," 7 Oct 1914, p. 9; "Innocent Man Serving Term In Prison?" 8 Oct 1914, p. 12; and "Board Allows Freedom To Eight Men," 9 Oct 1914, p. 8.

232 *The Rigby Star* (Rigby, Idaho). "C. W. Poole was an arrival," 8 Oct 1914. BYU Library. https://contentdm.lib.byu.edu/digital/collection/RigbyStar/id/31520/rec/1.

233 *The Rigby Star* (Rigby, Idaho). "Smith pardon request denied," 15 Oct 1914. BYU Library. https://contentdm.lib.byu.edu/digital/collection/RigbyStar/id/31615/rec/14

234 McDonald, Dylan J., Walker, Steve, and Crowder, David L. "The Moses Alexander Collection," Idaho State Historical Society, Boise, Idaho, (2002), p.6. Idaho State Archives.

235 *The Idaho Daily Statesman* (Boise, Idaho). "Splendid Record," 19 Jul 19 1903, p. 6.

236 *The Record* (Saint Maries, Idaho). "Splendid Record," 30 Oct 1914, p. 2.

237 *The Idaho Statesman* (Boise, Idaho). "Can Idaho Penitentiary Be Citizenship School?" 22 Oct 1916, p. 15.

238 *The Idaho Statesman* (Boise, Idaho). "Convict Writes Story," 9 Jul 1916, p. 17.

239 Murphy, Patrick C. *Behind Gray Walls*. p. 33-36.

240 *The Idaho Statesman* (Boise, Idaho). "Can Idaho Penitentiary Be Citizenship School?" 22 Oct 1916, P. 15

241 *The Idaho Statesman* (Boise, Idaho). "Snook Knocks Broxon Down," 28 Oct 1916, p. 1; *Evening Capital News* (Boise, Idaho). "Brutal Attack on Secretary to Governor," 28 Oct 1916, p. 1. Many Idaho newspapers published stories about the fist fight in the Capitol. *The Idaho Statesman* and the *Evening Capital News* provided contrasting perspectives on the fight and its fallout before and after the election.

No Forgiveness

242 Wikipedia. https://en.wikipedia.org/wiki/1916_Idaho_gubernatorial_election.

243 *The Idaho Statesman* (Boise, Idaho). "Prison Farm To Be Kept Up," 24 Nov 1916, p. 7; "Pardon Denied to O.V. Allen," 22 Dec 1916, p. 7.

244 *The Idaho Statesman* (Boise, Idaho). "Snook Resigns," 22 Dec 1916, p. 7; *Bingham County News* (Blackfoot Idaho), "Frank Dekay Is Slated," 21 Dec 1916, p. 1; "DeKay on the job," 28 Dec 1916, p. 1.

245 *Jackson's Hole Courier* (Jackson, Wyoming). "Wilson News," 1 Jul 1914, p. 1.

246 *The Idaho Statesman* (Boise, Idaho). "Utah Pioneer Dies," 17 Aug. 1916, p. 4.

247 "I'll Be a Sunbeam" (also called "Jesus Wants Me for a Sunbeam") is a popular children's Christian hymn composed by Nellie Talbot; it is sung to music composed in 1900 by Edwin O. Excell.

248 Lloyd, Carmen Neal, "Remembrances," an autobiographical essay. (Circa 1980). Family papers.

249 Family papers, originals in author's possession.

250 *Evening Capital News* (Boise, Idaho). "Coleman Will Not Be Given His Freedom," 3 Jan 1917, p. 3.

251 Neal, Mrs. D.S. Letter to Gov. Alexander, Jan. 27,1917. File 22, Box 14, AR2-11, Idaho State Archives.

252 Neal, May Lewis. Letter in pencil to the federal Land Office in Blackfoot, Idaho, Feb. 17, 1917. Family papers.

253 *Teton Valley News* (Driggs, Idaho). "Darby," 22 Feb 1917; and "Darby," 8 Mar 1917.

254 Neal, Mrs. D.S. Letter to Gov. Alexander, March 6, 1917. File 22, Box 14. State identifier 20180720132725729. Moses Alexander Collection, AR2-11. Idaho State Archives.

255 Pincock, Sen. John E. Letter to Gov. Alexander, March 3, 1917. File 22, Box 14. Moses Alexander Collection, AR2-11. Idaho State Archives.

256 Driggs, Don Carlos. Letter to Gov. Alexander, March 19, 1917. File 22, Box 14. Moses Alexander Collection, AR2-11. Idaho State Archives.

257 Rawlins, A. F. Juror-signed form letter to Board of Pardons, March 26, 1917. File 22, Box 14. Moses Alexander Collection, AR2-11. Idaho State Archives.

258 Smith, Ellington. "In the Matter of the Application of Ellington Smith for Pardon." Smith, Ellington, File number 1884, Box 2470, Records, Idaho State Penitentiary, 1869-1973, AR00042. Idaho State Archives.

259 *The Record* (St. Maries, Idaho). "Coleman Secures His Release," 27 Feb 1917, p. 1

260 *Evening Capital News* (Boise, Idaho). "Coleman Free," 22 Feb 1917, p. 1.

261 *The Kendrick Gazette* (Kendrick Idaho). "Miscarriage of Justice," 2 Mar 1917, p. 2; "That Pardon Board," 9 Mar 1917, p. 2; and "That Pardon Board," 13 Apr 1917, p. 2. Many other newspapers reported on the Coleman reprieve.

262 *The Idaho Statesman* (Boise, Idaho). "Prisoners To Get Out," 6 Apr 1917, p. 4; "13 Prisoners Get Pardons," 7 Apr 1917, p. 8; *Evening Capital News* (Boise, Idaho). Board Gives A Full Pardon to Walter Grant," 7 Apr 1917, p. 3.

263 Letter from Secretary of State W. T. Dougherty to penitentiary warden Frank DeKay, April 9, 1917. File 22, Box 14. Moses Alexander Collection, AR2-11. Idaho State Archives.

264 *Evening Capital News* (Boise, Idaho). "War Council of State," 18 Apr 1917, p. 8.; *The Idaho Republican* (Blackfoot, Idaho). "Idaho Mobilizes Resources," 23 Apr 1917, p. 1. The Black Canyon dam was completed in 1924 and remains in operation.

265 American Battle Monuments Commission. Accessed Jan. 27, 2025. https://www.abmc.gov/news-events/news/hometown-boys-idaho-information-and-statistics-about-wwi-service-members.

266 Davies, William, letter to May Neal, March 5, 1916. Family papers.

267 Darby Ward manuscript and historical reports, 1891-1971. LDS Church History Catalog.

268 Berntson, Mrs. P.W. Letter to May Neal, June 18, 1917. File 22, Box 14. Moses Alexander Collection, AR2-11. Idaho State Archives.

269 Smith, Ellington, File number 1884, Box 2470, Records, Idaho State Penitentiary, 1869-1973, AR00042. Idaho State Archives.

270 Certificate of Death, File No. 120 401, State of Montana Bureau of Vital Statistics. June 25, 1917. Copy in author's possession.

271 Excerpt from second 1917 citizen petition. File 22, Box 14. Moses Alexander Collection, AR2-11. Idaho State Archives.

272 *Dialogue: A Journal of Mormon Thought*, Vol. 26, No. 3, Fall 1993. P. 101-117.

273 *The Teton Peak-Chronicle* (St. Anthony, Idaho). "Commissioner Proceedings," 20 Apr 20, 1905, p. 6.

274 Driggs, B.W., *History of Teton Valley, Idaho*, edited by Louis J. Clements and Harold S. Forbush. Eastern Idaho Publishing Co., Rexburg, Idaho (1970). p. 186.

275 *Montpelier Enterprise* (Montpelier, Idaho), "Local News," 6 Jan. 1905; *The Post-Register* (Idaho Falls, Idaho), "Former Valley Resident Dies," 8 Feb 1938, p 3.

276 Letters and petitions supporting Smith pardon, File 22, Box 14. Moses Alexander Collection, AR2-11. Idaho State Archives.

277 Recorded conversation with David Lewis Neal and his wife Mona Neal, summer, 1984, in Island Park, Idaho. Tape and transcript in author's possession.

278 *The Idaho Statesman* (Boise, Idaho). "Pardon Board Releases 25," 1 Aug 1917, Wednesday, p. 6.

279 Dougherty, W.M. Letter to Warden Frank DeKay, Aug. 1, 1917. File 22, Box 14. Moses Alexander Collection, AR2-11. Idaho State Archives.

280 *The Jordan Times* (Jordan, Montana), quoting *Sumatra Record*, "Gil Dodge motored to Sumatra," 4 Aug. 1917, p. 1.

281 Certificate of Death, File No. 122 237, State of Montana, Bureau of Vital Statistics. Aug. 12, 1917. Copy in author's possession.

282 *The Idaho Republican* (Blackfoot, Idaho). "Speaks of Warden DeKay," 10 Sept 1917 p. 2.

283 *The Idaho Republican* (Blackfoot, Idaho). "DeKay's Road Builders," 8 Oct 1917, p. 8.

284 *The Idaho Statesman* (Boise, Idaho). "Do Returns Justify Costs of Using Prisoners on Highways?" 19 May 1918, p. 17.

285 *Evening Capital News* (Boise, Idaho). "Wants Good Horns," 24 Dec 1917, p. 5.

286 Warden Frank DeKay memorandum to Board of Prison Commissioners, 17 Dec 1917. File 22, Box 14. Moses Alexander Collection, AR2-11. Idaho State Archives.

287 *The Rigby Star* (Rigby, Idaho). "Fisher to Denver," 10 Jan 1918, p. 1.

288 Centers for Disease Control and Prevention. "History of 1918 Flu Pandemic." https://blogs.cdc.gov/publichealthmatters/2018/05/1918-flu/

289 *The Idaho Statesman* (Boise, Idaho). "State Board Opens Fight On Influenza," 9 Oct 1918, p. 1.

290 *The Challis Messenger* (Challis, Idaho). "Uncle Sam's Advice On Flu," 6 Nov 1918, p. 5. This advice from the U.S. Public Health Service was published in many Idaho newspapers.

291 *The Idaho Statesman* (Boise, Idaho). "Accident at the Pen," 12 July 1918, p. 5.

292 *The Idaho Statesman* (Boise, Idaho). "How Prisoners Knit," 17 Sep 1918, p. 7.

293 *The Idaho Statesman* (Boise, Idaho). "Ramirez Must Die February 8," 03 Jan 1918, p. 3; and "Pardons Given 22 Prisoners," p. 8.

294 *The Record* (Saint Maries, Idaho). "Will Give Prisoners A Chance To Help," 8 Mar 1918, p. .3

295 *The Meridian Times* (Meridian, Idaho). "Ex-treasurer Allen Wants to Help Build Ships," 8 Mar 1918, p. 1.

296 *The Idaho Statesman* (Boise, Idaho). "Dozen Prisoners Granted Pardons," 5 Apr 1918, p. 7.

297 *The Idaho Statesman* (Boise, Idaho). "Pardon Board Grants Freedom To Ten Convicts," 3 Oct 1918, p. 8. Also see *Clearwater Republican* (Orofino, Idaho), "Pardon Board Did Well," 19 Apr 1918, p. 4. Ellis was paroled in December.

298 Letter from Secretary of State W. T. Dougherty to Warden DeKay, Oct. 3, 1918. Smith, Ellington, File number 1884, Box 2470, Records, Idaho State Penitentiary, 1869-1973, AR00042. Idaho State Archives.

299 *The Idaho Statesman* (Boise, Idaho). "Nez Perce Is Stricken," 18 Oct, p. 5; and "Boise Hospital Capacity," 26 Oct 1918, p. 7.

300 *The Idaho Statesman* (Boise, Idaho). "Young DeKay Is Wounded," 26 Oct 1918, p. 7.

301 *The Idaho Statesman* (Boise, Idaho). "Murderer Uses Red Cross Yarn To Escape Prison," 18 Nov 1918, p. 3.

302 *The Idaho Republican* (Blackfoot, Idaho). "Influenza Over The State," 6 Dec 1918, p. 1

303 *The Idaho Statesman* (Boise, Idaho). "Two Prisoners Die, Victims of Influenza," 20 Dec 1918, p. 4.

304 *The Idaho Statesman* (Boise, Idaho). "Inmates Fire Buildings In Prison Disturbance," Mar 8, 1973, p.1.

305 Digital Atlas of Idaho. Idaho State University. https://digitalatlas.cose.isu.edu/geog/historic/histtxt/idpent.htm#.

306 Newberg, R.D. Letter to Mrs. Randall Foster, Jan. 25, 1973. Copy in author's possession.

307 Author's telephone conversation with Susan Foster, Nov. 5, 1918.

308 Penfold, Janet. Email messages to the author, Sept. 13, 14, 15, 2023.

309 Riley, Jim. Email message to the author, Sept. 21, 2023.

310 Smith, Joseph Fielding. *Teachings of the Prophet Joseph Smith*. The Deseret News Press, Third Edition (1942), p. 339-340.

Bibliography

PUBLISHED WORKS

Arrington, Leonard J., *Brigham Young: American Moses*. Vintage Books, Random House, Inc. New York, New York. (Copyright 1985; Vintage Books 2012)

Bigler, David L., *Forgotten kingdom: the Mormon theocracy in the American West, 1847-1896*, (*Kingdom in the West*; v. 2). Arthur H. Clark Company, Spokane, WA, (1998).

Bowen, A. W., *Progressive Men of Southern Idaho*. A.W. Bowen & Co., Chicago, (1904).

Brodie, Fawn, *No man knows my history - The Life of Joseph Smith The Mormon Prophet*. Alfred A. Knopf, New York, (1972).

Bradley, James L., *History of the Latter-Day Saint Church in the Teton Valley, 1888-1956* (1956). Theses and Dissertations. 4546. https://scholarsarchive.byu.edu/etd/4546

Deseret Sunday School Union, *Deseret Sunday School Songs*, (1937 edition; first published in 1909).

Doyle, Arthur Conan, *A Study in Scarlet*. Ward Lock & Co. London. (1888 in book form; taken from Baring-Gold, William S., editor, *The Annotated Sherlock Holmes*. Clarkson N. Potter, Inc. New York, (1967).

Driggs, B. W., *History of Teton Valley, Idaho*. Edited by Louis J. Clements and Harold S. Forbush; Eastern Idaho Publishing Co. Rexburg, Idaho (1970). Original edition by B. W. Driggs, 1926.

Ekins, Roger Robin, *Defending Zion: George Q. Cannon and the California Mormon Newspaper Wars of 1856-1857*. The Arthur H. Clark Co. (2002).

Forbush, Harold S., *Education in the Upper Snake River Valley – The Public Schools (1880-1950)*. Ricks College Press, Rexburg, Idaho (1992).

French, Hiram T.; *History of Idaho, A Narrative Account of Its Historical Progress, Its People and Its Principal Interests.* Vols. I, II, & III. Illustrated. The Lewis Publishing Company, Chicago and New York (1914). Facsimile copy from Scholars Select

Franzwa, Gregory M.; *Maps of the Oregon Trail.* The Patrice Press, Gerald, Missouri (1982).

Green, Dean H., *History of Island Park – a Pictorial and Written History from before 1890 to Idaho's Centennial Year 1990.* Island Park – Gateway Publishing Co., Ashton, Idaho (1990).

Hampshire, David; Bradley, Martha Sonntag; and Roberts, Allen; *A History of Summit County.* Utah State Historical Society and the Summit County Commission, Salt Lake City, Utah (1998).

Jenson, Andrew, *Encyclopedic History of the Church of Jesus Christ of Latter-day Saints.* Deseret News Publishing Co., Salt Lake City, Utah (1941).

Jenson, Andrew, *History of the Scandinavian Mission.* Deseret News Press, Salt Lake City, Utah (1927).

Johnstone, Rachel S., *Inmates of the Idaho Penitentiary 1864-1947: A Comprehensive Catalog.* Idaho State Historical Society, Boise, Idaho, (2008).

Klass, Perri, *A Good Time to Be Born: How Science and Public Health Gave Children a Future.* W.W. Norton & Company, New York, NY (2020).

Long, Everette B., *The Saints and the Union, Utah Territory during the Civil War.* University of Illinois Press, Chicago (1981).

Lukas, J. Anthony, *Big trouble: a murder in a small western town sets off a struggle for the soul of America.* Simon & Schuster, New York, NY (1997)

Mulder, William and Mortensen, A. Russell, editors. *Among the Mormons – Historic Accounts by Contemporary Observers.* A Bison Book, University of Nebraska Press, Lincoln, NE. (1973). First published in 1958 by Alfred A. Knopf, Inc., New York, NY.

Murphy, Patrick C., *Behind Gray Walls.* Caxton Printers. Ltd., Caldwell, Idaho (1920).

Nye, Bill, *Remarks.* (Edgar W. Nye) Thompson and Thomas, Chicago (1901).

Nye, George L., *Reports of Cases determined in The Supreme Court of the State of Utah including portions of the October Term, 1899, and February Term, 1900.* Vol. 21, Callaghan & Co. (1901). Google Books. www.google.com/books/edition/_/dQhIAQAAMAAJ?hl=en&gbpv=1

Park, Benjamin E., *American Zion – A New History of Mormonism.* Liverwright Publishing Co., a division of W.W. Norton & Co. New York (2024).

Peterson, Marie Ross, and Pearson, Mary M., *Echoes of Yesterday – Summit County Centennial History.* Daughters of Utah Pioneers of Summit County, Mountain States Bindery, Salt Lake City, Utah (1947).

Smith, Joseph Fielding, *Teachings of the Prophet Joseph Smith.* The Desert News Press, Salt Lake City, (Copyright 1938, Third Edition, 1942).

Stegner, Wallace, *Mormon Country.* Bonanza Books, a division of Crown Publishers, Inc. New York, NY. (1942).

Stratton, Laura Lynn Lewis, *From Old to New: The Life and Times of Daniel Lewis and His Two Wives Mary Davis Lewis [and] Karen Marie Sorensen Lewis.* Utah Printing Company, Salt Lake City, Utah (1995).

Turner, John G., *Brigham Young, Pioneer Prophet.* The Belknap Press of Harvard University Press Cambridge Massachusetts (2012).

Ulrich, Laurel Thatcher, *A House Full of Females: Plural Marriage and Women's Rights in Early Mormonism, 1835-1870.* Alfred A. Knopf, New York, NY (2017).

Young, Gary D., *Morgan Lewis of Kamas Valley, Utah.* Self-published. (1999) Available at Summit County Courthouse, Coalville, Utah.

Whalen, William J., *The Latter-day Saints in the Modern Day World.* University of Notre Dame Press, Notre Dame, Indiana (1964).

Wilson, Elijah Nicholas, *Among the Shoshones*. Bookcraft Publishers, Salt Lake City, Utah (1960). First published by Skelton Publishing Company, Salt Lake City, UT, 1910.

Wilson, Elijah Nicholas, and Wilson, Charles A., *The White Indian Boy and its sequel: The Return of the White Indian*, Charles Alma Wilson, 1985. The University of Utah Press (2005).

PERIODICALS, PAMPHLETS, AND ONLINE RESOURCES

Bashore, Melvin L., and Haslam, Linda L., "Mormons on the High Seas – Ocean Voyage Narratives to America (1849-1890)," *Guide to sources in the Historical Department of the Church of Jesus Christ of Latter-day Saints and Other Utah Repositories,*"Historical Department, The Church of Jesus Christ of Latter-day Saints (1990).

Cannon, M. Hamlin, editor, "The Prison Diary of a Mormon Apostle." *Pacific Historical Review*. Nov., 1947, Vol. 16, No. 4 (Nov., 1947), pp. 393-409, University of California Press.
www.jstor.org/stable/3635856

Coates, Lawrence G., Boag, Peter G., Harzenbuehler, Ronald L., and Swanson, Merwin R., "The Mormon Settlement of Southeastern Idaho, 1845-1900," *Journal of Mormon History*, Vol. 20, No. 2 (Fall, 1994) University of Illinois Press: Mormon History Association.
www.jstor.org/stable/23286599

Hansen, H. N., "An Account of a Mormon Family's Conversion to the Religion of the Latter Day Saints and of Their Trip From Denmark to Utah," *The Annals of Iowa* 41(1), (1971) p.709-728.
https://doi.org/10.17077/0003-4827.11120
Ibid. p.765-779.
https://doi.org/10.17077/0003-4827.11123

Holt, Kristin, blogger. May 31, 2018.
www.kristinholt.com/archives/15728

Idaho Legislature website, State Statutes.
www.legislature.idaho.gov/statutesrules/idstat/

Kipling, Rudyard, "The Betrothed." The poem first published in the *Pioneer and Pioneer Mail*, 21 November, 1888. The Kipling Society.
www.kiplinsociety.co.uk
accessed Feb. 15, 2025.

Lane, Anthony, "Anatomy of a Fall," *The New Yorker Magazine*, New York, NY, (Oct. 16, 2023).

Mackley, Jennifer Ann, and Harper, Steven C., *Wilford Woodruff Papers Project*. The Wilford Woodruff Papers Foundation.
www.wilfordwoodruffpapers.org/wives-and-children
accessed on Feb. 18, 2025.

McDonald, Dylan J., Walker, Steve, and Crowder, David L., "The Moses Alexander Collection," Idaho State Historical Society, Boise, Idaho (2002). Idaho State Archives.
www.idahohistory.contentdm.oclc.org/digital/collection/p265501coll4/id/543

National Park Service.
www.nps.gov.

Neal, L.G., *The Murder of David Steven Neal – A True Story*.
Self-published pamphlet, McCall, Idaho (2003).

Oyez.org, *Reynolds V. United States*.
www.oyez.org/cases/1850-1900/98us145

Newspapers.com, A subscription online service, the website provides access to more than 1 billion pages from newspapers from around the United States and beyond.
www.newspapers.com/about/

Park, John R., "Second Report of the Superintendent of Public Instruction of the State of Utah For the Biennial Period Ending June 30, 1898," Salt Lake City. (1899). Google Books, from the General Library of the University of Michigan. www.google.com/books/edition/Report_of_the_Superintendent_of_Public_I/mbqgAAAAMAAJ?hl=en&gbpv=1&dq=Summity+Stake+Academy+Utah&pg=RA2-PA52&printsec=frontcover

Savage, Julie Heming, "Hannah Grover Hegsted and Post-Manifest Plural Marriage." *Dialogue: A Journal of Mormon Thought*, Vol. 26, No. 3, (Fall 1993). www.dialoguejournal.com/wp-content/uploads/sbi/articles/Dialogue_V26N03_4.pdf accessed on Feb. 12, 2025.

Siefrit, William C., "The Prison Experience of Abraham H. Cannon," *Utah Historical Quarterly*, 1985, Vol. 52, No. 3, J. Willard Marriott Library, University of Utah. www.issuu.com/utah10/docs/uhq_volume53_1985_number3 accessed Feb. 18, 2025.

Smith, Eugene E., *Life Story of Eugene Ellington (Enoick-Nick) Smith*, Typed copy, (1985) Teton County Museum, Driggs, Idaho.

Smith, Jr., Octavus, "A history of my life," *Family Search*. www.familysearch.org/en/tree/person/memories/KWCH-VJ6 accessed Feb. 20, 2025.

U.S. Census Bureau, "Thirteenth Census of the United States Taken in the Year 1910 – Statistics for Idaho." Reprint of the supplement for Idaho (1913). https://www2.census.gov/library/publications/decennial/1910/abstract/supplement-id.pdf, accessed on Jan. 28, 2025.

University of Utah, "Annual of the University of Utah including the State School of Mines and the State Normal School, Salt Lake City, 1901-1902." (1901).

Utah History Encyclopedia. www.uen.org/utah_history_encyclopedia

Woods, Fred E., editor; Everett, Joseph B. database curator; and Ellingson, Brent, IT product manager. *Saints by Sea – Latter-day Saint Immigration to America*, selected data reformatted by permission from the Mormon Immigration Index CD, copyright 2000, in collaboration with the Church History and Family History Departments website, copyright 2010-2025, Brigham Young University. https://saintsbysea.lib.byu.edu/

ARCHIVES, HISTORICAL SOCIETIES, LIBRARIES, AND MUSEUMS

Brigham Young University, Harold B. Lee Library, Provo, Utah.
https://guides.lib.byu.edu/universityarchives

Ibid. L. Tom Perry Special Collections.
https://lib.byu.edu/

Ibid. Library archives.
http://archives.lib.byu.edu/

Cumberland University, Vise Library, The Stockton Archives, Lebanon, Tennessee.
https://library.cumberland.edu/archives

Idaho Falls Public Library, Idaho Falls, Idaho.
https://www.ifpl.org/

Idaho Historical Society, Boise, Idaho.
https://history.idaho.gov/

Idaho State Archives, Boise, Idaho.
https://history.idaho.gov/archives/

Jackson Hole Historical Society and Museum, Jackson, Wyoming.
https://jacksonholehistory.org/

Research Center for the Utah State Archives and Utah State History, Salt Lake City, Utah. http://historyresearch.utah.gov

Teton Valley Museum, Driggs, Idaho.
https://tetonmuseum.com/

University of Utah, J. Willard Marriott Library, Salt Lake City, Utah.
https://lib.utah.edu/

Upper Snake River Historical Society, Rexburg, Idaho.
https://www.rexburghistoricalsociety.org/

Daniel Neal

Utah Division of Archives and Records Service.
https://archives.utah.gov/

NEWSPAPERS

Bingham County News, Blackfoot, Idaho
Blackfoot Optimist, Blackfoot, Idaho
Box Elder News-Journal, Brigham City, Utah
Caldwell Tribune, Caldwell, Idaho
Challis Messenger, Challis, Idaho
Clearwater Republican, Orofino, Idaho
Coalville Times, Coalville, Utah
Daily Utah Chronicle, Salt Lake City, Utah
Deseret Evening News, Salt Lake City, Utah
East Oregonian, Pendleton, Oregon
Evening Capital News, Boise, Idaho
Evening Standard, Ogden, Utah
Idaho Republican, Blackfoot, Idaho
Idaho Statesman, Boise Idaho (aka *Idaho Daily Statesman*)
Jackson's Hole Courier, Jackson, Wyoming
Jordan Times, Jordan, Montana
Kamas Courant, Kamas, Utah
Kendrick Gazette, Kendrick, Idaho
Meridian Times, Meridian, Idaho
Montpelier Examiner, Montpelier, Idaho
Morning Examiner, Ogden, Utah
Ogden Standard-Examiner, Ogden, Utah
Park Record, Park City, Utah
Record, St. Maries, Idaho
Rexburg Standard, Rexburg, Idaho
Rigby Star, Rigby, Idaho
Salt Lake Herald, Salt Lake City, Utah
Salt Lake Telegram, St. George, Utah
Salt Lake Tribune, Salt Lake City, Utah
Teton Peak-Chronicle, St. Anthony, Idaho
Teton Valley News, Driggs, Idaho
Wood River Times, Hailey, Idaho

LDS CHURCH PUBLICATIONS AND OTHER RESOURCES

The Doctrine and Covenants of the Church of Jesus Christ of Latter-day Saints, The Church of Jesus Christ of Latter-day Saints, Salt Lake City, Utah (1952).

The Book of Mormon, Translated by Joseph Smith (1830). Copyright 1963 by David O. McKay, trustee in trust for The Church of Jesus Christ of Latter-day Saints, Salt Lake City, Utah.

FamilySearch, operated by the Family History Department.

Hymns, The Deseret News Press, Salt Lake City, Utah (1948).

International Genealogical Index (IGI), FamilySearch database. https://familysearch.org/ark:/61903/2:1:9V15-T5S

The Children Sing, Deseret Book, Salt Lake City, Utah (1951).

The Church History Catalog, https://catalog.churchofjesuschrist.org/

Church History Library, 14 E. North Temple Street, Salt Lake City, Utah. www.history.churchofjesuschrist.org/landing/church-history-library?lang=eng

The Relief Society Magazine, *A Legacy Remembered, 1914–1970*. Deseret Book Co., Salt Lake City, Utah (1982).

Saints by Sea, "Latter-day Saint Immigration to America." https://saintsbysea.lib.byu.edu

www.ingramcontent.com/pod-product-compliance
Lightning Source LLC
Chambersburg PA
CBHW040301170426
43193CB00021B/2971